THE
SHATTERED
BADGE

THE
SHATTERED
BADGE

The Story of Ed Donovan, Stress Cop

by

BILL KANKEWITT

ⓝ METHUEN

Toronto New York London Sydney Auckland

Canadian Cataloguing in Publication Data

Kankewitt, Bill, 1943-
  The shattered badge

ISBN 0-458-80460-6

1. Donovan, Edward C.   2. Boston Police Stress
Program.   3. Police — Job stress.   4. Police —
United States — Biography.   I. Title.

HV7936.J63K36 1986   363.2'092'4   C86-094421-2

Excerpt from SIGNAL ZERO by George Kirkham
copyright © 1976 by George L. Kirkham.
Reprinted by permission of Harper & Row,
Publishers, Inc.

Printed and bound in Canada
1 2 3 4   86   90 89 88 87

In memory of
GEORGE B. MCCLELLAN
Commissioner of the Royal Canadian Mounted Police
1963–67

*"And whosoever of you will be the chiefest,
shall be servant of all."* Mark 10:44

Happy are those who dream dreams
and are ready to pay the price to
make them come true.

L.J. Cardinal Suenens

CONTENTS

PREFACE

"Eddie Donovan saved my life." Charlie Gilham's comment was typical of the police officers I talked to in the United States and Canada about Ed Donovan and the Boston Police Stress Program. "Either you love him or you hate him and often it's both," Gilham said.

There was something special I sensed about the officers I met who'd been helped by Donovan. After each visit to Boston I returned home to Edmonton feeling touched by their openness and sincerity. I felt closer to them than to friends I've had for twenty years. They had a piece of something special and Ed Donovan had a gift — to find out what it was became the challenge of researching this book.

Most of the material you're about to read came through situations I witnessed first hand, the rest through interviews with Donovan and the officers and wives involved. The willingness of those officers to talk candidly about their feelings and problems was amazing.

Why is a Canadian who lives two thousand miles from Boston writing this story? Because it is a story about police officers everywhere and the work of Eddie Donovan has reached police forces in all corners of the world.

My deep thanks to those who at critical stages believed in me and the book: Ron Reinhart, Bernie Goedhart, Barb and Mike Valois, Barb Johnston, Gwyneth Runnings, and Tanya Long. To Edmonton Police Chaplain Bruce Cowley who first told me about Donovan. To those special friends who stuck by my side during the tough times, took interest in the project and helped with the manuscript. To Leigh, Zan and Zoë for the light they brought to my life each day and for understanding their father's preoccupation with the book. And especially to Miriam—my wife, best friend and writing partner who worked with me line by line from research to final manuscript and who provided me with encouragement and insight.

This is a true story. The names of some police officers have been changed and certain incidents disguised to protect the confidentiality of the Boston Police Stress Program. Incidents occurring in the small cities surrounding Boston have been given fictional city names.

BILL KANKEWITT

THE
SHATTERED
BADGE

PROLOGUE

Summer, 1969

It was a hot, humid summer afternoon, and Boston's Fenway Park was alive with the sounds of baseball.

The old-fashioned brick and steel ballpark was filled to capacity with 34,000 zealous fans jammed into every available seat. The beer flowed freely as the restless fans combatted the afternoon heat and egged on their beloved Red Sox. And the Sox needed egging. They'd lost two in a row to the hated New York Yankees, and a loss in this afternoon's game would seriously hurt their pennant hopes.

Today's game hadn't gotten off to a good start. The Sox were down 3–0, and the Yankees, with runners on first and third, were threatening to score more in the top of the fifth.

The notorious left field "boo birds" were unleashing their wrath on the home team.

"Come on, pull the damned pitcher."

"Williams, you couldn't manage your way out of a paper bag!" They saw themselves as the true Red Sox baseball fans. Hard-drinking, tough-living blue collar workers, they sweated and fought to earn a living, and they expected the same from their team. They played no favourites and had little compassion for any of the local ballplaying heroes who dared to let them down. They had booed the legendary Ted Williams for most of the nineteen years he patrolled left field in front of them.

Current Red Sox super star Carl Yastrzemski was faring no better in the left field jungle. He was mired in a six-week batting slump and had been treated viciously by the boo birds. Today, he had come up with his own way of dealing with them. He had stuffed huge balls of cotton in his ears. It was his way of silencing his critics and saying "screw you," as well. This only served to aggravate the boo birds, drawing out more of their venom.

"You suck, Yastrzemski!"

"Why don't you put some in your mouth too!"

"Yeah, and stick some up your ass!" An empty whisky bottle flew through the air and landed five feet in front of the startled Yastrzemski.

The pace of the trips to the beer concessions quickened and the tension of the game and the insults to Yastrzemski picked up. The left field fans prided themselves in their ability to pack the suds away.

A double play ended the Yankee threat, and the Sox were ready to redeem themselves in the bottom of the fifth. Thirty-four thousand sets of eyes were now intently focused on the Red Sox hope, lead-off hitter Billy Conigliaro.

"Come on Billy! Hit the bloody ball!"

"Let's get going."

High up in the left field stands, behind the last row of shouting fans in Section Thirty-six, a uniformed cop stood vigilant at his assigned position. He was paid to watch for trouble, but the only trouble he saw was his own. He was crying. Large reflective sunglasses hid his watery eyes. Two salty tears rolled down under the glasses and onto his cheeks. With deft moves of his sleeves and his shoulder, he subtly managed to blot them away.

He needn't have worried. No one looked or cared. All 34,000 fans were intently digging in, licking their lips, and rolling their shoulders in rapt empathy for their hitter, "Billy C," while he did battle with the Yankee pitcher.

For the crying cop, Ed Donovan, this was crowd control detail, and he dreaded it. He flinched every time the crowd roared its disapproval. His stomach churned with every hurled insult. He panicked and looked away when the whisky bottle was thrown at Yastrzemski. The crowd scared him.

He felt it was a monster ready to turn on him at any moment. The people would take out their rage on him because he was a cop and everyone hated cops.

"What's the matter with me?" he begged to a God he no longer believed in. "Am I a coward, a weakling, what's the matter with me?"

He'd been a tough cop — a street cop with a special assignment — a police photographer. A ten-year veteran of snapping the ugly side of life and death. Capturing the grim reminder of shattered dreams; each day shooting on film the victims of brutal murders, car accidents, rapes, and suicides. Thousands of pictures of death. Now the one that haunted him the most was his own. He was a basket case. Burnt out, pushed to the limit, and unable to take it any more.

Police forces usually rotate their photographers after a few years, because most can't take the constant presence of death. Ed Donovan was cool — too tough to let it bother him. Now it had him trapped. He was cracking up. He was like the victims he had so often frozen in his lens. His subjects didn't smile, and, now, neither did he.

"Ball four." Conigliaro walked. The fans roared their approval. Donovan breathed a short, desperate sigh of temporary relief. He knew the crowd could turn ugly again in the instant it would take to hit into a double play.

Reggie Smith stepped up to the plate. The fans urged him on.

"Come on Reggie, you can do it."

"It's up to you. Come on, Reggie baby."

"Please hit it, Reggie," Donovan silently prayed to himself. "Cool the crowd down. Keep them off my back. Make them happy. Let me get out of here. God, I don't want to be here."

Donovan was on duty because he needed the money. Special detail paid extra. With a wife and seven kids to feed, Donovan always needed more money. Some people pumped gas or drove a cab for extra cash. Cops worked riots and crowd control. For Donovan, special detail had taken its toll.

Student uprisings and the anti-Viet Nam riots had raged violently in Boston for the past three years, and Donovan had been on duty for most of them. In full riot gear, he had been face to face with enraged mobs. He had wanted to run from their taunts and projectiles. He was afraid, but he was even more afraid to run. Cops weren't supposed to run.

In some riots, he was in plain clothes, assigned to take pictures of the conflict. That was even worse. He had been harassed and beaten by over-anxious cops who thought he was the press. He couldn't win. Now he was at a simple baseball game, and he couldn't even take this anymore.

The tears were getting into his mouth now, and his hands began to tremble as he tightened them around his night stick. He let his right hand go for a second to find the security of his revolver. His palm massaged the gun butt in a sensual, circular manner. Like a little child with his blanket, Ed Donovan clung to his defences, trying to cope, afraid at any minute the crowd would turn on him.

He was a street cop; despised and hated. Society didn't care if he lived or died, and, right now, neither did he. He wanted to run, but he was trapped: the yelling fans in front of him, his back to the cold brick stadium wall. As far as anyone at the ballpark knew or cared, there he arrogantly stood for all to see. Big daddy. The cock of the walk. The bully in blue.

But inside, Donovan felt like a wasted, empty corpse. He imagined dozens of fat little rats sucking his body dry. He heard their harsh and mocking voices, taunting him. "Scaredy cat, scaredy cat, Eddie is a scaredy cat."

"Strike three." Reggie Smith struck out. Donovan sagged. Yastrzemski was now the batter. The crowd booed and hurled more insults.

"Strike one." Yastrzemski almost toppled out of his shoes

as he swung wildly at the pitcher's first offering. The crowd's anger began to rise.

Donovan moved slightly to his left, steadying himself on a pillar. He was drenched with sweat now and wanted to puke. Any moment the crowd would see his facade and turn on him. The game would stop and all 34,000 pairs of eyes would be looking at him. There'd be stone cold silence. Eddie Donovan on display — the scared cop, the Librium junkie, the boozer, the coward who couldn't cut it. Crying like a baby at a baseball game.

A few muffled snickers came from the crowd. Soon, all of them would roar with laughter at him. Ed Donovan was a joke.

He turned his face toward the pillar and sobbed out loud.

The crowd let out a deafening cheer. Yastrzemski had stroked a single, and the Sox had runners on first and third.

"Way to go, Yaz. We love you!"

Long shadows filled the empty Fenway parking lot. The game had ended two hours earlier. Ed Donovan sat silently in his car at the far end of the lot. He looked nervously down the barrel of his service revolver.

Put it in the mouth and pull the trigger. Neat and quick. No chance of being a vegetable. No messy corpse for the relatives to identify.

Ed Donovan had photographed too many suicides to not know how to do it. "Christ, if you were going to do it, do it right," he had always thought. It surprised him — the distasteful way so many of his fellow officers did it.

Like the retired officer who shot himself the week before. Did it in the public crapper at the library. Right in a stall. Shot himself in the temple to boot, to make it real messy. Donovan didn't like that one little bit. There the old man was, pants down, slumped against the side of the stall. The blood had oozed down to form a single large puddle on the floor. Donovan had to step in it to take the final close-ups.

"What for?" he thought. He knew the cause of death would be listed as a heart attack. The administration always covered up cop suicides. Can't let the public know that cops do this sort of thing. Doesn't suit the image. Poor public relations.

The cops at the scene had said little. No one in this tough-guy business was going to say what he was thinking. But to a man, you can bet they had the same thoughts going through their heads as Donovan had through his, "Is this how I'm going to end up? Is all the abuse worth it if this is the final pay-off?" What they had said out loud would shock the uninitiated:

"I know that constipation is annoying, but this is ridiculous."

"Strange place to clean your gun."

"That's the worst heart attack I've ever seen."

Gallows humour they call it. It isn't that cops don't care. They joke about it as a way of keeping sane. It's a release from the horror of some of the scenes they must face every day. Donovan hadn't felt like joking about it that time.

Donovan's vision of the body in the washroom stall dissolved to the picture of his own suicide in the Fenway parking lot. His head was exploding now. He put the gun in his lap and cradled his head in his hands. Leaning against the steering wheel, he started to cry again. This had to end.

The drugs hadn't helped. The booze didn't do it. The booze and drugs together didn't do it. The pain only got worse and worse. The horrors he had seen on the job the past ten years destroyed his faith in God. Once a staunch Catholic, he now no longer believed in anything. Suicide was the only way left to him.

He gripped his pistol and slowly put the barrel in his mouth. It tasted bitter and oily as his tongue touched the strange object. His teeth clenched the barrel. He squeezed his eyes shut as every muscle in his body tightened to its maximum. His finger slowly started to pull on the trigger.

Memories of childhood raced through his mind in a millisecond. His finger tightened further. His wife, the kids, fleeting glimpses of them all raced by.

A note!

He should leave a note. He owed at least that to his kids. The gun slid from his mouth as his muscles went limp.

Paper? A cigarette package will do. A pen, "Where's my fucking pen?" Donovan said out loud as he fumbled through the car looking for something to write with.

He was sweating again and his hands began to tremble. There's the pen. He tried to pick it up. His hands were shaking uncontrollably. He wanted his kids to know that he loved them. They had to know that. It wasn't their fault. He loved them dearly, and he wanted to tell them.

His hands were shaking too violently to write. His crying turned to hysterical wailing. He beat the steering wheel with his fists. Eddie Donovan wanted it all to end, but he couldn't do it.

He was a god-damned failure, even at suicide.

He frantically tried to get his hands and fingers to work well enough to open the pill container he kept in his glove compartment. No luck. He managed to gnaw off the plastic top and swigged the container to his mouth like a shot glass to swallow the three Librium tablets left in it.

Darkness had settled over the parking lot. Donovan curled into a crying, shaking ball in the front seat of his car and sobbed until he fell into a troubled sleep.

Nine Years Later, Spring, 1978

Ed Donovan rocked nervously back and forth in his chair, fidgeting with his hands. Alone in his office at the stress centre, he had done nothing for the past hour but stare periodically at the phone that sat on the side of his cluttered desk. Should he make the phone call?

He was afraid, but it was nothing like the fear he had experienced during his down and out days. This was an intense fear of rejection. He had been fearless when it came to setting up the Boston Police Stress Program, knocking on doors, fighting the establishment, or speaking his mind. But this was different. It was like phoning God. That's almost what Hans Selye was to those who studied stress.

Hans Selye, C.C., M.D., Ph.D., D.Sc., the president of the International Institute of Stress, the guru, the founder of stress studies and treatment as it exists today. The man, Alvin Toffler said, who "knows more about stress than any other scientist alive." The author of over 1,600 papers and a dozen best-selling books, the gospel for those who work with stress.

Donovan looked at the phone again and thought, "How can I, Ed Donovan, street cop and former drunk, phone someone like that? How dare I? He probably won't even accept the call."

Asking Senator Edward Kennedy and author Joseph Wambaugh to serve on the board of his new International Law Enforcement Stress Association (ILESA) was easy in comparison. Somehow a "no" from them wouldn't have hurt Donovan, a "no" from Dr. Selye would. Donovan wanted him badly, to serve on the board and on the editorial committee of *Police Stress Magazine*.

Donovan had reached for Dr. Selye's books during his recovery. They helped him then, and they helped him now to run the stress program. If ILESA were to have any clout on a worldwide basis, Dr. Selye's involvement would make the difference.

Donovan battled his reluctance to make the call. "God damn it, Donovan, make the bloody call," he muttered. He glanced at the phone on the corner of his desk. This time he stared at it intently, then swallowed slowly, took a deep breath, reached over, and picked up the receiver. Very carefully, he dialed Selye's office number at the University of Montreal.

"Good morning, International Institute of Stress," said the efficient voice of a woman.

"I'd like to speak to Dr. Selye, please," Donovan said, as he hunched over in tension.

"I'm sorry, but Dr. Selye is busy at the moment. Who's calling please?" Donovan thought his worst fears were coming true, that he wouldn't be able to get through to Dr. Selye. He'd be screened out at the lowest level if he didn't give it his all.

"My name is Ed Donovan, and I run a police stress program in Boston, and I want to talk to Dr. Selye to arrange a meeting with him to get his help with a worldwide police stress group I'm setting up." The words rolled from his lips in his Boston accent at a machine-gun pace. The controlled manner, carefully rehearsed in his mind, was replaced by desperate scrambling.

"A stress program for whom?" The voice sounded puzzled.

"For police officers," Donovan fired back. "They suffer from severe stress problems."

"And what is it you want from Dr. Selye?" The voice asked guardedly.

"His help and advice in setting up a stress organization for police all around the world," Donovan said, starting to get a little frustrated and impatient with the voice.

There was a long moment of silence. "And you want Dr. Selye to help set up a stress organization for police?"

"Yes," Donovan quickly answered. Another silence.

"I'm afraid Dr. Selye has a very busy schedule. He receives many requests that he'd like to help with, but he has simply no time," the voice said politely but firmly.

This time it was Donovan who was quiet for a moment. "It's the kiss-off," he thought.

"But all I'd like is a short appointment with him. It wouldn't take much of his time, just fifteen minutes, that's all I need," Donovan said, in a pleading tone.

Now it was the voice's turn for silence. Donovan knew she realized he wasn't easily discouraged. He jumped in.

"Look," he said. "I'm sorry if I'm being a bit pushy, but I think Dr. Selye would be very interested in what I do. I'm a former alcoholic cop who had a complete nervous break-down. I read Dr. Selye's books, and they were a tremendous help in my recovery. Then I started a program in Boston for other cops who have problems. Police suffer a terrible amount of stress. It affects their work, their health, their marriages, and their families.

"There's no one who understands their problems enough to help them. My Boston program is really working well, and now I want to help police officers all over the world. Something has to be done. Just a little bit of advice from Dr. Selye would be a big help. I'd only take a few minutes of his time."

Donovan slumped back in his chair. He was drained. He had said his piece and done his best. If this didn't work, well, you could only do so much.

The voice was silent. Whatever decision she was going to make had been complicated by Donovan's pleading. "Just a moment," she finally said.

Donovan pivoted his chair nervously from side to side. His energy had returned quickly, and all the adrenalin he was generating had to go somewhere. His left hand, tightly gripping the phone to his ear, was beginning to perspire. "Come on, come on. Get him to the phone," he said under his breath. Donovan prayed the next voice he'd hear would be Dr. Selye's. It seemed forever, and Donovan was wild with impatience.

"Mr. Donovan," said the voice. Donovan's heart was in his mouth. "If you can come to Montreal this Saturday morning at 10:00 A.M. Dr. Selye can see you for fifteen minutes."

"Great," bubbled Donovan. It wasn't as much time as he needed, but it was a foot in the door. After all, he hadn't expected to make it this far. The voice gave him the details of where to find the office, but Donovan barely listened. With excitement dancing in his Irish eyes, he plunked the phone receiver back into the cradle, jumped to his feet, drove his right fist into the air, and let out a bloodcurdling scream of delight. He did a little staccato dance and whooped with joy a few more times.

Donovan was panicky. He was late, and you do not keep important people like Dr. Selye waiting. The cabbie had taken him to the wrong university. Now, they sped through the dreary Montreal rain, trying frantically to make up for lost time.

Donovan's heart felt like it was going to explode in his chest. He wrung his hands anxiously, apprehensive because of the stature of the man he was about to meet and because he was now ten minutes late.

"Son of a bitch," Donovan muttered, fighting back the temptation to choke the cabbie. Not an appropriate action, just before meeting the "father of stress studies."

The cab skidded to a halt in front of the main entrance of the University of Montreal's *Pavillon Principal*. Donovan thrust the fare — no tip — into the cabbie's hand, then bolted from the back seat. He raced up the stairs, two at a time, into the building's foyer. Long corridors stretched out in every direction. Which way to go? He didn't know French, and here he was looking for the *Institut de médecine et chirurgie expérimentale* where Dr. Selye's office was. All the signs were in French. It was a quiet Saturday morning, there was no one around to help him, and he'd completely forgotten the voice's instructions.

Like a rat in a maze, Donovan paused, hesitated, and then raced down the nearest corridor. It was 10:16 A.M., and the fifteen minutes allotted for his appointment had expired. Down the second corridor he veered in frenzied pursuit of the right door. Then he spotted the worn lettering:

Dr. Hans Selye
President
International Institute of Stress

The hall clock showed 10:17 A.M. Would Selye still see him? Donovan's temples joined his heart in pounding out a bass drum duet. His red hair was a ruffled mop and he was sweating now. "Not the place to have a heart attack," he thought, imagining the irony.

He took a deep breath, straightened his tie, smoothed his hair over his ears, and knocked on the door.

"Come in," he heard. Donovan entered but saw no one in the elegant book-lined study. Slowly, a huge, stuffed, brown swivel chair on the far side of the office turned to face him. The small, hawk-nosed, white-haired man in the chair raised his head and looked sternly into Donovan's nervous eyes.

"Ed Donovan, you are late." Hans Selye spoke with a firm voice, heavily laced with a Viennese accent.

"I'm sorry, Dr. Selye. The cab driver took me to the wrong university."

Donovan paused anxiously and looked for some sign of forgiveness from Dr. Selye. Selye let a trace of a smile escape and rose to shake Donovan's hand.

"You're a very determined man, Mr. Donovan, and it sounds like you have an interesting story to tell me." Donovan smiled weakly. Selye motioned him to sit, then sat down himself. He looked at Donovan expectantly. Donovan realized there'd be no small talk.

He started telling his story, slowly and carefully at first, but as he sensed Dr. Selye's interest and saw the gleam of fascination in the old man's eyes, he started to relax and speak from the heart.

Selye listened, only asking questions to clarify some parts of the avalanche of information Donovan was giving him. The fifteen-minute meeting stretched into thirty minutes, then an hour, then two hours as Hans Selye listened, enthralled by the story of Donovan's work and the problems faced by police officers.

"Of course I will. Something has to be done!" was Selye's quick and blunt response to Donovan's request for help with ILESA and *Police Stress Magazine*. He called an associate into the room to meet Donovan.

"I want you to meet Ed Donovan, the stress cop. We're going to be doing some work with him." Donovan beamed his broad Irish smile. The meeting had exceeded his wildest dreams. He thanked Dr. Selye and left to catch his flight back to Boston.

The ride back to the airport was much more enjoyable for Eddie Donovan. The rain had stopped, and bright sunshine illuminated the historic old Montreal streets as the cab picked its way through traffic. Donovan thought of the unofficial slogan of Canada's famous Mounted Police, the RCMP, "We always get our man."

He smiled. Today, he got his.

The two worked closely over the next year, consulting frequently over the phone as Donovan formed ILESA and *Police Stress Magazine*. One day, late in August, 1979, Selye called Donovan at home.

"I want to talk to you, Eddie," Selye said. "Can you come up to Montreal?" Intrigued, Donovan caught the next available flight. This time, he enjoyed the cab ride to the University of Montreal for his second face to face meeting with Dr. Selye. With an air of confidence and curiosity he marched up the stairs of the *Pavillon Principal* and in the door through the foyer to the rat maze. Smiling at his distress during the previous visit, Donovan walked down the long corridor to Dr. Selye's office. The door was open, and Donovan saw Selye was on the phone. Selye motioned him into the room.

"I've got someone I want you to talk to, Ed." Not knowing what to expect, Donovan took the phone from Selye.

"Hello, this is Ed Donovan," he said hesitantly.

"Ed, this is Linus Pauling,"

Donovan was astounded. He'd heard of the Nobel Prize winner, famous for his theories on vitamins and stress and couldn't believe this was happening.

"Ed, I understand you're coming to Monaco with us," Pauling said. "I'm looking forward to meeting you and hearing what you have to say. Hans has told me a lot about you." Not really understanding what was going on, Donovan mumbled some cordiality to Pauling, then handed the phone back to the grinning Dr. Selye. The composure Donovan had brought to this meeting turned to stunned amazement. What had he gotten himself into? He was going to Monaco, and he didn't even know where it was. Selye finished his call with Pauling.

"November in Monaco, Ed. A symposium on the management of stress. We want you to be one of the speakers," Dr. Selye said. "It will be attended by medical doctors from around the world."

"Who else is going to be speaking?" Donovan asked.

"Some well-known scientists, like Hans Krebs and Roger Guillemin who've won Nobel prizes, Jonas Salk, Linus and myself," Selye added.

Donovan almost floated from the room when it came time for him to leave. "Me! A patrolman from Boston," he thought, "sharing a podium with Nobel Prize winners. Boy, if my buddies from the drinking days could see me now."

Donovan wondered if he looked scared. He'd been nervous about this day for the three months since he first found out about the Monaco Stress Symposium. Now he was sitting at the speakers' table, waiting for his turn at the podium.

The main conference room at Loew's Hotel looked like a scaled-down version of the United Nations General Assembly. Nearly all the 500 plush seats were occupied by doctors from all over the world, anxious to learn more about stress from the experts: Roger Guillemin, Linus Pauling, Christian de Duve, several other renowned scientists — and Eddie Donovan.

Donovan looked out over the hall. Flags from the nations of the world framed the room. High above the speakers' platform, a bank of interpreters sat in glass-enclosed booths, while over a hundred magazine and newspaper journalists filled the press section. Television and film cameras were set up on both sides of the room. Like a bouquet of flowers, an arrangement of twenty-five microphones sprouted in front of the podium.

Donovan wrung his hands under the table. His heart and temples were pounding that all too familiar tune, and his stomach churned in complaint. "Please God," he thought, "just let me give my speech without fainting, then I'll go home quietly to Boston where I belong." He fought to keep negative thoughts from his mind: "Will the audience accept me? Will they listen? Who am I to be here? I'm not a doctor or a scientist."

All the heavy hitters were taking their turns at the podium: Selye, Krebs, Salk. Donovan was scheduled to speak at mid-afternoon. "The audience will be drained," he thought. "They won't want to listen to me."

It was all so ironic. Here Donovan was, racked with tension and stress, while the world's greatest experts talked about it, but he really didn't hear a word until the moderator introduced him. It was a short introduction, just Ed Donovan, the stress cop from Boston. He had no letters, titles, or honours to recite after his name.

Donovan walked cautiously to the podium. He placed his notes carefully in front of him to hide his nervousness, but he didn't plan on using them.

When the scars of experience have touched every inch of your body, when you've tasted the barrel of a cocked .38 revolver in your mouth, and when you've lived your own story, you don't need to use notes. Donovan spoke from the heart.

The audience, still full from lunch, shifted uncomfortably in their seats. Who was this person in the green plaid jacket who looked so out of place?

Donovan took a deep breath. Then, firing up his Boston twang and rapid-fire delivery, he charged into his story:

"More and more people are unloading their frustrations on the police. The officer in uniform has become the focus of misplaced hatred, the punching bag of society — the very society the officer is sworn to serve and protect. Men and women who become officers feel they will help to serve society and make their communities safer places to live, but this concern for society backfires in their faces. The officer is placed in the firing line every day and asked to maintain law and order at any price, even at the expense of his own life or mental well-being.

"Do you know in which incidents policemen get killed the most? Everyone thinks it's the shootout with the bank-robber or the bang, bang chases you see on television every night. It isn't. The average cop rarely in his whole career gets involved in a shoot-out.

"The number one killer of cops is the stopping of cars for routine checks or minor violations and the number two killer is domestic disputes. The average cop faces these situations every day, but how do you know when there's gonna be a kook with a gun waiting to blow your brains out? What kind of stress is that going to cause?

"The job builds human time bombs and if nothing is done to defuse those bombs, they're going to blow up right in the face of the administration, but the general attitude of most police departments is if you can't stand the heat, get out. That's wrong. We need prevention and treatment before we're in a crisis situation.

"But you know what they do in a lot of police depart-ments to help combat stress? They spend thousands of dol-lars equipping gyms with exercise equipment and running tracks." He paused for a second and then boomed em-phatically, "Big help! What do they tell a cop who's divorced, alcoholic, sick and suicidal? Go run five miles a day."

The words, thoughts, and emotions poured from Donovan. The audience was enthralled; they sat stone still, leaning forward to absorb his message. This was not rheto-ric or the academic theory of previous presentations. Just Ed Donovan telling his own story.

Donovan looked out at his audience. He knew he had them. Encouraged by their acceptance, he quickened his already rapid-fire delivery. The words literally jumped from his mouth.

Suddenly a note was slipped in front of him by someone from the head table.

"Slow down, Ed," it said, "you're doing fine, but the interpreters can't keep up with you."

Donovan took a deep breath and a quick sip of water. He slowed down, but the more relaxed pace only served to heighten the force he put into each sentence.

"An officer is often confronted with situations other people can walk away from. We cannot, however, leave the scene where some kid has been crushed by the tire of a truck, or mangled by a freight elevator, or where an entire family has been murdered by a deranged father. We have to control our emotions so we can deal with the situation at hand.

"How many times can you see dead bodies and deal with domestic disputes before something has to give? As an officer you have to insulate yourself from becoming emotionally involved, a difficult task for any human being. We're only human, and we have the same strengths and weaknesses as everyone else, yet we have to go into people's homes and settle their problems. At the same time we're not allowed to have any of our own.

"We are not made of stone."

Donovan paused briefly and glanced over at Dr. Selye. The proud doctor beamed back at his protégé and flashed the thumbs-up sign. Donovan went back to the task at hand. He had only thirty minutes, and he still had a lot to say.

"The policeman thinks he's supposed to be the problem solver for the world. He's taught to hold it in, to adapt. When the other helping professions — doctors, social workers, priests — have their backs to the wall, they call a cop. Who does a cop call?

"We need more stress training in all areas of law enforcement. Officers must be taught to recognize the onset of stress and how to cope with it in a constructive rather than a destructive manner. They must be made to realize they will experience fear on the job, and this is normal. Officers must be shown it's not unmanly to cry and be encouraged to seek outside help for a problem they feel they can't handle.

"Police officers need a place to turn in their time of need."

Donovan, damp with perspiration, his eyes moist from the emotions his story stirred, had finished.

The audience rose as one to give the patrolman from Boston a standing ovation. He had not only opened their eyes to the problem, but had provided the ray of hope in his one-man battle to overcome it.

The applause continued. Dr. Seyle rushed over to embrace Donovan.

"I'm proud of you, Eddie. You did the best job here."

CHAPTER ONE

FULL CIRCLE

Wednesday, 10:00 A.M. Spring 1985

Life seemed to have come full circle for Eddie Donovan. Once a victim of his job, he had gained control of his life and become a world-renowned police stress expert, but he now felt himself losing control and becoming the victim again.

His constant crusade to save other cops from the forces that had almost killed him fifteen years ago was taking a toll. The weight of the work load he was carrying and the administrative battles he fought daily were wrecking his health and undermining his spirits.

Despite the worldwide recognition he'd been getting for six years, and the dozens of programs around the world modelled on his Boston success, Donovan's own police department hadn't been supporting him. His budget had been slashed, and where he once had two full-time counsellors, he'd been on his own now for the last three years. The strain of being on call twenty-four hours a day, combined with the lack of support and hassles from some of his Boston Police bosses, had caught up with him. His health problems had mounted over the past few years so that he now had chronic headaches and, for the last month, a severe pain in his left side. Donovan worried he had cancer. His doctor had booked an ultra-sound appointment for him for the coming Monday.

Depressed and angry, Donovan steered his black Ford LTD toward work and the Boston Police Stress Center in Mattapan, on the city's southern boundary. Coming from his home in Plymouth, thirty-eight miles south of the city, Donovan turned off the freeway and headed cross-country for the final few miles. He drove up and around the winding wooded hills on Chickatawbut Road in the Blue Hills Reservation until he reached the summit. He slowed and pulled into a viewpoint nestled in a park among towering trees high above the freeway and madness below.

In the distance, Boston could be seen like a sleeping giant, lying mellow beneath the quiet haze of the mid-morning sun. The peace and beauty made Donovan feel he was looking out on the world from the edge of heaven, despite the pain that tugged in his gut.

This morning was particularly tough for Donovan. He had had to have his dog, Suzanne, put to sleep. In the range of life and death situations he'd experienced at the stress program, the death of his dog shouldn't rate — but it did, and to know why was to understand much about policemen.

A reporter interviewed Donovan recently, and the topic came up of men, particularly policemen, being unable or unwilling to show their true feelings. The reporter's father was a tough New York cop, and she said, "You know, it's funny, the only time in twenty-five years I ever saw my father cry was when his dog died. When his mum and dad died, he didn't shed a tear, but for weeks after the dog died, he cried at the mention of her name."

"That," Donovan said, "is the whole problem with cops in a nutshell. Most don't know how to unburden their feelings; they think crying is unmanly. So they keep it in, and it kills them. Something about the death of a dog opens up the only chink they'll allow in the armour."

The loss of this dog carried a special significance for Donovan. A gift from his mother when he first sobered up, the white toy poodle had been his faithful companion for fifteen years. She symbolized his rebirth and new-found zest for life, and she was the security blanket he clung to in moments of vulnerability.

The turmoil of his stress counselling, and now the loss of Suzanne, made him want to stop the treadmill he was on and take a look at what was happening to him. Stopping at the park would give him some time to think.

It was early spring, and there was a special crispness, freshness, and hope in the air. It was an atmosphere of birth rather than death. Donovan thought of the irony of this as he stepped from his car and walked toward the opposite side of the park. He had stopped here many times with Suzanne. Instinctively, he glanced back to make sure Suzanne hadn't wandered onto the road. His heart sank as he thought, "How long will it take for me to stop doing that?"

Donovan looked young for his fifty-three years and the many battles he'd fought. His wiry body was lithe, the age only showing on his vein-corded hands and laugh-lined face. His full head of red hair, ruffled by the breeze, had rusted a bit with age. His light blue eyes were piercing and sad. Five feet, ten inches tall, the freckle-skinned Donovan had weighed a skinny 135 pounds when he originally wanted to join the Boston Police. He had force-fed himself bananas and lifted weights to make the department weight limit. Now, twenty-eight years later, he was a lean 150 pounds of nervous energy, always on the go, always seemingly able to find some reserve strength and energy when exhaustion threatened to drag him down.

Donovan briskly crossed the park, a solitary figure in the bright morning light. He walked with his upper body tilted forward, moving in a knife-like manner as if he were battling a headwind. He was an emotional contradiction. Excitable, dynamic, energetic, a natural extrovert, Donovan talked a mile a minute in his South Boston "Southie" twang and laughed in a staccato manner but was able to shut up and listen when he counselled. He knew most problems could be helped if you just closed your mouth and opened your ears and heart while a person talked about their problems and feelings. That was the basis of the whole stress program: get people with the same problem together and talk about it. There was nothing fancy or scientific about it, it just worked.

Donovan had always had a helping nature, but he had never had confidence in himself or his abilities. After the summer of 1970 when he became sober, he stayed in ID and Photography for a year and a half, and on his own time gradually became more involved with AA and with helping troubled cops. Two patrolmen, Joe Ravino and Gus Guthro, approached Robert di Grazia, the new commissioner of the Boston Police Department (BPD), with the idea of a stress program. Because di Grazia was an outsider, brought in from St. Louis to shake up the department, he welcomed the innovative idea. If nothing else, it was good PR for him, and would upset the status quo. He transferred Ravino and Guthro into training and research in the summer of 1972 to study the viability and need for a stress program. Late in 1972, they noticed the work Donovan was doing with alcoholics and asked him to join them. Donovan was reluctant; determined to show he was a good cop, he was busy taking courses and studying for advancement to a supervisor's position.

But the chance to help others attracted him, and for the next year and a half he worked with Ravino and Guthro in the pioneer stages of the program, while still taking courses to become a supervisor. Sucessfully handling his studies and the challenging work on the stress program showed Donovan he had abilities. His self-confidence grew. At this critical time, he read Selye's books and studied his philosophy of stress.

After Gus Guthro died of cancer in 1973, Ravino and Donovan carried on the research. At this time, they sent a letter surveying all major police forces throughout the United States regarding stress. Responses showed 95 percent had no program, and only a few had department chaplains or psychologists. Philadelphia and New York had an in-house alcohol program, as Boston had had for years, but no one was dealing directly with stress.

During this same period, Donovan and Ravino started lecturing an hour every second day at the police academy to in-service training classes, telling them about stress and about the proposed stress program. For Donovan, his knees knocking and heart pounding, going in front of his peers was a traumatic experience. The classes weren't receptive, but he persevered, talking candidly about his own problems. His sincerity relaxed their defences, and they began to listen. Once Donovan felt their acceptance, his confidence soared.

"We'd ask the classes, 'How many of you would seek help through a shrink? How many would go to a chaplain or an outside agency?' Ninety-nine percent said they would never go outside. Most didn't believe in God and trusted no one. It was the cop's disease: paranoia. A few on their last legs would go to the alcohol program. Yet privately, they'd admit they had problems and needed help. They were relieved others felt the way they did, because they thought they were going nuts."

After the lectures, cops from the class would corner Donovan and Ravino and say:

"Too bad you didn't have this three years ago when I got divorced."

"They needed this five years ago when my partner committed suicide."

"I wish they had had this eleven years ago when I was studying for sergeant and fell apart."

"The classes saw our sincerity and openess and trusted us because we'd been there," Donovan says. "As a result we were getting people asking us where they could go for help. They'd want to meet us afterwards, to have coffee with us — anything to talk to us. They'd give us the names of policemen who were hurting or had problems, and we'd go out and track them down. We were in business before we even got started. It showed us peer counselling was the right approach."

They were ready to start the stress program officially, but police brass and the union opposed it. Commissioner di Grazia had been shaking up the department since his arrival, forcing out his foes. Few who remained trusted his motives, and the stress program was regarded as his baby.

The union fought by threatening to throw Donovan and Ravino out. "He's just using you guys. As soon as he finds out who the problem officers are, he's going to fire them," a union official told them.

"Joe and I drew up a draft of the program," Donovan said. "We showed how it would operate, pointing to its confidentiality, and presented it to the union, but they would holler and scream and walk out of the meetings." Trying to develop a set of guidelines for the program acceptable to both union and police brass proved impossible. Donovan and Ravino kept rewriting the proposal and trying again, but each time the union rejected it, banged their fists on the table and left. The brass looked at the proposal coldly and always found holes in it. They feared losing their power to discipline or fire problem officers. "No," Donovan insisted, "we're only here as a counselling service to help police officers and their families. We don't do discipline — that's your job — to supervise and discipline. The union looks out for the legal aspects and protects the job. We look out for the officer's mental and physical well-being." Donovan and Ravino fought for the program for over a year, while more and more officers heard about the centre by word of mouth and sought their help.

Ravino and Donovan wanted the program to be autonomous of police headquarters. Not even the top police administrators would have access to the centre's files or know who used the program. Donovan established a simple record keeping system of three-by-five-inch file cards with as little information on them as possible. Donovan knew any officer who came for help and saw notes being taken would be suspicious, so mostly he carried the cases in his head. Gradually, the program earned the cops' trust, and reluctantly the union agreed to the operation of the stress program on a trial basis.

Commissioner di Grazia issued the general order for the program to open officially on July 1, 1974. At this point, Donovan made a commitment to the program and dropped his ambitions to be a supervisor. Di Grazia ordered the entire command staff to meet with Donovan and Ravino and hear about the program. Di Grazia told command staff they were no longer to transfer a problem officer elsewhere, or cover up his problem but were to send him to the stress program.

"It would have been wonderful if it had happened that way but it didn't," Donovan said. "They didn't like it one bit. They didn't like listening to two patrolmen telling them how to do their job. They felt the program usurped their power. Two of the upper echelon felt if an officer had a problem, he should be fired outright. Ironically, both of them came to the program for help later for family members. It changed their whole attitude about the program."

The program moved into space in an office building a few blocks from police headquarters. The department chaplains, the hospital liaison officer, and Joe Kelly from the alcohol program were ordered to be part of the stress program. Eventually, the alcohol program was absorbed into the stress program, while the chaplains and the hospital liaison officer, never happy at being grouped with the program anyway, went their separate ways. The program was partially funded at this point by a small grant from the Law Enforcement Assistance Agency, a federal agency that no longer exists. Some of the funds were used to start a volunteer component to the stress centre, allowing twenty-nine officers to take a Boston University extension course on counselling skills.

Donovan's compulsive nature turned to a thirst for knowledge about stress and counselling. He joined all sorts of groups and organizations to learn about stress and the services available in the mental health community. He attended suicide conferences, marital conferences, addiction conferences, anything there was in the Boston area, whether it was a course at Harvard or just a small community meeting. He studied psychology and read voraciously, even women's magazines because they had many articles dealing with emotions and coping. He learned all he could about the medical side of stress by taking courses and studying physiology, pharmacology, and psychopharmacology. He took courses on transcendental meditation, yoga, visualization, and biofeedback. He sought out people who ran self-help groups and programs and learned that what the stress program was trying to do was right on course.

However, much of what he had to learn wasn't available in books or lecture halls. Donovan had to develop his own counselling philosophy and techniques, using his experience, his common sense, and his feel for people.

He knew he couldn't wear a three-piece suit and sit in an office waiting for cops to come to him. He'd have to be a motivator, a salesman selling mental health and well-being, so he operated like a new business trying to carve out a market share by working harder, smarter, and longer than anyone else.

He saw police men and women as little kids in grown-ups' suits. They became cops for idealistic reasons, to help people and catch crooks, but after finding out what police work was really like their fears, doubts, and disillusionments were trapped inside them by the uniform and the image that went with it. The result was early burn-out and a variety of medical and personal problems. There was no doubt the job changed them; Donovan heard that from every police wife who had known her husband before he was a cop.

Donovan saw some cops reach out for help, but most retreated into the problem, making the same mistakes, afraid to change. If he couldn't crack their barriers, they'd never be helped. Donovan had to convince them it was a sign of strength to reach for help rather than a sign of weakness. He eventually developed a repertoire of tricks and ploys to get them in the door of the stress centre.

Once in the door, the group sessions broke down the final barriers to accepting help. "In a peer group, he's talking to people who've been through the same thing. As a result," Donovan would say, "he can't bullshit them like he can others. He's forced to deal honestly with his problem."

By nature, Donovan wanted people to like him, but what often worked best for him in counselling cops was being "Mr. Prick." He goaded them, angered them, pushed them to the wall, anything to make them talk, but he was also a highly skilled and talented communicator. A friend's mother once remarked, "Eddie, you have the ability of making people talk to you whether they want to or not. It's a God-given gift."

Donovan developed a "paper towel system" of counselling: if one approach didn't work, throw it away and try another one. He was always reading, talking to others, listening to new ideas, and willing to risk trying something new.

He learned that timing was crucial. If an alcoholic cop called begging for help at four in the morning, Donovan would convince him to be admitted to a detox hospital, then drive over, pick the man up, and deliver him to the hospital. Donovan knew if he waited till morning, or sent someone else, the man would change his mind. "Marrying them" he called it, "forming a bond at a critical moment. If you didn't, it might take weeks to get him back to the same point."

He was plugged into the police grapevine, with friends in every department and every sub-station. "When a situation goes down," Donovan said with satisfaction, "I know exactly what everyone is thinking."

As the program grew, Donovan saw the need for preventive measures and convinced the department to let the stress program educate brand new recruits for a day before they hit the street. The classes were held in the stress centre's living room, so the rookies knew where the stress centre was and what the atmosphere was like. From his success with the rookies, Donovan coined the phrase "blue inoculation," and police forces all over the world followed his lead. "Instead of getting a man over forty, on his third marriage and a fullfledged alcoholic, we get the young guy before the problems are irreversible. With rookies, the biggest problem is their fear of the street. You can see it in their body language. In class we plant the seed of seeking help and many would call months later saying, 'I thought what you said was bullshit, but it's happening to me now. Can you help me?' "

Donovan held spouse training sessions for the rookies' wives. What most departments called spouse training was allowing the wife to ride around in a police car and shoot the gun at the range. Donovan thought that was "bullshit." "They've got to learn about the emotional side of the job, the stress and what it can do to their husbands and how it affects kids and marriages and what to do about it." They held the groups in the stress centre and brought in experienced police wives to talk to them. In the following months and years, a rookie's wife would often call for help for herself or her reluctant husband.

Cops, fearing recognition, were still reluctant to come to the stress centre's downtown location. This spurred Donovan and Ravino, in 1976, to find the house at the Mattapan Chronic Hospital grounds. They fixed up the old place, giving the stress program a real home. The privacy of the new location dramatically increased the flow of officers. When Joe Ravino retired in 1979, Donovan took complete control of the program with two full-time counsellors working for him.

But from the start, the heart of the stress program was its system of volunteer counsellors, and Donovan is quick to give them the credit they deserve. The full-time people could not reach everyone. The more people in the trenches who could take a troubled officer aside at work and point him in the direction of help, the better. Donovan trained them, and, when there were funds available, some took university counselling courses.

In 1981 a tax-cutting measure, Proposition 2½ caused crippling lay-offs on the already shorthanded 1,600-man force. The administration put Donovan's two full-time people back on the street and told him he was next. Eventually, six hundred officers were laid off. The result was many troubled people: those who were laid off and those over-worked and demoralized officers who remained. Donovan and the few volunteer helpers he had phoned as many laid-off officers as they could and wrote to the rest. Mary, the woman Donovan lived with and would soon marry, spent hours at the stress centre answering the phone and counsel-ling troubled officers and wives as Donovan ran from crisis to crisis.

More officers were laid off and the situation worsened. Donovan asked Commissioner Joseph Jordon for permis-sion to recruit more volunteers and have the department recognize their efforts so the supervisors wouldn't think the volunteers were being unproductive when they stopped their regular duties for a moment to help a troubled officer.

Jordon gave Donovan the permission he needed. The thirty volunteers worked mainly on their own time, often at great sacrifice to themselves and their families, but the program, despite many serious problems, survived the lay-offs.

Eventually everyone was hired back, but because of the opposition to the program by some superintendents, Dono-van never got back his full-time counsellors. The volun-teers who stayed on were the pieces of glue that held the scattered structure together. But while they were always well intentioned, sometimes there were problems.

When Donovan went out of town on a speaking engage-ment, someone would take his beeper and handle emer-gency calls. One time the officer covering for Donovan was a dispatcher working the turret, the communications con-trol centre. A suicidal officer, Bert Gee, with gun in hand, phoned the stress centre number begging for help. The dispatcher knew the officer but was very busy with police calls.

"I can't take it any more . . . " the man said, but the dispatcher had to interrupt.

"Hang on Bert, I've got to take a call." Twenty seconds later he returned to Bert, but Bert spoke about three words and the dispatcher had to interrupt again for another call. Suddenly over the phone the dispatcher heard "Bang." Then silence.

"Bert . . . Bert . . . are you okay?" he shouted into the phone.

"Bang . . . bang." Two more shots, then he heard nothing. He quickly dispatched two squad cars to the house. The officers ran into the house and found Bert, the smoking gun still in his hand, sitting at the kitchen table eating a tuna fish sandwich. Next to him was a suicide note written on a brown paper lunch bag. The officer picked up the dangling phone still connected to the turret and told the anxious dispatcher, "Bert's okay, but he's just killed his dishwasher." The frustrated Bert had blasted three bullets into his portable dishwasher, which now sat mortally wounded, in a pool of water on the other side of the kitchen.

Two volunteers from the stress program rushed over and calmed Bert. They smoothed things over with his wife and children who had arrived home in the meantime. The next day the volunteers came by and took Bert and the dishwasher to a neighbourhood appliance store. The store owner offered Bert twenty-five dollars for his machine. Not about to look a gift horse in the mouth, Bert accepted and went home happily with a new dishwasher.

The old one now hangs suspended over the main counter in the appliance store. On it is a sign. "IF WE CAN'T FIX IT, YOU MIGHT AS WELL SHOOT IT."

When Donovan returned from his trip, he convinced Bert, an alcoholic for twenty years, to be admitted to an alcohol treatment centre. He dried out and in the two years since, has been a highly respected attender at the group meetings and one of Donovan's ablest volunteers. The volunteers are all people who came to the program with problems and who, in turn, now help others.

Donovan had a concise description of the stress centre's work. "We save marriages, careers, and lives . . . Jesus, it's so fucking simple. All you need is a few people who care."

Donovan could easily have quit to go to a better paying and more rewarding job elsewhere, but his roots and commitment to the BPD went too deep. During this difficult period, he was hospitalized several times for stress-related problems.

But Donovan was a survivor. He was three parts Irish, which gave him toughness, character, and humour, and one part German, which gave him the stubbornness to hang in. He was a tattered and battered rebel — a Don Quixote tilting at establishment windmills. Now back on his horse, he jousted with the unions, the police commissioner, and the psychologists, whose established way of dealing with stress-related problems was to ignore them or cover them up.

Donovan reached the far side of the park, sat on a bench, threw his head back, took a deep relaxing breath, and studied the magnificence of Boston from afar. The city looked tranquil, peaceful, and beautiful, like a sleeping giant. Donovan felt much better now. The vitality in the air and the grandeur of the view were awakening him to the continuing challenge of his work, and he did have a busy day ahead of him. He also had a plan to get some help for the program.

Donovan turned off River Street into the winding driveway that arced around the barren grounds of the Mattapan Chronic Disease Hospital. Its ancient, poorly maintained brick buildings, some abandoned, sat far back from River Street, giving it the depressing look of a prison. Donovan drove slowly around the narrow driveway to the far side of the grounds where two large, old, white frame houses stood. Forty years ago they were elegant doctors' residences; now they were weatherbeaten reminders of the better days of the hospital. The least attractive of the two, badly rundown and in need of a paint job, housed the stress program. In front of the house, a crude sign with the lettering, "Boston Police Stress Program," burnt in wood, hung precariously from a rotted post. Unkempt grass, brush, trees, and vegetation of all kinds attacked the house from three sides. The only usable entrance to the house was the side door on the fourth side. Next to it, two abandoned cars sat forlornly on a concrete parking pad. Donovna pulled in behind the cars, glanced at the battered house, looked at the mess around it, and then silently thanked God that he at least had this.

Donovan climbed the three steps to the side entrance, unlocked the door, and went in. "God-damned slobs, they're worse than a bunch of kids," Donovan said when he saw the mess of paper cups and filled ashtrays littering the tiny kitchen and the large main meeting room that had been left by a group who used the house the night before. The program didn't have the luxury of hired help.

Donovan was the whole program, its one paid employee, chief cook and bottle washer, and right now the janitor as he scurried around cleaning up the mess for the group due in ten minutes. Donovan and some volunteers had recently knocked out a wall on the main floor to join the ground floor living room and dining room into one large area, big enough to hold the thirty or forty who now attended the major group meetings. The sides and one end of the room were lined with surplus metal stacking chairs. At the far end was a table. On the tattered walls around the room were a few plaques, newspaper clippings, some cartoons, and an abundance of hand lettered slogans: "Build bridges, not walls."

A sitting room, connected to the living room by a wide archway, provided a cozy meeting area at the back of the house. A staircase in the corner led to the second floor where Donovan had his office. The sitting room had the luxury of an old chesterfield and a battered coffee table in addition to some mismatched chairs. An old but workable fireplace and some faded wood panelling gave the room an air of warmth. A rack in the corner of the sitting room was stuffed with health care literature. Donovan held the smaller group meetings in the sitting room, just as he would a few minutes from now. He needed the relaxed atmosphere the room provided for his more difficult groups, for example those meetings for cops who'd killed and for those who'd been shot or seriously injured. This morning's eleven o'clock meeting was for an even tougher group. Just thinking about it made Donovan edgy.

He cursed at the dilapidated coffee urn as it balked at his initial attempts to brew the coffee for the meeting. Finally outwilling the machine, he hurried upstairs to his office to check the telephone answering machine and plan his hectic day. After the group this morning, he had his weekly lecture at the police academy in the afternoon, then the regular Wednesday night stress meeting. In between, he'd fit in numerous phone calls, individual counselling, ILESA and *Police Stress Magazine* business. Any moment, the beeper he had at his side twenty-four hours a day could come to life, signalling another crisis for him to handle. It usually did several times a day; often in the middle of the night.

Donovan was always at the ready. On his desk were his stacks of three by five cards, neatly arranged, which served as his notes for each case he handled. His office was neat and efficient, and the two phones on his desk rang continuously. The walls were covered with memorabilia, awards, and treasured photos: Donovan with Joseph Wambaugh, Donovan with Steve McQueen, Donovan with Hans Selye.

Down the hall from Donovan's office was a network of small rooms. One contained a donated photo copier, another *Police Stress Magazine* material, another a sitting room with uninviting, dusty furniture, then a tiny room where Donovan kept a cot for his catnaps, and another small room where the real cat napped. Donovan had the program's pregnant cat and resident mouser locked there. He'd had her for three years now and was afraid she'd head up to her favourite perch on the roof to have her litter, due any day. Next to Donovan's office was the washroom. The building had sagged so much, the doorframe hung at an angle so it automatically swung wide open. As a result, the wives' groups had developed tremendous kidney power.

The sound of cars in the parking lot, the back door opening, and voices filtering up from the kitchen told Donovan the men were here for the meeting. He quickly finished with his notes and instinctively reached under his desk to give Suzanne a pat. He slowly looked down to see her blanket, still twirled and bunched into that comfortable kind of nest that dogs love to make. He looked sadly at it for a minute.

"Hey, Donovan, you hiding up there?" boomed a voice from the sitting room below.

"Hold your horses," Donovan bellowed back. He slowly rose and swallowed the lump in his throat. He was almost at the door, then stopped, went back, picked up Suzanne's blanket and neatly folded it into a compact bundle. His eyes moistened as he tightly clutched it to his sore side, breathing in for the last time what remained of the faint smell of Suzanne in the blanket.

"Hey Donovan, you got a woman up there? There's a bunch of customers down here that need your help."

CHAPTER TWO
LONNIE

Wednesday, 11:15 A.M.

"This fucking job killed him, it killed my boy," shouted Charlie Gilham between sobs. He was crying uncontrollably. The burly, six-foot, 220-pound, forty-year-old detective buried his head in his massive hands and rocked from side to side.

The six men seated around the battered coffee table in the stress centre's sitting room looked at Gilham compassionately, tears welling up in their own eyes. They knew what Charlie was going through. Each of the others in the room had lost a child through suicide. One month before, Gilham's fifteen-year-old son Lonnie had taken his dad's service revolver and blown his brains out.

From his chair opposite Gilham, Eddie Donovan surveyed his small group and silently thanked God this was one common police tragedy he had been spared. He looked down at the table, its surface bearing mute testimony to the hundreds of groups Donovan had led. Dozens of burn marks from cigarettes forgotten in moments of agony spotted the surface. Donovan had seen the table pounded on, kicked, and cried on while he urged, begged, and prodded his fellow officers to bare their feelings and let out the hurt. Groups of alcoholics and addicts, those who had been shot and those who were suicidal, all battled their problems round this old table. But no group was tougher for Donovan to run than this one.

For these cops, the stresses and strains of their jobs reached past their own lives and affected their children, the innocent victims of society's contempt for their fathers' job. Donovan repeatedly saw these suicides tear away the hearts

35

and souls of police officers and their families. He wished these deaths were isolated occurrences, but cops from patrol officers to police chiefs shared this pain. It had no respect for rank. If the Boston area was any indicator, each year more than 500 children of police officers in the United States and Canada kill themselves. Sometimes, the botched attempts were the worst: a misplaced bullet to the head, leaving the kid a vegetable. Some parents did not seek help, so the child attempted suicide again and again. And Donovan had to handle the ugly consequences. There was no one else to do it. At least, no one a cop would talk to. Donovan was currently counselling twenty cops who were going through this hell, and he had no idea how many more there were whom he hadn't heard about. The previous week, the six men who were at the suicide group meeting had recalled 102 children of officers they knew of who had committed suicide in the past five years in the Boston area.

Charlie Gilham's behaviour after the suicide followed an all too familiar pattern. He resisted all offers of help. Donovan knew from experience that Charlie was questioning his competence as a man and as a father, and was feeling responsible for his son's death — almost as if he had pulled the trigger himself.

Charlie refused to talk to his superiors, refused psychological services, wouldn't talk to his priest or even his wife about his feelings. He wouldn't even visit his son's grave. The loss cut too deeply. He became depressed and aloof, causing his family and friends to worry about him. Four days ago he had submitted his resignation to the department. The chief didn't want to lose Gilham or see him throw his career aside, so he called Eddie Donovan asking for help. It had taken Donovan two phone calls and a personal visit to convince the reluctant Gilham to attend today's group session. Donovan wanted to be sure it went well.

From the twenty cops he was counselling, Donovan carefully chose six for this group. The right mix was important, because today's meeting could be a matter of life and death.

If all went well, Gilham would be put on the road to accepting and living with his son's suicide. Otherwise, Donovan
knew that Gilham, too, might commit suicide. Donovan
had seen this happen a number of times.

If anyone could get through to Charlie Gilham, it would
be this group. Physically, the six men were very different,
but one thing was the same — they were cops — cops who
shared what is probably the worst tragedy that can befall a
parent. Their eyes mirrored a sadness and hurt the years
would never erase.

Joe Lenthome's fourteen-year-old daughter had slashed
her wrists in her parents' bed while they were out of the
house. Ray Mazetti's seventeen-year-old son jumped to his
death from an apartment balcony. Darren Onchar and
Wayne Gashman both had sixteen-year-old sons who had
killed themselves with their fathers' guns. Harvey Allen's
thirteen-year-old daughter took a drug overdose, and Gord
Weise's fifteen-year-old boy hanged himself.

Donovan knew each suicide carried the same message
loud and clear: "Fuck you and fuck your job, Dad." It
wasn't easy being a cop's kid. It often meant that you had
an authoritarian, demanding father who was obsessed with
his own children's safety because he regularly had to, for
example, pull the bodies of drunken teenagers from twisted
car wreckages. You might be mocked and teased cruelly at
school because of your father's work. And your neighbourhood might be no better. Neighbours often won't associate with the cop or his family.

Donovan looked over at Gilham, who was being com-
forted by Lenthome and Mazetti. They had their arms
around the big detective and were gently giving him encouragement. After a few minutes, Gilham straightened in
his seat, shook his head sadly, then looked at the faces
around him. Donovan sat up straighter as he sensed an
opportunity to make Gilham talk. He wanted Gilham to
tell the story of what happened to his son. It might be cruel
to put him through this process, but it worked. "Venting,"

it's called. Talk about it, talk about your feelings and fears, talk about what's bothering you, get out all the pent-up emotions. You can talk to a brother officer about things you might not tell your wife, a priest, or a police department psychologist. Another cop had been there. Another cop would understand.

Charlie took a long, slow, deliberate drink from the glass of ice water in front of him. He swished a second sip around his mouth for a few seconds before swallowing it, then put the glass down and dipped two fingers into the glass to bathe his bloodshot eyes. He took two tissues from the box on the table and methodically wiped the tears, water, and sweat from his face.

He looked at the patient but expectant faces around the table and nervously cleared his throat. Everyone in the group knew that if Charlie's life was ever to mean anything again, he had to talk. They waited. Slowly, for the first time, Charlie Gilham began talking about the hurt he had been living with for the past month.

"He was such a good kid," Gilham said. "Good marks, a help at home, loved to play ball with me. He was my best friend, my pal, but the job killed him. Who'd want to be the kid of a cop? The crap he heard at school: 'Your old man's a pig. Who's paying him off now? I hear he has a different hooker every night down on the drag.'

"How can your kid hear that every day at school or out on the streets and not be affected by it?" Charlie's eyes were glazed with frustration and anger.

Charlie Gilham was a good cop. Seventeen years on the Danville Police Force. Two meritorious service awards. Proud to be a detective. No desk job for him. He joined the police force for the action and challenge, and that's what he got: five years on patrol, ten years in criminal investigation, and the last two years in juvenile. He asked for the switch to this unit when his own kids were growing into their teens, because he loved kids and wanted to help them with their problems. He knew the teenage years were the toughest, so he felt he could do the most good as a policeman by working in juvenile.

He was a tough father, but what cop wasn't. He loved his children, particularly his eldest, Lonnie, because there was a strong affinity between the two. Charlie saw a lot of himself in the boy.

Lonnie felt the normal pressures of being a policeman's kid; the odd insult here, a cruel remark there, but he seemed tough enough to handle it.

Charlie's well-intentioned switch to juvenile tested Lonnie's toughness. Danville was small enough that people knew who did what to whom. If Charlie made a drug bust, the kids knew it, and Lonnie had to pay. One day a gang from school cornered him in a downtown confectionery store, knocked him down, and poured quarts of milk over him. He was harassed again and again, and eventually he became ostracized from the rest of the kids. Blaming his father, he struck back the only way a kid knows. He rebelled. He joined the "bad" crowd. He smoked more, drank more, and started stealing. Soon, Lonnie was in trouble with the law and causing his Dad embarrassment in front of his fellow officers. They didn't say anything, but Charlie knew what they were thinking: "What kind of a father is he anyway?"

The week before his son died was a particularly rough one for Charlie: hassles with the job, hassles with Lonnie at home. He was mentally and physically exhausted when he finished his final shift of the week, Friday afternoon.

No one was home as he trudged wearily up the stairs to the bedroom. His wife and two girls were out shopping. Lonnie was at a friend's. That suited Charlie just fine. He wasn't in the mood to talk to anyone. He just wanted to get out of his suit and into some jeans and a sweat shirt and sit down with a beer.

"Ah, Christ," he muttered under his breath. Things were getting to him. He had forgotten to leave his gun at work, a Colt. 38 service revolver. He never brought it home. Charlie was almost paranoid about that. He made a clear division between home and work, because he'd seen too many cops flaunt their guns to their family and their neighbours. For Charlie, the less his family saw of the tools of his trade, the better.

Charlie unbuckled the shoulder harness that held his revolver tightly to the side of his chest. He took it off and hung it in the back of the closet, thinking it would be safe there until Monday.

Downstairs, Charlie opened a beer and settled in front of the television for an hour of rest and relaxation. Later, he and his wife were to spend the evening at a neighbour's playing bridge, but Charlie didn't want to go. He thought momentarily about cancelling, but knew it wouldn't be fair to his wife. She looked forward to the weekend and social occasions that didn't revolve around Charlie's job and other policemen.

Despite Charlie's apprehension, the evening went well. The card game and idle chatter helped him put his problems aside for awhile, and he even managed to enjoy himself. He was up first thing Saturday to go across town and help his brother-in-law lay a new concrete driveway. Charlie welcomed diversions like these from Lonnie and the fights they now had so frequently. Charlie wasn't one to skirt trouble, but he didn't have the emotional energy to deal with any tension this weekend.

Charlie felt tired but cleansed by the hard work of the morning when he arrived home in the early afternoon. Again, everyone was out. Charlie wanted to get out of his dirty clothes and wash up, but before he had a chance, the phone rang.

It was Barbara Demeter, the mother of Lonnie's best friend.

"Charlie, I don't want to alarm you, but something strange is happening with Lonnie. He's going around to all his friends and saying goodbye. You're not moving, are you?" Charlie slammed the phone down. His policeman's instincts told him what was happening. He ran up the stairs to the master bedroom, his heart pounding. The gun was gone. "Jesus Christ—no, no, no." In a flash, Charlie bolted down the stairs, out the back door to the driveway, and into the car.

Charlie floor-boarded his beat up Pinto. He knew exactly where to find Lonnie. "Come on, you gutless wonder," he screamed at the Pinto. Charlie clenched his teeth until the muscles in his jaw bulged. His race to the community playground, a mile from the house, seemed to take forever. "Lonnie, you've got to be there," Charlie prayed. Lonnie always went there when he was happy or when he was upset or depressed. It's where Charlie had taught him how to play ball, where he proudly watched him hit his first little league home run.

Charlie burst out of the Pinto and ran toward the play area in the centre of the park. His professional training had taught him again and again that people are creatures of habit. "Please be there, Lonnie, please be there," he urged.

Then he spotted Lonnie, sitting on top of the playhouse he used to love hiding in as a kid. Lonnie's head popped up at the sight of his father running towards him. Charlie slowed slightly when he saw the .38 in his son's right hand.

Lonnie jumped down and started to run away aimlessly.

"Lonnie, wait, Lonnie, stop." There was no response as Charlie tried to pursue his son.

"Lonnie, I love you, please stop. I'm not going to hurt you. Wait I love you!" Lonnie was a hundred feet ahead of his father and running effortlessly.

"Lonnie, please stop, I beg you. I forgive you. I'm sorry." Charlie was breathing heavily. He realized he wouldn't be able to catch the boy.

Suddenly, Lonnie stopped. Like a slow-motion replay on television, he turned to face his father. Lonnie slowly raised the gun and pointed it to his right temple. Charlie stopped immediately, about thirty feet away from his son.

"No, no, no, don't do it. I love you. I love you." Charlie

was close enough to see the pained expression in Lonnie's eyes. It said, "Fuck You, Mr. Cop."

Lonnie pulled the trigger. Fifteen years of love, nurturing, and hope crumpled at Charlie's feet into a lifeless, bleeding corpse. The type of corpse Charlie had seen so often as a cop. Now it was his son, his flesh and blood.

He kneeled over Lonnie, frantically trying to shake some life into him. He removed the gun from his son's limp hand.

"Please live Lonnie, please live. I'm sorry, I'm sorry." Lonnie's lifeless eyes stared blankly at Charlie. He shook him some more. The cop in Charlie knew Lonnie was dead but the father in him clung to a thread of hope that Lonnie would begin to breathe again.

The kick to Charlie's head toppled him to his side. Two strangers kicked and punched Charlie into semi-consciousness. He didn't know what was happening. He saw people running at him from all sides.

"This bastard just shot the kid. Call an ambulance. Call the police." Charlie's face was forced into the dirt, moist with the blood and liquid from his son's head. His arms were wrenched behind his back. Someone jammed his own gun, its barrel still smoking, into the back of his head.

"You big fucking coward."

Two more kicks to the head drove Charlie into unconsciousness. He welcomed it. The pain was too much. All this happened a month ago, but here in Eddie Donovan's group the pain was as if it happened yesterday. Charlie sobbed lightly as he finished his story.

"My job killed him," Charlie whispered. Then, more forcefully, he said, "Being the son of a cop killed him." He looked up at the other group members and then turned to Donovan.

"Why?" he asked. "Why?"

Donovan had no simple answer. Nothing was going to bring back Lonnie or the other kids. But Donovan knew he could save Charlie Gilham, save him from the same fate that claimed his son. Crying and unleashing his feelings was a major step, and Charlie had also seen there were others who suffered just like him. Donovan really couldn't do much more today, but in subsequent meetings Donovan and the group would tackle Gilham's feelings of guilt and his reluctance to visit the grave.

CHAPTER THREE
POLICE ACADEMY

Wednesday, 1:00 P.M.

Donovan still had a big chunk of day ahead of him as he hustled upstairs to his office, leaving Charlie Gilham and a few others talking downstairs. He had half an hour to squeeze some work into the day's busy schedule of meetings. He stood and sorted his mail while taking phone messages from his answering machine. Then, sitting at his desk, he returned the most important calls while reading his mail and making notes. When his other phone rang, he put his pen down and worked both phones at the same time like a busy stockbroker.

Donovan had four other groups like the kids' suicide group this morning that met regularly for specific stress problems. There was a group for officers who'd been shot or injured that met Thursday mornings, another for cops' wives on Thursday evenings, one for alcoholic cops on Monday evenings, and a group on Tuesday mornings for officers who'd killed or injured suspects in the line of duty.

Tonight's general meeting for a variety of stress-related problems had the largest attendance and was the focal point of the week. Many of the officers who attended counselling in the specialized groups also came to this meeting. Attendance at all the meetings was voluntary, but cops with problems were encouraged by their supervisors or fellow officers to come. However, Eddie Donovan's understanding of the word encouragement had stronger connotations. "Kick ass" more accurately described his interpretation as he picked up the phone to call some officers who missed the last few meetings.

"Ron, it's Eddie Donovan calling. Where've you been the past few weeks?" Donovan drummed his fingers impatiently on the desk as Ron gave his excuse.

"You know my phone number, you could have given me a call. How are things going?"

Pause.

"Doesn't sound so terrific to me."

Pause.

"Yeah, well I finally realized I couldn't do it myself. Who the hell are you? The Lone Ranger doing it on your own? Even Tonto comes to our meetings."

Pause.

"Are you gonna get over here tonight?"

Pause.

"Bowling! Screw bowling. What're you gonna do, bowl ten lines and think your problems will go away? I haven't heard of that cure before."

Pause.

"Look brother, I've been talking to a few people at the station, and I haven't heard too many good things about how you're doin'."

Pause.

"You just get your ass over here tonight, and you'll find out. Come over here and take your medicine like a man."

Pause.

"I'll see you at 7:30 sharp."

Donovan slammed the receiver down and dialed again. He finished the calls at 1:30 P.M. and slipped out for a quick sandwich on the run at the neighbourhood diner. He drove the few miles from the stress centre to the Boston Police Academy in nearby Hyde Park, where he lectured to new recruits and veteran cops at in-service training classes. His visits provided him with a special opportunity — they gave him the chance to practise preventive medicine.

Donovan spent most of his time firefighting — dealing with problems after they'd taken their toll on a career, on a marriage, or on physical or mental health. Donovan's ambitious plans for the stress program emphasised preventive measures: get to the cop before he had a problem, teach him to recognize trouble signs and to learn what to do about them. He wanted to visit every roll call, have classes for wives, for female cops, even help for the gay and lesbian cops, now a significant number on most police forces. He also wanted to run health and nutrition seminars and teach biofeedback and other stress reduction techniques. But to do that he needed a budget and manpower. Most of his time now was spent on crisis intervention, salvaging what he could from bad situations.

Consequently Donovan valued the opportunity the academy presented. Rather than handing out life jackets and throwing out life lines, he was teaching cops to swim in the turbulent sea they would face. The rookies with their wide-eyed naivety were shocked by his revelations of the situations they'd encounter and the havoc the job could cause. They were easy for him to reach and teach.

What Donovan relished most though was facing the tough-nut vets, the twenty-year cops who were still patrolmen and would be for their entire careers. Their arms would be crossed and their proud chests puffed out in defiance when Donovan entered the classroom. They didn't want to be there. What could they learn? They could take all the crap and hand it back two-fold, because they'd been on the street for their entire working lives, and that was the classroom that counted.

Getting them to listen was a challenge, and Donovan loved it. It wasn't his style to pussyfoot around in a situation where much of the audience was potentially hostile. He knew you had to flush out the toughest, hardest case then confront him and put him on the spot. It was like a duel, but the weapons were words and the ammunition was raw gut feelings. Right now, however, his biggest task was mustering the energy to give today's lecture. The suicide group had drained what little energy he had started with in the morning.

Donovan turned in to the parking lot behind the academy, once a concrete playground filled with kids and basketballs, now cluttered with police cars and spotted with oil stains. He parked at the back of the lot, hoping the walk around to the front door of the academy would refresh him.

"Hey, Donovan, we don't need any today," someone bellowed from a second floor window. The bright sunshine reflecting off the windows blocked Donovan's view, but he grinned and flashed the finger sign at his buddy, Harry Prefontaine, an instructor at the academy. Five years ago, Harry's shout would have represented the academy's unofficial policy toward the stress program. Now they were one of the few U.S. police academies incorporating stress training into their recruit and in-service programs.

When Donovan entered the building, Harry had some welcome news for him. His audience today would not be rookies or vets but senior officers in supervisory positions. They'd be a receptive audience, more open to Donovan's message, because they dealt directly with burnt out cops.

He waited impatiently in the hallway outside the classroom, listening to Harry introduce him to the class. Through the partially open door, Donovan saw some of the supervisors shuffle their feet and look around bored as Harry, carried away with his introduction, seemed intent on raising the status of Donovan to sainthood and of the stress program to divine intervention. Donovan couldn't take it any longer and burst into the room.

"Cut out the bullshit Harry, it's time to get the show on the road." Harry, red-faced, quickly exited. Donovan took a deep breath and surveyed his audience. He wore his customary slacks, open-necked shirt, and a sporty leather windbreaker. By contrast, most of the supervisors, thirty men and one woman, were in uniform or suits and ties.

"Now that I've got your attention, I want to ask you a

question." Donovan looked around at the faces in the room. "What is stress?"

"This group will be easy," he thought, watching them search for an answer. As supervisors, they were familiar with the stress their subordinates faced, but they also had their own problems and were under a lot more stress than those they supervised. They were squeezed from the top and the bottom: from a headquarters that demanded results and from the union-protected troops in the trenches they had to motivate and discipline.

"Okay, you've thought about it," Donovan said. "What's stress?"

"Something that concerns you," someone said uncertainly.

"Pressure," another joined in as Donovan nodded encouragement.

"Anger you can't get rid of."

"Problems you take home from work."

"Family problems."

"You're each right," Donovan shot back. "Even a newborn baby feels stress. You clap your hands to make a loud noise and the baby jumps. That's you every day on this job."

The class didn't know what to make of this dynamo who spoke in a machine-gun patter, but he certainly had their attention.

"Everyone has stress; the question is, how do you handle it? It's not the stress that's damaging," he told them, "but the destructive response to it. That's distress. It's what happens when you don't know how to open up to anyone. The macho tough guy image that cops carry around is a killer. God, I wish we could just take some paint remover and scrape it off." Donovan walked slowly to the side of the room, then whirled and said, "Have you noticed the ages of your brother officers who are dying from supposedly normal causes?" Donovan could see the supervisors, although outwardly controlled and disciplined, sag a bit and shift in their seats. "Most who are dying are in their late fifties. A white male is supposed to live till he's seventy-four. Why don't cops? There's new statistical evidence that shows being a cop could take twelve years off your life span."

The supervisors didn't return Donovan's piercing stare. "Gotcha," he thought, watching some fumble with the blank paper in front of them, or others look down to count their feet. Donovan sat on the edge of the instructor's desk, interlocked his fingers, adjusted his legs and then scrutinized the faces in front of him.

"How long does it take you to come down after you've had a tough call?" he asked. Some stared vacantly ahead as they considered the question.

"An hour," said the woman supervisor.

"Six quick beer."

"A day."

"As long as it takes to get home and jump into the sack with my wife," said a smirking detective at the back. Everyone chuckled but Donovan.

"You may think you've come down but you're only fooling yourself. What about the call to a sudden infant death? You get there ahead of the ambulance and the parents are screaming for you to do something for their child. You see she's dead, but they keep screaming at you. You pick up the dead child and press your mouth over hers and pretend to try mouth-to-mouth resuscitation. You feel the coldness of the limp body right through your lips down to your feet and you think of your own children.Every moment the parents' terror-filled eyes are on you hoping their precious child will live. You keep up the facade till the ambulance arrives five minutes later. Then you listen to their screams of horror when they finally realize their child is gone. They look at you angrily and their look says, 'Why couldn't you have done more?' How long does it take you to forget a call like that?" The supervisors, somber faced, some with eyes slightly moist, were silent.

"Never," one finally replied quietly.

For the next two hours, Donovan continued to hammer home his message about stress and its effects. He told them about his own background — his problems with drugs and alcohol, the difficulties in his marriage, his attempted suicide. He outlined the development of the stress program and indicated the things he felt still needed to be done. He quoted studies and statistics that showed that police had one of the highest rates of divorce, alcoholism and suicide of any occupation. One study showed that retired policemen had a suicide rate eleven times greater than the general population.

"Everyone talks about cops as being the strong, silent, macho John Wayne types," Donovan said, injecting his characteristic note of humour, "but you know, John Wayne's characters always knew it was okay to be afraid." His eyes sparkled, as he prepared to do his John Wayne imitation.

"He was coming ashore on Iwo Jima with Martin Milner and Milner said, 'I'm afraid.'

"John Wayne looked at him and said, 'You better be, pilgrim, I'm always afraid.'" Everyone laughed. Donovan had always wanted to be an entertainer, a comedian. Now he used those talents to bring life to his lectures. No one slept in his classes.

"How do your release your feelings, how do you keep from going nuts?" Donovan asked. "What do you do when there's a bunch of cops standing around a grisly scene?"

"We use humour," said the detective at the back. Everyone looked back at him, expecting a wisecrack, but he just shrugged his shoulders. "Stinkers and crispy critters," he finally said, "a partially decayed body is a stinker . . . burnt bodies are crispy critters."

"I remember when I was a rookie cop," Donovan said, "and I was called to my first death. This guy had had a fatal heart attack in a private playing room at a posh bridge club. He was sitting perfectly upright, nattily attired at the table with the cards still in his hands. The first two officers on the scene sat at the table with cards in their hands. One looked up at me as I walked wide-eyed into the room and said, 'For Christ's sake, kid. It's about time you got here. Sit down! We need a fourth.'" The supervisors laughed. "That's right," Donovan said. "Laugh, it's a release, it's a coping device.

"Do you know what happens to stress if you don't let it out? You end up hiding pain with pain. It goes to the weakest point of your body. Backache, headache, ileitis, colitis, ulcers." Several class members twisted uncomfortably in their seats as Donovan continued. "The way you handle stress determines how long you live. Your body tells you when your lifestyle sucks. You wake up tired, you have to drink, you have constant headaches, backaches, you can't sleep, you have recurring nightmares. You could be slowly committing suicide." Donovan looked long and hard at his captive group. "You don't have to die to be dead. There are a lot of walking wounded out there who need help badly. The macho image keeps them from getting it. You have to teach cops to ask for help."

Donovan told them about Dr. George Kirkham, a young Florida State University criminology professor who subscribed to the prevailing academic theory that police work attracts men who are basically insecure, hostile and authoritarian. Therefore better screening was needed — find the most psychologically stable, best-educated and most compassionate men whose sole professional aim would be to help protect their fellow man, men who would not need the power symbolized by a gun or a nightstick.

"So much for the theory," Donovan said. "He decided to put his money where his mouth was." Kirkham took the training and become a cop in a major U.S. city for four months to see the problem first hand. Donovan went on to tell the group what happened to the professor. Kirkham wrote about his experience in the book *Signal Zero*:

I had always personally been of the opinion that police officers greatly exaggerate the amount of verbal disrespect and physical abuse they get. I quickly found that my badge and uniform . . . only acted as a magnet which drew me toward many individuals who hated what I represented.

. . . The same kinds of daily stresses which affected my fellow officers soon began to take their toll on me. I became sick and tired of being reviled and attacked by criminals who could usually find a most sympathetic audience in judges and jurors eager to understand their side of things and provide them with another chance. I grew tired of living under the axe of news media and community pressure groups, eager to seize upon the slightest mistake made by myself or a fellow police officer.

. . . My wife was quick to notice the changes in me. I seemed so different, she said. Like some other person much of the time. Tense and restless, irritable. My language was incredibly profane. She could not recall ever having seen me take a drink to get to sleep at night.

. . . As we checked off duty, I was vaguely aware of feeling tired and tense. My partner and I were headed for a restaurant and a bite of breakfast when we both heard the unmistakable sound of breaking glass coming from a church and spotted two long-haired teen-age boys running from the area. We confronted them, and I asked one for identification, displaying my own police identification. He sneered at me, cursed and turned to walk away.

The next thing I knew I had grabbed the youth by his shirt and spun him around shouting, "I'm talking to you, punk!" I felt my partner's arm on my shoulder and heard his reassuring voice behind me, "Take it easy, Doc!" I released my grip on the adolescent and stood silently for several seconds, unable to accept the inescapable reality that I had "lost my cool."

My mind flashed back to a lecture during which I had told my students, "Any man who is not able to maintain absolute control of his emotions at all times has no business being a police officer."

As a police officer myself, I found that society demands too much of its policemen: not only are they expected to enforce the law but to be curbside psychiatrists, marriage counselors, social workers and even ministers and doctors . . .

I have often asked myself the questions: "Why does a man become a cop? What makes him stay with it?" . . . The only answer to this question I have been able to arrive at is one based on my own limited experience as a policeman. Night after night, I came home and took off the badge and blue uniform with a sense of satisfaction and contribution to society that I have never known in any other job.

"This job changes you," Donovan said, "and if you don't find a way to ventilate the feelings it causes, the job will kill you." Donovan felt his headache and the tension in his arm ease. He had done his own ventilating while talking to the group.

"I know a guy on the tactical squad who's trained to talk down jumpers and hostage takers. He's one of the best. He came home one day exhausted and didn't want to talk to his son until after he'd had a few beer to settle down from his day. His boy said to him, 'Dad, you'll spend three hours talking a man out of suicide — how come you won't spend thirty seconds with me?' " Donovan walked slowly to the side of the room and then turned to face the class.

"I just came from a meeting with six cops who've had a son or daughter commit suicide," he said, pausing. "How's your relationship with your kids? How are you and the wife or husband getting along? How's your health?

"You've got a tough job and the stress program is here to help you. Thank you." The class enthusiastically clapped their thank you to Donovan. He wanted to get out of the smoky classroom to the fresh air outside but a number of the supervisors cornered him with questions and comments.

"When you're a recovered alcoholic, what do you do when someone tries to force a drink on you?" someone asked.

"That's easy," Donovan said. "Usually it happens in someone's house, and they say, 'Just have one, it won't hurt.'

"I say, 'Okay, I'll have one, but I better warn you, if I drink I'm liable to puke on your carpet and try to get into your wife's drawers.' That usually gets the point across."

There'd be many more questions, but Donovan didn't mind, it was good for business.

CHAPTER FOUR
STRESS GROUP

Wednesday 7:00 P.M.
Well ahead of the 7:30 P.M. starting time, participants in the regular Wednesday evening stress session began to arrive. Each settled in for the meeting in the way most suited to his personality and mood. Some stood and talked animatedly around the coffee urn in the kitchen or in small groups in the corners of the main room. Others sat together and talked quietly. Several solemn figures, oblivious to the others, stared silently at the floor, their vacant eyes and downturned closed mouths were signals of the hurt and depression within. A pretty Chinese woman, the lone female among the several dozen males, flitted from group to group at the far end of the room. Laughter erupted frequently, as did the hard-nosed profanity that was second nature to a cop.

Everyone wore a different mask, but they were all there for the same reason: something about their mental and physical well-being had gone awry. Gradually, under Donovan's careful guidance, the masks would be taken off to expose the scared, hurt souls inside. It was a painful process — to expose the real person. For a few it would happen at the first meeting, for most it would take several sessions, and for some it would never happen.

Newcomers, who could be identified by their nervous glances and shocked looks when they saw a familiar face, tried to decide where to sit. The large circle of chairs ringing the long meeting room was now almost filled with police officers young and old, black and white. Most were dressed casually. Others, on duty, coming from or going to work, were in uniform and equipped with the tools of their trade:

guns, cuffs, radios, night sticks, mace, bullet pouches, flashlights, all clipped or belted to their bodies.

Donovan insisted on starting his meetings on time. At 7:30 on the dot, he strode from his office, proceeded down the stairs, and began to work his way to the opposite end of the room. He moved quickly but acknowledged almost everyone.

"How you doin' brother? Glad to see you, Ernie. Hey, did you see me on TV last weekend? Those bums at city hall did it again. . . ." He had the knack or carrying on one-sided running conversations with everyone.

"Good house tonight," he thought, seeing the crowd sitting two and three deep. "And headquarters says there aren't any problems." When Donovan sat down, those standing rushed to find a chair.

"Ed Donovan, Boston Police," he said, taking control immediately. "Jim Craven, Milton Police." "Leo Deschamps, BPD." In rapid-fire fashion, each officer introduced himself. As well as people from the Boston and area police, there was a New Hampshire sergeant sent to study the stress program for possible use in his own force, a prison guard, one retired officer, and Dr. John Barry, the program's consulting psychologist. "Dr. John," as he was called by everyone, sat quietly and calmly, as he did every week, at the opposite end of the room from Donovan, his lanky frame draped over a chair, one large hand wrapped around a cup of coffee, the other around his pipe. The strong aroma of his tobacco mixed with the smoke of cigarettes, rose in a curling white mist above the group, mingling with the pungent smells coming from the coffee urn in the kitchen.

Donovan was usually careful to choose a long-time member of the group to speak first, because he wanted the newcomers to relax and see how things worked. Tonight was different.

"Brad, tonight is your first time here. Could you tell the group why you've come?" Donovan asked. Brad Molineaux looked scared. Fiftyish, with curly grey hair, he had a youthful, dashing look, but heavy lines and dark shadows under his eyes were gradually eroding his good looks. Brad was a lieutenant, the highest ranking officer in the room, and his rank would create a barrier separating him from the group. Donovan wanted to break down that barrier quickly, so he wanted Brad to start the meeting.

"As a superior officer, it was very hard for me to come here," Brad said nervously. "I wondered what some of you guys who worked for me would think and maybe what you would say to others." Brad looked straight ahead avoiding eye contact with those around him, his face red and tense with embarrassment.

"Brad, anything that's said in this room doesn't go beyond these walls. Everyone here felt the same the first time," Donovan said, seeing his discomfort. Tears welled up in Brad's eyes as he struggled to continue.

"I got myself into a situation that's tearing me apart, and I'm afraid it will kill my marriage and turn my kids against me," he said.

"What's the problem?" said one of the officers.

"I've been charged with sexual harassment on the job," he said in a low, halting tone.

"Do your wife and family know?" another asked. His guilt or innocence would not be questioned by the group. Their concern was for Brad and what the situation was doing to him.

"No, not exactly. They know I have a problem, but they don't know what it's about. The story's been on television, but they didn't use my name, and it hasn't been in the papers."

"Are you going to tell them?"

"I don't know," Brad said.

"Better you tell your wife than she find out from a neighbour, or your kids hear about it at school," someone else said.

Brad rubbed the tears from his eyes. Before coming to the meeting he knew he had two choices: Tell his family or blow his brains out. The pressures, fears, and cold reality of that position drove him to swallow his pride and seek help.

"How's all this affecting you personally?" someone asked.

"Oh, it's bothering me."

"Are you drinking more?"

Brad looked back down at his feet. "Yes."

"Is that going to solve your problem?" another queried. Brad didn't have to answer. The tears ran down his cheeks as he raised his eyes to look at his brother officers. Rank was unimportant. He was just another cop with a problem, and he somehow sensed that although the questions were tough, there was care and concern behind them. Here he could unload his burdens. Donovan knew it was time to move on to someone else. Brad would be taken aside by a few officers at the end of the meeting and offered some specifics on handling his problem.

"Becky, how are you feeling this week?" Donovan asked. Becky looked more like a model than a policewoman. Pretty, slight of build, with long, flowing, silken black hair, she wore a skirt and blouse that begged for attention. Donovan thought, "With the problems some of these guys have, the last thing they need is a broad flaunting her body." But just as some of the men had their tough-guy exteriors masking the hurt inside, Becky was covering hers in the only way she knew how. One year ago, while trying to arrest a woman shoplifter, she had been severely beaten. Since then, Becky had been off work with back pain and severe headaches. She looked worried and drawn, the pre-meeting tease gone from her eyes.

"My back is still giving me problems, and the headaches just don't seem to want to go away," she said. "I keep asking the doctors why I still have the problem, but they can't tell me."

"Do you want to go back to work, Becky?" George Leehan asked. Leehan was a senior volunteer whom Donovan was grooming for a full-time counsellor position if he ever got the funding.

"Sure, but how can I work with these problems? I can hardly do the housework."

"But Becky, the doctors say your injuries have healed."

"You tell that to my back and headaches," she snapped. A few of the men observed her intently. Some looked out into empty space, listening to the proceedings or struggling with their own thoughts, maybe questioning the origin of their own pains or comparing their situations with Becky's.

"Becky, are you afraid to go back?" George asked again.

"No way. I want to go back, but my injuries won't heal." No one in the group was buying her protest. They'd had this argument with her before. George tried to help out.

"It's all right to be afraid. There isn't one person in this room who hasn't been scared shitless to go back on the street at one time or other. If they tell you otherwise, they're lying to you and themselves," George said.

"Becky, the problem is in your head, not in your back. You don't want to go back to work because you took a beating. I don't blame you, but until you admit it to yourself, you're going to keep having problems."

"I'm not scared. I like my job, and I want to go back to work," she replied.

Donovan stayed out of the discussion as much as he could, letting the group work on each other's problems. They were doing a good job with Becky. She wanted sympathy but wasn't going to get any. She had told the group about her divorce and the difficulties her thirteen-year-old daughter was giving her, but Donovan knew Becky was still holding back. She had been sexually abused as a child, was a battered wife in a short and tragic marriage, and had a serious alcohol problem she refused to acknowledge. Like many women police officers, she suppressed her emotions and played the macho role but took on the problems that went with that role. Donovan knew Becky had to face her fears and talk about them, or they would destroy her physically and mentally.

Jim Duffield spoke up from across the room. "I've had four back operations and used to live with constant pain.

For the last three years my back has been terrific. Yesterday, my younger brother had open-heart surgery, my only grandchild was diagnosed as having cystic fibrosis, and I had to go to court on a serious personal matter. Today, I've had backpain and a splitting headache all day, and this afternoon my left arm went numb. You tell me that wasn't stress." His comment did little to convince Becky. She sat there defensively, with her arms crossed, and a defiant look on her face.

Donovan figured Becky had been on the spot long enough, so he turned his attention to a worried looking Tommy Branigan on the other side of the room. "How's it going, Tommy?"

"The not drinking is going fine. I'm going to one or two AA meetings a day, and that's helping me get through each day, but now I've got all sorts of health problems surfacing." Tommy had been a heavy drinker for thirty years and had dried out only three months ago. A pleasant, chubby man of sixty, he had the sincere, compassionate look of a doting grandfather. Only a slight redness in his face and the prominence of bloodvessels in his nose hinted at his problem. It was a miracle he had managed to sober up, but now he was paying the price of years of alcohol abuse. He talked about the medical tests he had gone through that day and all the upcoming tests he was facing.

"Are you afraid you're going to die, Tommy?" Donovan asked.

"You're damn right. I'm scared. For thirty years, I tried to kill myself with booze. Now that I'm sober, I see a lot of things I want to live for and enjoy: my wife, my kids, my grandchildren. I've got so much to make up for," he said, his voice breaking as he clasped his beefy hands together to squeeze out the pain.

As the parade of speakers continued, several windows were opened to air out and cool the room, hot and stuffy from body heat and smoke. Latecomers added to the group's size. At opportune moments, people slipped quietly to the kitchen for more coffee or upstairs to use the washroom. A

loud discussion started in the kitchen but stopped abruptly
when Donovan yelled, "Keep it down." Donovan knew the
focus had to be on the speakers. What they needed most to
solve their problems was someone to listen, care, and
understand.

Not everyone who came to the meetings had sincere
intentions. There were always a few malingerers who
wanted to use the program as a lever to help them get on
disability — either they weren't really sick, or they just
didn't want to get well. Donovan could always spot them
because they rarely contributed to the meetings. When they
did talk, their fairy tales sounded like they came from the
same broken record. "What bastards they are," Donovan
thought. "I've got dozens of officers who could get disability legitimately fighting to get back to work, and here these
parasites are, with hardly anything wrong, trying to take
the easy way out." Donovan wanted to tell them to beat it,
but he knew he had to take the bad with the good. He liked
to stare right through each one of them until they were
forced to look away. Some staged remarkable recoveries
after he scored them with his evil eye.

Dr. John was a familiar figure to those at the meeting.
His patient face topped with grey hair and glasses and his
low-key, friendly manner gave him credibility with the
groups, a credibility that was strengthened by his ties to the
police community. His father had been a life-long cop, and
his brother was a recently retired deputy superintendent.
Many in the room were in counselling with him, usually
with their wives. Donovan encouraged this practice.

Dr. John and other trained professionals were a vital part
of the stress centre's treatment program. Donovan was like
a country doctor, the all-encompassing general practitioner
with the big heart and twenty-four-hour-a-day dedication,
always willing to come, always willing to search out those
who refused help. The medical and mental health professionals in their clean offices with the nine to five hours were
the specialists.

By coming to the meetings and holding office hours at

the stress centre once a week, Dr. John made it easier for those in need of his help. He wasn't threatened by Donovan's work with peer counselling as were some psychologists and psychiatrists. He was comfortable taking his weekly seat in the meeting to see first-hand how Donovan and his group accomplished what medical and psychological science couldn't. Universities didn't teach balls and heart.

There were others waiting to talk so Donovan picked up the pace of the meeting by turning to Kenny Atkins, a clean-cut type who looked more like an accountant than a cop. A sergeant on a small town police force, Kenny had his masters degree in criminology and specialized in rape prevention, lecturing and making training films on the topic. Two weeks previously, his seventeen-year-old daughter had been raped at 8 o'clock in the evening, only two blocks from home. Devastated, and filled with poisonous, conflicting emotions, Kenny had come to last week's meeting for help but couldn't talk, broke down, and had to be taken upstairs to see Donovan privately. Tonight he was more composed, telling the group about the rape and the anger he felt.

"That son of a bitch raped my baby, and I want to kill him," Kenny said bitterly. He paused for a moment. "But I also feel like a failure, like I let my girl down. Here I am telling others how to prevent rape, and I let my own daughter get raped, almost at our back door. What kind of father am I?"

"It wasn't your fault. You can't bodyguard her all the time," Tommy Branigan said. Kenny squirmed in his chair as he grappled with his feelings.

"What will you do if you come face to face with the rapist and you have your gun on?" Tommy asked.

"I'd want to shoot the bastard, but I don't know if I could. Justice is hard to rationalize when your own kid gets hurt. He scarred her for life." Donovan looked at the somber faces around the room, each contemplating what he'd do if he were in Kenny's boots. Kenny would need more meetings to defuse his rage and accept the situation.

It was difficult for many to gather the courage to speak out in front of others, but Donovan had his tricks. He looked slowly around the room, knowing that eye contact often nudged a reluctant speaker to words. To the others it would appear they spoke on their own initiative; it saved face and gave them the control a cop liked. Donovan's glance settled for a long moment on the face of a stranger, a latecomer to the meeting.

"I wasn't going to say anything this evening," he said, "because it's my first meeting, but I had something happen to me today that I want to talk about." The regulars at the meeting exchanged "Who is he?" glances when no one recognized the tough-talking newcomer sitting at the far end of the room behind the first row of seats. About five feet ten inches tall, weighing close to 300 rock solid pounds, he was the stereotypical image of a mean, hard motorcycle cop. His face was bulldog square, and he had a small leather cap perched on the top of his head. Reflective sunglasses covered his eyes, and a toothpick hung from the corner of his mouth. His massive arms were crossed on his chest. His voice, while hard and tough, had a well-spoken, confident air to it.

"My fourteen-year-old daughter tried to commit suicide today," he said without a trace of emotion. "Her ex-boyfriend was moving to another school and gave her a note yesterday that said she was a dumb bitch. When my back was turned this morning, she stole some booze from the house, took it to school, drank it there, and then slashed her wrists." He spoke methodically and efficiently as if he were testifying in a courtroom.

"I get a call at work and rush over to the hospital," he said. "There were all sorts of mess-ups there as to whether she should be admitted, whether she should see a psychiatrist, or what. Finally they refused to admit her, so we brought her back home."

"How bad were the cuts?" someone asked.

"When I got to the hospital I peeled back the bandages to

look, and they were just chicken scratches. She's got exactly what she wants. All her friends are calling to ask how she is. She's in her glory. Her friends think she's a hero now. Just before I left for this meeting, she asked if she could go over and stay at a friend's house tonight. I said no way.

"Now, for the last few days, she's had a new boyfriend, but his father and older brother have both committed suicide. Her girlfriend, the one she wants to stay with tonight, her father committed suicide two weeks ago, and the girlfriend has tried to commit suicide four times."

"Holy shit, what kind of people do you associate with?" someone gasped. People were shaking their heads around the room. No matter how much you'd seen, there was always something new.

"What kind of relationship did you have with your daughter prior to today?" asked a more composed group member.

"Good, we got along really well."

"Were you tough with her or ever hit her?" the speaker probed.

"Only once — I slapped her last week for lying to me," he said, surprised at his own answer.

"Do you hug your daughter and tell her you love her?"

"Not exactly, but I do love her, and I show it in my own way. She knows I'm not an emotional, touchy-feely person." Val Devany, sitting next to him, had heard enough. His Irish temper and outspoken disposition were starting to take control of him.

"I've got something I'd like to say to you. I'm not going to pull any punches, and you might end up wanting to hit me." Val leaned forward trying to gauge the man's mood by peering through the reflective sunglasses, but all he could see was himself peering back. Val hesitated for a moment, then straightened in his seat and said, "You come across like a marine drill sergeant, and it sounds like that's the way you run your house. Total control — no nonsense."

"Yes, I do," he said, taking Val's statement as a compliment.

"It seems to me your daughter was just trying to get your attention," Val continued. Silently, expectantly, everyone waited for the father's reaction, heads nodding in agreement with Val.

"No, I don't think so," he said coolly and slowly, but everyone could tell the wheels were turning in his mind. He swished the toothpick back and forth in his mouth. It was as if the group had slashed a switch-blade through his tough exterior, exposing the vital organs beneath. No one was about to twist the blade, though; he'd already been given plenty to think about. Several of the other cops who'd gone through the same thing with their kids would corner him after the meeting.

Joe Cody, a fifteen-year career patrolman, jumped in to talk about his day. He was angry at the courts, the union, and the world in general as he started to bitch about a run-in at the courthouse that day.

Cody wasn't in the group's good books. Donovan had sent him to Parkview detoxification hospital to dry out a month ago, but he had left after a week, saying he didn't need it anymore. Donovan wasn't happy with his outburst; union politics didn't have a place in the meeting. Cody hadn't finished his bitter tirade before Jim Kunas abruptly interrupted.

"Were you drinking before court, or was it after?"

"No."

"No, you didn't drink before, so you drank after?" Jim asked, trying to trap him.

"No, I didn't drink at all," Cody said irritably.

"How much did you have to drink before tonight's meeting?"

"Not a drop, I didn't have any booze today." Cody was convincing no one.

"Are you still doing barroom details?" Sam Echevaran asked. On these details, a cop in uniform is hired by a bar owner to guard against trouble, but Donovan knew from experience that the cop could be the biggest drinker and potential troublemaker there.

"Yeah, I enjoy doing them, and the drinkin' don't bother me," Cody said.

"You're an alcoholic, and you say that doesn't bother you?" Kunas said in exasperation. "Boy, you're sure a lot tougher than anyone else in this room. You're like a sex maniac standing guard at a nudist beach, and you tell us you don't get a hard-on? Who are you trying to kid?" Cody, muttering something about a conspiracy under his breath, escaped to the kitchen to get some more coffee.

Donovan did one last check around the room to make sure he hadn't missed anyone. "What about you, brother?" he said to a black cop who, Donovan knew, had serious problems.

"Not tonight," came the quiet reply. Some, like this black cop, found just listening at the meeting was medicine enough. With time they would open up.

"Well, that's it for tonight," Donovan said. Quickly, a couple of kitchen pots were passed around the room for donations to the coffee fund and for flowers and cards for those in hospital. As everyone slowly stretched and got to their feet, George Leehan shouted out the nightly reminder to please clean up ashtrays and cups before leaving.

"Remember, Eddie's not too keen about cleaning up your trash," he said over the rising voices. Donovan sprinted for the peace and quiet of his office. He needed to talk to George about a couple of things and didn't want to get cornered by anyone downstairs. He wanted them talking to each other and working out their own problems. Many he counselled grabbed on to him as if he were their lifeline, and, while they needed it at the start, if he let them cling too long, they became dependent.

He sank into his office chair and took several deep breaths to ease his tension and cleanse his lungs. Donovan heard George outside his closed office door, but someone had him cornered in conversation. He knew who that would be; Vinny the vampire.

Vinny was an alcoholic who had dried out two years ago

and had been coming faithfully to the stress meetings ever since. But he was like a vampire sucking dry Donovan, George, Dr. John, and anyone else he could corner. Manic depressive, he would sit through the meetings bent over with his head in his hands, elbows on his knees. He would never speak or acknowledge what was going on.

Donovan, Dr. John, and other doctors tried to persuade him to take anti-depressants to help control his moods. He refused. He continually burdened them with his problems but wouldn't take any advice. It was hard, but Donovan had to abandon him. He could only spend so much time with someone until he said, "The hell with them . . . there are others out there that need our help more, and they might be willing to meet us half way." He wouldn't stop Vinny from coming to the meetings, but his presence angered Donovan.

"George, come on in here. I need to see you right away," he shouted through the door. He knew George was too nice and easy going to lose Vinny quickly. Vinny talked on. Donovan leapt to his feet, charged over, and swung open the door. "George, I need you now," he said, yanking George inside and slamming the door in Vinny's face. "Get lost, Vinny," Donovan muttered through the closed door just loud enough for Vinny to hear.

"George, you can't let him bother you like that. He'll suck you dry."

CHAPTER FIVE
THE EARLY
YEARS

Thursday, 7:32 A.M.

Donovan rubbed his eyes, then squinted, trying to focus on the bedside clock. He'd barely had two hours sleep. The sounds of breakfast being made and female voices filtered in from the kitchen. He lived with Mary Rasmussen, and she was getting her thirteen-year-old daughter, Anne Marie, off to school.

Donovan and Mary had been together four years. They were a unique contrast in personalities that had somehow drawn together: he, dynamic, energetic, gregarious; she, serious, shy, reserved. Mary, now thirty-seven, had had polio as a child and spent most of her youth in a body cast. She was slim, long waisted, with graceful fingers, inquisitive eyes, and long blond hair. Numerous operations enabled her to walk with a noticeable limp, although she moved like a courageous crippled swan. She had had a short, unhappy marriage to an alcoholic and had spent twelve years on her own raising Anne Marie and supporting herself with a variety of jobs that had to be interrupted with more operations on her legs and long recovery periods. In 1984 she had gone to school, graduated from a licensed practical nursing program, and planned to work full-time in the fall.

Behind Mary's tough, almost defensive exterior was a caring, warm person. Her adversity had given her a strength and will to survive that she shared with Donovan. They were a big help to each other: he driving her to develop

68

confidence and overcome her shyness; she the unpaid force behind the stress program. For the last four years, since the lay-offs and Donovan's loss of his counsellors, she was frequently at the stress centre, answering the phones, writing letters, and when Donovan was away often doing individual counselling. This summer she and Eddie were going to get married, and Donovan was as excited as a little kid about it.

Donovan rolled onto his back and propped some pillows behind his head. He'd gotten home from last night's meeting at 11:00 P.M., talked to Mary till midnight, then read for a couple of hours before falling asleep. His beeper had jarred him awake at 3:00 A.M. A depressed detective from the west end was threatening to commit suicide. Donovan called him and talked him down, but it took an hour, and when he finished, he was so pumped up he couldn't sleep. He read until fatigue finally overtook him.

"What time'd you get to sleep?" Mary asked irritably as she entered the room.

"Five."

"You're crazy. You're going to kill yourself. Is it worth it?"

"I'm gonna see the commissioner pretty soon and get some help."

"How many times have they promised you that?" Mary said.

"You coming to the meeting tonight?" Donovan said, changing the subject. It was the wives' regular Thursday meeting, and Mary usually attended.

"Yeah, I guess." Mary blew him a kiss and returned to the kitchen to make his breakfast before he rushed off.

Donovan sat up in bed, with several pillows behind his back, to clear his head and get the cogs and wheels turning. He didn't mind the call and the lack of sleep, but Mary was right. He was killing himself trying to keep the program alive, but he knew when it counted, he couldn't say "no."

Surviving and helping came naturally to Edward Charles Donovan. Born on December 14, 1931, in the working class district of South Boston, the red-headed chubby baby was nicknamed "Buster" by his mother, and that's what everyone called him for the next seventeen years. While his father, a Boston-born Irishman, was travelling the countryside in search of work, his mother, Dorothy Donovan was left on her own through the Depression years to raise eleven kids. Eight of her children would reach adulthood; the others died at ages three, four, and five, within three days of each other from different communicable diseases. Of the eight who lived, Buster was number five, with one older brother; the rest were girls. When his parents eventually divorced, Donovan developed very strong ties with his mother.

Small and slight of build, Dorothy Donovan was the backbone of the family, with a tough, feisty, fighting spirit inherited from her German father and Irish mother. For years, she worked for the telephone company as an operator, but during the war they gave her a blackjack and made her the front door security guard to check ID and watch for potential troublemakers or saboteurs. "Can you imagine her bouncing drunks?" Donovan said recently, looking proudly at his tiny mother, now in her eighties, crippled with arthritis, and in a wheel chair. "She had guts doing a man's work."

With his mother working long hours, young Eddie Donovan had to pitch in with his brother and sisters in running the home. It was tough, but there was always food on the table and love in the household. Their house, an unusual three-storey duplex with two rooms on each floor, was crowded with kids and pets, but clean. Donovan developed his fascination for pets, and, at one time, even had a monkey in the house.

When he was eleven, a blind man moved in next door. Donovan watched neighbourhood kids play jokes on the man, stringing ropes across the sidewalk, and putting excrement where he would walk. Donovan became the man's friend, then his seeing eye dog as he accompanied him frequently to the Perkins Institute for the Blind where the man worked making mattresses. Donovan became a fixture there and a friend of most of the workers. He learned how to laugh at adversity when his blind friends would hit him with lines like, "See you later, Buster."

The sister closest in age to Donovan was deaf from a childhood bout of measles. Donovan was the only one in his family who learned sign language to communicate with her, although he wasn't above playing innocent jokes like answering a phone that wasn't ringing and telling her the call was for her.

Like most kids in the neighbourhood, Eddie Donovan was basically good but no angel as he advanced into his teens. He stole vegetables from gardens, scrounged spilled coal, and in high school went for joy rides in stolen cars, although he wouldn't actually steal them himself. In his biggest scam, he broke into an ice cream parlour with some friends and ate the loot. He hated bullies and dirty fighters, got into a few fights himself, and, when he did, fought fair and usually lost.

South Boston teemed with Irish, Germans, Lithuanians, and Italians — most were labourers, many firemen and policemen. The hard-living, hard-working ethics and culture rubbed off on Donovan. The times taught him good values: if you wanted something, you had to work for it, but working for the family came first. You also respected authority. To Donovan, cops were people you feared: "Either they'd kick the shit out of you if you were bad, or they'd take you home to your mother who'd kick the shit out of you." That left him with a healthy respect for the police, but he never dreamed of becoming one himself.

Donovan struggled to get through high school. "I felt I was an ugly dummy, and who the hell would like me with my skinny body and big ears?" He clowned and joked to cover his feelings of inadequacy. Some innocent drinking with the kids on the beach when he was fifteen showed him he could talk and feel better when he had a drink in him. He tried enlisting in the service to go to war but was turned down because of his age. When he graduated from high school he had no money for college or trade school, so at seventeen he joined the navy; it promised the excitement and action he craved.

Boot camp at Great Lakes, Michigan, introduced him to a reality he hadn't really seen in South Boston. His upbringing had fostered some bigotry in him toward blacks, but boot camp was his first real exposure to them, and he was shocked at how they were treated. In one incident, a young black mate of Donovan's had made plans to be married on the weekend, but a spiteful drill sergeant scheduled him for "punishment." Punishment for those in the bad books was torturous rifle drills and callisthenics done in the evening. Donovan told his friend to sneak off and get married, then took his place in the ranks to do his punishment. When they called out the black's name, Donovan, from the middle of the back row answered, "He . . . ah," in the best southern accent he could muster.

The smartest guy in Donovan's whole group was black. Jimmy Cotter had the best test results, highest IQ, and was a solid, likeable person, but unofficial policy prevented blacks from going to technical school to learn the more skilled trades. Donovan himself was lined up for electronics school, at that time a new field and a desired placement. The black policy angered him. When he spoke his mind, the brass told him to be quiet. Donovan said, "no way." It was his first real fight with the establishment, and he lost. His posting to technical school was cancelled, and he ended up a bosun's mate for several years, chipping paint and washing decks with his new black friends.

Fascinated with photography since he was eight, Donovan managed to advance into photography work with the Office of Naval Intelligence (ONI). There he learned fingerprinting and carried out criminal investigations as a photographer in Key West, Florida, doing undercover surveillance work, secretly photographing foreign ships. The ONI interacted with the FBI, and Donovan got a taste of police work dealing with sabotage and intelligence. "I liked the challenge of going after the bad guy and solving crimes, I thought that was what police work was all about."

When he left the navy to return to Boston in 1953, Donovan, only twenty-two, had five years of exciting memories and a desire to be a photographer with his own studio. He also had a young wife, a baby, and one more on the way. For the next three years he worked at dozens of jobs: autobody worker, machine shop helper, factory worker, warehouse worker, and salesman. He hated them all and quickly quit each one. He still dreamed of being a photographer. Finally, he landed a job with a photo company, but it was in the darkroom developing someone else's pictures. The pay was on a piecework basis. Donovan noticed that the women who worked with him were given the more time-consuming, lower-paying batches to work on. He'd seen his mother battle sexual discrimination at the phone company, so he'd come to work early and switch bags, giving the women some of his more lucrative jobs and taking their poorer ones in return. The women never knew; Donovan wasn't looking for a reward or a pat on the back, but he had the satisfaction of putting one over on the system. Somehow, he always seemed attracted to the underdog's battles and wanted to help.

The photo lab wasn't the answer; like his other jobs, it lacked the action and challenge he'd been used to in the navy. He saw many of his navy friends go into police work, and that sparked an interest. He put a police radio in his car to listen to calls and sometimes raced to the scene of incidents with his camera hoping to shoot a prize-winning picture.

With naive ideas about police work, and the desire to do undercover work like he did in the navy, he applied to the Boston Police Department. He drank a fair amount while he was in the navy but stopped when he wanted to become a cop. The standards to enter were high, so he went to evening school, taking classes to build his credentials. This, combined with his navy and fingerprinting experience, made him an excellent candidate, except for one thing: his size. Scrawny and weak, he didn't weigh enough, so he supplemented his diet by eating bananas and pumping iron to build himself up to the 140-pound limit. He made it, and was called to report to the academy. It was only a four-week course in those days, but Donovan still worked an evening job while in the academy to help support his wife and two kids with a third en route. On July 10, 1957, he graduated and was sworn in as a Boston police officer.

Rookie patrolman Edward C. Donovan, Badge Number 1011, was a sight. His skinny, banana-honed physique, the fierce red freckles on his baby face, and large jug ears holding his oversized cap out of his eyes were not intimidating. He looked seventeen and couldn't fight his way out of a paper bag. But Donovan, with his new uniform, gun, nightstick, and handcuffs, felt like superman come to rid Boston of scum. His large heart and turbocharged spirits compensated for his physical shortcomings. He was a dynamo ready to be unleashed as he awaited his first posting. But then devastation; he was assigned to Station 17, which was out in the residential boondocks where nothing ever happened.

Teamed with a veteran officer on his first afternoon on duty, they pulled up to an old municipal building and went down to the boiler room. Donovan's partner pulled out a bag from behind a storage shelf, took his civilian clothes out of it, changed into them, and told Donovan, "Stay here kid, I'll be back in a few hours." The officer then went home and took his wife shopping while Donovan cooled his heels.

Despite the inauspicious start, Donovan volunteered for everything, ran one-man cruisers, and made good arrests. He worked hard and had initiative: stopping suspicious looking cars, finding stolen goods, and solving crimes before people even knew what had happened. Eddie Donovan

Donovan at five months
with mother in 1932.

The Donovan kids, from
left to right, Helen
(hidden), Peggy, Dotty,
Winnie, Eddie, Louise
and Sonny.

New sailor and mother in 1950.

Navy photographer, circa 1953.

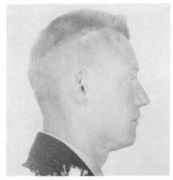

Rookie patrolman, 1957, twenty-six years old.

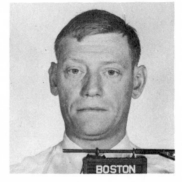

Gag mug shot, ten years later, 1967

Donovan photographing a homicide in 1964.

"Ace photographer"—clowning masked the hurt inside.

In full uniform, on hospital grounds.

Sherlock Donovan.

Donovan with nurses—
more clowning.

Reading a grim headline.

Donovan in full uniform,
late 1960s.
"Distinguish yourself."

Special detail, bodyguard
to the stars. Donovan
with Steve McQueen on
movie location in Boston,
early 1960s.

With Jimmy Durante,
1961.

was enthusiastic and compulsive about anything he tackled.

Veteran cops told him, "Slow down kid, you're making us look bad." When the Miranda law was passed, it took the fun, zest, and initiative out of Donovan's sails. The Miranda Law, which is still in effect, prevents police from stopping anyone without good reason and requires that arresting officers read suspects their rights. "You couldn't do anything," he said. That's when he made a move to return to photography. He worked out of headquarters but soon saw the politics of police work. "The fair-haired boys and ass kissers got the easy jobs, like photographing the chief's speeches," he said. "Me, I got the bodies and the dirt, and that went on for twelve years."

During his first year on the police force, Donovan didn't drink at all. His only vice was cigar smoking, a carry-over from his navy days. Like many cops, he started to drink at "choir practice" (after shift drinking parties). It was the sixties now, with its riots and protests and the rebellion against the authority his uniform represented. The people he was sworn to help resented him. His drinking became excessive, while his cynicism and fear grew and his enthusiasm and idealism died. In the riots, he feared for his life, and during his regular job photographing bodies, he feared death.

"I was a good cop, always in the front where the action was. I'd go and photograph a black leader at a protest rally and end up marching with them. Suddenly there'd be no more whites around, and they'd say to me, 'Get lost or grow a new colour.' "

Eventually, Donovan noticed that his drinking was a problem, so he went to see the family doctor about it. The doctor said, "Naw, you're just drinking beer. Stop drinking, and I'll give you some tranquilizers." The doctor gave him Librium, just new on the market, and Donovan actually stopped drinking. But once he wasn't drunk all the time, he saw an Eddie Donovan he didn't know and didn't like. He felt isolated and depressed. He went back to the doctor who this time gave him anti-depressants. A few weeks later, Donovan was back again unable to sleep; the doctor gave him a prescription for sleeping pills. When Donovan became anxious from all the pills, the doctor gave him anti-anxiety pills. Valium came on the market, and the doctor prescribed that.

Donovan continued this way, without drinking, for four years, but he was always depressed and fatigued. He kept huge quantities of pills loosely jammed in a front pants pocket, stuffed in place with a large wad of cotton batting. He'd be battling students in the middle of a riot and reach into his pocket to gulp down a handful of pills.

Donovan did some part-time photography work for a man who was running for the governor's nomination. At a party following an important victory, Donovan had a beer. It didn't do anything for him, so he took another, and he started to feel good for the first time in four years. He took more and more, and the next day he had no hangover and felt terrific. But he also kept using the pills. Donovan kept up his dual addiction for six more years not realizing that the booze accentuated the pills' effects up to threefold. He had blackouts when he lost days at a time. He was always scared, afraid of cracking up, afraid of committing suicide, and afraid of being found out.

During one blackout, he turned blue and was rushed to a county hospital. The week he was in hospital no one asked him about his drinking until the final day when a doctor said, "Your wife tells us you drink a lot."

"Oh no, I don't, that's not true," Donovan said.

"Okay. Well, why don't you try to cut back a bit," the doctor said. Donovan got out at 3:00 P.M. and by early evening was drunk again. He had many more bouts with dual addiction. If he needed pills and the doctor was away, he'd write his own prescriptions. He chain-smoked cigars, inhaling the smoke and chomping on the end, not realizing the cigar juices drained to his stomach and helped trigger his anxiety attacks. "I was crying all the time, felt life sucked, and thought I was cracking up."

Police officers were low paid, especially in those days, so financial pressures forced Donovan to work overtime, extra details, and other jobs. He did private photography for weddings, bar mitzvahs, and live theatre where he met and drank with many famous people.

By now Donovan had six kids, four boys and two girls. He tried to spend as much time with them as he could, even taking the older ones on details with him to hockey, baseball, and basketball games. On the job, he saw the results of beatings, mutilations, and accidents involving kids which made him paranoid about his own. He feared a calamity was going to happen to them; he became overprotective and monitored their every action. "I didn't see straight kids, just the bad ones," Donovan said. "I thought, 'Oh my God, is there anyone good left?' "

His marriage never had any real substance. He was twenty-one, she was sixteen and pregnant when they married, and whatever glow there was soon wore off, but somehow they endured through sixteen years and, eventually, seven kids. Finally, Donovan's wife called Gus Guthro and Joe Kelly, who ran the alcohol program for the BPD, and told them about her husband's drinking problem. They approached him, but Donovan bluntly told them to get lost.

Two more years of hell lay ahead for Donovan. Thoughts of suicide dominated his mind, and he made subtle attempts at it. In panicky anxiety attacks, he'd race his cruiser at ninety miles an hour, aim it at a tree or a light standard, but pull out at the last second. He wanted his death to look like an accident, so not to hurt his kids, but was frightened of becoming one of the disfigured, mangled corpses he'd photographed so many times. He'd put a gun in his mouth, but couldn't pull the trigger. After the incident at Fenway Park, he lived in fear he would do it in a moment of sudden impulse, so he started carrying an unloaded gun and was even fearful of other officers' guns, afraid he'd grab one out of a holster and blow his head off in front of them.

"I realized I wanted to die but didn't know how to do it. I couldn't do it. I couldn't let my kids down." Donovan had an inkling then of what he knows now: the person who commits suicide isn't the victim; the people left behind are. They're the ones who hurt. The person who pulls the trigger holds the gun to his family's head as well as his own.

Donovan's home life deteriorated to the point where one afternoon, on duty, he arrived home in a drunken rage. His wife accused him of trying to kill her and called the police. Two cops tried to take him out of the house, but he wrestled them down a flight of stairs, resisting until one finally had to club him over the head, cutting him so that he needed five stitches. He was handcuffed and dragged out of his house, a bloody, cursing mess, and loaded into a paddy wagon in front of the whole neighbourhood. "I was humiliated, then locked up in my own jail with friends poking their heads in all night. 'Eddie, is that you?' "

Donovan managed to squirm out of the predicament but immediately went back to drinking. By now, he was separated from his wife and living with another woman. A few months later he went by his home, had an argument with his wife, and fired a shot from his service revolver into the living room ceiling. This time he had to face the music. He was allowed to work restricted duty in headquarters but had his gun taken away, and was scheduled to face a police trial board. He continued living with the other woman. She was his escape, a neutral element, away from the frustrations and responsibilities he faced at work and home. But by escaping, he wasn't facing himself.

The cries for help that eroded his body and gnarled in his guts for twelve years finally exploded in the main lobby of police headquarters on the way to work one morning. The thread of life and sanity that Eddie Donovan clung to snapped: "I was sick and tired of being sick and tired." At the time he didn't realize it was an AA slogan. He said, "The hell with it, I'm not going to work." He didn't want to face life or work. He screamed at everyone in the large main lobby, telling patrolmen, sergeants, captains, and deputies to go fuck themselves. Suddenly he was quiet. He looked around at the shocked faces in the lobby. Donovan raised his arms as if to speak, then lowered his head and his arms at the same time. Eddie Donovan was through fighting. He called Gus Guthro, not realizing the real fight for his life had just begun — a long and hard one. Guthro and Joe Kelly arrived within minutes and committed him to a hospital for detoxification.

Ironically, Donovan had been in the hospital only four days when a counsellor rushed into his room saying they needed his help in admitting. A Boston cop who tried to cut his throat was just brought in and was refusing to stay. Donovan said, "You've got to be crazy. I want out of here, too." He refused to help, but before he knew what happened, they brought the cop to his room. He looked like the wild man of Borneo. He stood six-feet-four inches tall, his hair was shooting all over the place, and his eyes had the look of a crazed animal. Large, blood-soaked bandages were wrapped around his neck like an orthopedic collar. Donovan thought, "Holy Mother of Christ, he reminds me of me." Donovan made him sit down, shooed the attendants and counsellor out of the room, and sat next to the man.

"Hey, you'd be crazy to leave here," Donovan said, "this place is terrific; it's the best thing that ever happened to me." Donovan raved on about the institute and what it was doing for him, and how bad he was before he came in. To Donovan's amazement, the cop listened and stayed. That incident rekindled Donovan's long-suppressed desire to help others which had been numbed by booze and pills for twelve years. Ten days later, when Donovan was released from hospital, sober and dried out, he realized his battle was just beginning.

It was mid-summer, 1970, and Donovan went to live with his mother in Wrentham, a small city ten miles southwest of Boston, away from anyone who knew him as a policeman. He felt he was an embarrassment to the force and an embarrassment to himself. As an alcoholic, he felt like a leper: misunderstood, unwanted, shunned.

The summer heat was oppressive, and Donovan's room was so hot he could hardly breathe the air, yet he'd wake up in a shivering cold sweat, screaming. He was in the midst of withdrawal symptoms from alcohol and drugs but wasn't told this in the hospital. A week later, Donovan returned to work at headquarters in ID and the darkroom, still without his gun and awaiting the trial board on his shooting incident.

Joe Kelly kept telling Donovan's mother he'd get Eddie and his wife back together. "That was a real pain in the ass," Donovan said. It taught Donovan that in counselling you guide people but let them make their own decisions. Kelly's pressure to mend the marriage made Donovan avoid him.

Donovan related to Gus Guthro and his brand of counselling. Guthro was tough, honest, and blunt. When Donovan got depressed and wanted pity, Guthro attacked.

"What do you mean you can't forgive yourself? Are you playing God, you idiot?" Guthro would say.

"If God can forgive you, who the hell are you that you can't? Get your head on straight first; you don't need that bullshit."

Donovan would later say, "That's my kind of man."

Donovan was afraid of life sober. He had to learn how to make love sober, face the world sober, talk to people, and be assertive. He'd never done those things without the help of alcohol or pills. Real life was something for which the counselling at the hospital did not prepare him. His superiors allowed him to keep his job on condition that he go to at least three AA meetings a week, but Donovan went every day and sometimes twice a day, fighting for life and sanity. "If I didn't make it then, I knew I never would." His girlfriend, with whom he was to form a nine-year relationship, urged him to go to the meetings and was very supportive. Donovan hung on the fringes of the AA groups he attended, not really participating in the discussions or sharing his feelings. He was too nervous to speak, too afraid of what he'd say.

He spurned other avenues of help: "I thought most priests

were drunks and fags; all they'd do is sprinkle holy water on you. I no longer believed in God. I wouldn't go to a psychiatrist; I thought they were all pill pushers." But Donovan stayed with AA because he saw people he identified with laughing at their past. "My motive for going to the AA meetings was survival. I was afraid if I drank I'd kill myself, and now I was afraid to die.

"If there's one thing I got out of AA it was hope — there was hope for me. Everything I have today I owe to AA. I owe my life to the two policemen who dragged me there."

When his mother saw the profound changes in him, she gave him an unusual gift. She had a toy poodle who had pups but was unable to nurse them. She gave all the pups away to be bottle fed except one. Giving it to her son, she said, "Now that you're sober, you can accept this responsibility." Donovan hated wimpy, fluffy little dogs, but he nursed the puppy through her first few fragile weeks of life. He named her Suzanne, and she came to symbolize his new shot at making something of his own life. For fifteen years, the dog was to be his constant companion.

Fellow cops saw the same changes in Donovan his mother did and started coming to him for help. Two years later he joined forces with Joe Ravino in the pilot stages of what was to become the stress program. But Donovan also wanted to prove to the force he was a good cop and determined to become a supervisor. He put three years of studying and hundreds of dollars in course fees toward developing his candidacy at the same time he worked on the stress program. The program had finally been approved, and Donovan was offered a full-time posting there at a patrolman's rank and salary. But he had just taken the supervisors' exams and topped the lists. He had to make a decision between the two: the advancement, status, and pay of a supervisor, or the long hours, poor pay, and uncertainty of running a stress program.

It was an easy decision for Eddie Donovan to make.

CHAPTER SIX

KEVIN

GUNNED DOWN OFFICER CRAWLED FOR HELP
A heroic Boston police officer was shot in the leg yesterday during a supermarket hold-up in Brighton and crawled up a flight of stairs to phone for help as the young thug emptied the safe.

Said Officer Ernie Walsh, 60, "I wish I could have done more, I'll tell you that."

In fair condition at St. Elizabeth's Hospital in Brighton yesterday, surrounded by family and buddies from the force, Walsh considered himself a lucky man.

Thursday, 10:30 A.M.
Ernie Walsh wasn't thinking about the shooting as he drove his wife's Ford Escort south along Washington Street toward the stress centre. The sixty-year-old patrolman who looked like a Norman Rockwell characterization of a kindly small town policeman, had driven the busy Boston street thousands of times on duty and off in his thirty-two years on the Boston Police Force. However, he hadn't driven down this particular street since he had been shot four weeks ago doing special detail guarding a supermarket on south Washington Street. That night, a twenty-year-old black male jumped the veteran cop from behind and in the struggle ripped off Walsh's holster with its .38 calibre revolver. Taking the gun, he fired one shot into Walsh's leg, then ordered the store manager to empty the cash register and safe. Once he had the money, the robber fled.

Walsh, now recovering at home after two weeks' hospitalization, was heading to an 11:00 A.M. meeting with Ed Donovan and a group of fellow officers who'd also been shot. As he guided the Escort mechanically down the street, his mind was two hundred miles away thinking of some spring fishing he was going to do up north. Suddenly, he realized he was passing the store where he had been shot; his heart skipped a beat. Then the distinct smell of gunpowder filled his nostrils. He broke into a cold sweat, his heartbeat quickened, then raced, as the incident flashed through his mind in vivid, frightening detail. His hands shook as he fought to hold the steering wheel with moist and slippery palms. Afraid to stop, he managed to drive slowly until the vision passed. Shocked and puzzled, he didn't know what had happened; while the wound in his leg was healing, the wound in his mind was just opening. Now his real fight to recover was about to begin.

To Eddie Donovan, there was nothing more challenging than working with cops like Walsh who suffered, whether they knew it or not, from the phenomenon called "post-traumatic shock syndrome." The term applies to anyone who, after experiencing a life-threatening situation or witnessing a tragic event, develops psychological problems. Cops who kill, those who are shot or injured, those who work a horrible car accident or a plane crash, particularly those who deal with women and children who've been savagely mutilated, are all potential victims of post-traumatic shock. Research shows that of police who experience such events, one-third will have minimal problems, one-third will have moderate problems, and one-third will have severe problems, such as mental or physical disabilities leading to quitting or being fired from the job, and serious problems at home. Walsh's flashback, complete with the actual sensations and bodily reactions, was normal, but with the care and counselling he'd receive at the stress centre, the complications he might suffer could be forestalled.

Having seen hundreds of Ernie Walshes, Donovan believed the cause of their distress was simple and obvious. Policemen are human beings, but the public, police administrators, and even cops themselves tend to forget it. Law enforcement is an occupation which demands that police be objective, stay emotionally uninvolved, and hide such feelings as fear or sorrow. But those feelings exist, and as Ernie Walsh was finding out, if they aren't expressed, they manifest themselves in other ways.

The argument that cops who crack up shouldn't have been cops in the first place angers Donovan. He's frequently seen bad cops mishandle gruesome situations because they aren't as compassionate, caring, or responsible as good cops should be. The good cops—the solid citizens with the right psychological profiles and records of exemplary service—are often the ones with stress problems. Because they care, they're more likely to suffer when they have to cut down teenagers who hang themselves, pull a suffocated baby out of a garbage can, or kill a deranged father of six.

Outsiders often say to Donovan, "Look at the bad things doctors have to see and do." "Yeah," he replies, "look at their divorce, alcohol, and suicide rates. They're almost as high as the police, and yet they're better trained, more socially accepted, and make five times the money a cop does."

At about the time Ernie Walsh became involved at the centre, Donovan had seen a powerful example of a severe post-traumatic reaction in a most unexpected situation. Frank Harrington, a BPD patrolman, was brought by a concerned friend to the regular Wednesday night meeting. For two years, the twenty-seven-year-old Harrington had suffered insomnia which led to heavy drinking, then work problems and marriage breakdown. He didn't know why he was self-destructing until he told his story to the Wednesday group. The group probed and peeled away his defences, exposing feelings that led back to an incident that had happened two years before. Harrington had been sitting in his parked cruiser filling out an accident report, when he looked up and saw an old priest crossing the street. A speeding car came out of nowhere and hit the priest while the horrified Harrington watched helplessly. He ran to the mangled priest and tried everything he could to save him, but the old man died in Harrington's arms clutching his bible.

Before joining the Boston Police Department the previous year, Harrington had spent five years as a paramedic, seeing hundreds of smashed bodies and every gory injury imaginable. He always coped well and was rated as one of the best paramedics in Boston. As a paramedic, and in other police incidents, he always arrived after the injury or death, took control, and did his job successfully. Witnessing the priest's death, and being a Catholic himself and not able to save him, left Harrington feeling helpless, inadequate, and guilty. When the group helped him unleash those feelings, he broke down and cried, finally recognizing what was destroying him from within. In his subconscious mind, he felt responsible for the priest's death; guilt led to insomnia (he feared he'd dream about the incident) and started the drive to self-punishment and destruction.

Donovan knew that cops have to depersonalize people and situations in order to cope. Usually, a policeman builds a wall, the "blue wall," around his feelings. The priest's death caught Harrington with his guard down. When Donovan called him the day after the meeting to follow up, Harrington said he'd had his first good sleep in two years. Even though he hadn't been shot, his wounds were deep, and Donovan wanted him to come to the same weekly trauma group as Ernie Walsh.

Several generations of cowboy and police shows have shown sheriffs and cops heroically killing bad guys as a matter of course. Therefore, we don't generally expect a cop simply doing his job to be bothered by death and dying. They're given a uniform, a badge, and a gun and are expected to handle our dirty laundry every day and avoid any problematic feelings. They're expected to do their duty, even though they may be second-guessed by internal investigations, trial boards, law suits, and a media that thrives on sensationalism and anti-cop feelings. Donovan sees the person behind the headlines and knows what the media, the investigations, and the policeman's own self-doubts do to him. It happens everywhere, and Donovan has the newspaper clippings to prove it, but, more importantly, he knows the story the papers don't tell.

In an eastern Canadian city, a welfare mother calls the police because her delinquent twenty-year-old son with a history of violent behaviour and crime is trying to take the family TV to his house. The son hits the mother and threatens his four younger brothers and sisters. Two officers respond to the mother's frantic call for help, but the son refuses to leave the house. They try to arrest him, and a scuffle breaks out. Now, the mother and kids scream taunts at the police. Although he is only five feet six inches tall and 140 pounds, the son is in a frenzy and gains the upper hand on the two policemen who have refrained from using their guns or night sticks. The son tries to grab an officer's gun; the officer shoots and kills him in the process.

The son becomes a saint in the papers; the mother sues. Every TV and radio station features interviews with the family who have gone from being welfare bums to martyrs. Even fellow policemen wonder why these two large, well-trained men couldn't subdue a punk kid. The newspaper stories don't reveal two more victims in this tragedy. The cop who killed the son breaks down within days. Three years later, his partner, the picture of macho strength and strong will, has difficulties directly related to the post-trauma of the shooting.

The story is repeated daily in Boston, Calgary, Belfast, or Melbourne. Because the readership of his *Police Stress Magazine* is worldwide, Donovan receives newspaper clippings and calls for help from police officials all over the world. Donovan sees police as being in a lose-lose situation, criticized if they do their job, criticized if they don't, and trapped by an image that denies their feelings. He has seen the damaging effects for over twelve years, and that's why the post-trauma groups are his favourite challenge.

He can't stop the shootings, but Donovan is determined

to keep the cop from becoming the victim. In Boston, whenever a cop shoots someone in the line of duty or is shot or injured himself, the police dispatcher is under orders to contact Donovan immediately. Donovan assesses the situation, goes to the scene if necessary, and makes sure the officer is in the hands of someone who understands post-trauma. In the first few critical hours after a shooting, little things are important, such as having the officer tell the story as few times as possible and having someone not involved in the incident sit with him and be his "buddy" while he waits to give statements back at headquarters.

Donovan then calls Paul Martin, a volunteer who co-ordinates the stress program's trauma teams. A team consists of four or five cops who have themselves experienced similar incidents. Donovan briefs Martin on the nature of the incident, then Martin goes over his lengthy list of officers who've been through the stress program, choosing those who best match the situation. A meeting is set up, sometimes as soon as the next day if need be. If the need is less pressing, the person will attend the next regular post-trauma meeting. Donovan has two regular post-trauma groups: Thursday mornings are for officers who'd been shot or injured, Tuesday mornings for officers who'd killed or wounded. Donovan used to call them shooting groups, but with more non-shooting post-trauma incidents occurring, such as Frank Harrington's, he decided that calling them trauma groups was more accurate.

Donovan and his volunteers regularly scan the Boston and area papers for any incidents involving police. When they find one in a department that doesn't have a stress program or shooting procedure, they call to find out how the officer is doing. That's how Kevin Miller came to be heading north on Highway 28 toward Boston and the stress centre at the same time Ernie Walsh was approaching from the opposite direction along Washington Street.

These men had entered police work from opposite directions, too. Walsh was typical of many Boston cops; he came from a police family. His older brother and father were policemen before him, and he turned his childhood fascination with doing good and chasing bad guys into a lengthy career.

Miller had had no such childhood ambitions. A university grad in sociology, he had spent three years managing a fast food restaurant, then three more years running a record store, both in a large mall. Periodically, police were called to the mall to quell minor disturbances, and Miller watched with growing interest their skill as negotiators and communicators. At the age of twenty-seven, Miller put aside aspirations to open his own business and joined the police force in the small city just outside Boston where he had grown up.

Two years later, during an evening he'd never forget, he was driving his cruiser down Main Street in suburban Rockcliff. He was glad he had made the career change. Despite long hours of boredom and the frustration of shift work, he loved police work. It was challenging, more satisfying than pushing hamburgers or records, and he felt he was helping people. He worked at keeping his five-foot eleven, 180-pound frame in top shape and ran five miles a day. He was ruggedly handsome with an athletic face, piercing steel-blue eyes and neatly trimmed blond hair. Two months earlier he had married his long-time girlfriend, and he was working on a master's degree in criminal justice.

At 1:30 A.M. he turned his cruiser onto a major residential street in a middle-class area where there had been reports of teenagers creating some Friday night mischief. He had driven for a few blocks down the quiet, tree-lined street when suddenly he heard a bang on the trunk of his cruiser. He hit the gas and cranked the wheel, spinning the cruiser around to illuminate the trouble, then slammed on the brakes. There was no one in the bright glare of his headlights. "Probably kids," he thought, "chucking a rock or brick and running for the hills." A man standing in a driveway nearby appeared to have come out of his house to see what was going on. Miller wondered if he should call for a back-up for such a trivial occurrence. He paused, then called. He stepped out of his cruiser and walked toward the man in the driveway to ask if he had seen what happened. Straining to see in the dim glow of the streetlight, Miller eyeballed the man carefully; he was white, fortyish, dressed in a blue windbreaker, blue cap, and grey slacks, his face expressionless, his hands hanging idly by his sides.

"Did you see what happened?" Miller asked as he reached the end of the driveway. No response. Miller walked slowly up the driveway toward the man, holding his bright 20,000-candle power flashlight in his left hand, shining it in the man's eyes to blind him and get a better look at him.

"Did you see what happened?" Miller repeated. No answer, no facial reaction, hands still limp at his sides. Miller instinctively reached down with his right hand to unsnap his holster. Maybe the man was retarded or deaf, Miller thought, stepping closer for a better look. Miller was now twelve feet away from him. Suddenly, the man pulled a 380 Baretta from the back of his belt and fired two quick shots toward the blinding light. No longer involved in a routine incident, Kevin Miller was about to fight for his life.

Miller felt one shot rip into his left shoulder, the other into his left arm knocking the flashlight to the ground. Facing death set off a strange time clock in Miller's mind. A second had a thousand parts and a hundred thoughts in it. Some thoughts, like "dive for cover," were geared to survival. Others were flashes of triviality, "Geez, no wonder they trained you to hold your flashlight out to the side in your off hand." That critical piece of training saved his life.

Miller instinctively rolled for the shelter of a car parked to the left of the driveway. Another shot shattered his right knee as the gunman's eyes began to adjust to the light. Miller saw the gun being raised and a bead being drawn on his head as he tried frantically to squirm further behind the car, at the same time struggling to get his gun out. But he couldn't. "I'm dead," he thought.

Then, just like the cavalry in the old movies, Miller's

back-up arrived, siren screaming, tires smoking. Seeing the dim silhouettes of Miller lying behind the car and a man fleeing around the back corner of the house, Dennis Creehan screeched his cruiser to a stop.

In one motion, Creehan grabbed his shotgun with his right hand, opened the door with his left, bolted out of the cruiser, and charged up the driveway toward his friend. Miller had a huge hole in his right leg where the hollow-point bullet had exploded into bone. The wounds in his shoulder and arm gushed blood. Creehan leaned over him. "I'm okay," Miller shouted, his hearing impaired by the gunshots. "Let's get the bastard." He gasped out a quick description of his assailant for Creehan.

Crouching over Miller to shield him, Creehan yelled into his portable radio, "We've got a guy down, send help, an ambulance. Suspect: white, heavy set, five-foot nine, moustache, blue jacket and hat." The flash and sound of four more shots came from behind a back corner of the house followed by silence.

"That's seven," Miller grunted. Creehan nodded. Their minds thought as one. They knew the clip was probably empty. Did he have another one? Would he run away? Should they move?

"Why the fuck is he shooting at us?" Creehan exclaimed. If their lives hadn't been on the line, the question would be funny. This wasn't regulation cops and robbers; this wasn't a criminal or prankster caught with his hand in the cookie jar. How the hell could they do something logical when there was no rhyme or reason to this?

It didn't matter. In the five seconds they had to act, the man ran around the house and came out right behind them. Miller saw him first. Before he could yell, a shot tore through Creehan's back, another hit Miller's portable radio knocking it off his hip. Miller tried frantically to squirm for cover but couldn't move. Temporarily stunned by the shot in his back, an entry and exit flesh wound, Creehan recovered and wildly fired off three rounds, then grabbed Miller by the seat of his pants and the back of his jacket collar and dragged him to cover around the side of the car. Creehan couldn't see the man in the dark, but fired back at the muzzle flashes still coming from his blazing gun.

The blaring sirens of approaching cruisers and ambulances rose above the gunfire. Then the gunfire stopped; the man had fled. The next thing Miller remembered was being lifted onto a stretcher and the attendants rolling him down the driveway to the waiting ambulance. He looked over and saw Creehan being placed in another ambulance.

A few hours later, their attacker was captured. It was his driveway he had been standing in, outside his own house, and when his day in court came he pleaded insanity. For whatever reasons, he had decided to kill a cop. Kevin Miller was in the wrong place at the wrong time; he was alive, but a probable post-trauma victim.

Donovan first heard of the shooting of Kevin Miller on the morning news. Two hours later, Donovan stood beside the young policeman's bed, looking down at his unconscious face and the massive bandages covering the bullet wounds in his shoulder, arm, and knee. Donovan knew the physical wounds would heal with time; what concerned him more was the damage inside. He looked at Miller's once robust face, now drained of color and limp from drugs, then placed his business card on the bedside table and left.

Kevin Miller was not unaware of Donovan and his work. While he hadn't met Donovan, Miller had heard of him down at the station and was inspired to write a paper on police stress for a criminology course he was taking toward his master's degree. He quoted Donovan extensively in his paper, but when he was shot down, Miller had no use for Donovan; he considered that Donovan's program was for the weak. Besides, no two shootings were the same; this was a private matter, and Miller figured he could handle it on his own.

Like a patient fisherman, Donovan kept angling to hook Miller into counselling: another visit to the hospital, several phone calls after he got out, all with no success until he baited his line with the "how's your partner doing" lure. While many cops wouldn't acknowledge their own problems, they did worry about their partners, and Miller was concerned about Creehan. His back injuries had healed, and he was ready to go back to work, but Miller feared that Creehan felt responsible for his being shot, for not doing enough to help when he came to the rescue. Donovan seized on Miller's concern and convinced him to bring Creehan to the stress centre. Creehan agreed to come only because he thought Miller needed the help. As far as Donovan was concerned, both would benefit. By talking to them together for an hour, Donovan exposed the bitterness and frustration burning below Miller's intense controlled exterior. Creehan was actually fine and returned to work with no problems. Kevin Miller agreed to come to the post-trauma meetings. Eddie Donovan had caught his fish.

Now, six weeks after the shooting, Miller nervously took his seat at the battered coffee table in the sitting room where the regular weekly meeting of the trauma group was held. Around the table sat Donovan, Ernie Walsh, Frank Harrington, Louie Gabarro, Manny Gomez, and Paul Martin. Walsh and Harrington were attending their second meeting. Gabarro, the senior member of the group, had been shot two years ago and had been coming to the meetings for the last year. Gomez, stabbed in the back a year ago, had been coming to the meetings off and on for six months but hadn't been to a meeting in several months. All were Boston policemen except Gomez and Miller.

Paul Martin was a natural choice to co-ordinate the trauma groups. The forty-one-year-old undercover detective, husky, gruff-looking, and bearded, sounded like he looked with a coarse, deep voice that was raspy from too many cigarettes. His tough exterior and profane street talk disguised a heart of gold and a sharp mind. Six years earlier he had had serious problems. Trained to expect the worst of others, his cop's paranoia had spilled over into his personal life and brought him to the point where he trusted no one. Depressed and drinking heavily, he had to be prodded to go to the stress centre because he had been suspicious even of it. The meetings and counselling broke down his barriers. He became a regular attender, then one of Donovan's busiest and most able volunteers. Three years later, he shot a kidnapper. His partner, who narrowly escaped injury and death in the incident, suffered as though he actually had been shot, refused help from the stress program, and experienced problems. Martin, because he was already in the program, handled the consequences of the shooting fairly well. Eventually, Martin convinced his partner to join the program.

Donovan was about to start the meeting, but Louie Gabarro was already holding court. Forty-five years old, bald, with large devilish eyebrows and an expressive face and hand movements, the talkative west end detective was a natural storyteller. He was talking about the problems a plain-clothes officer sometimes has in identifying himself to the public. Donovan sat back letting Gabarro go on for a few minutes, it would give Miller and Harrington a chance to feel more comfortable.

Gabarro told about a recently appointed superintendent who ten years ago had wanted to crack down on book-making. "It was a joke," he said, "the department wanted this bookie — a real oldtimer — who was using retired guys as runners and mainly dealing with senior citizens. A real over-the-hill gang. They weren't hurting anyone, but the department wanted them busted."

For a few days, Gabarro watched the dignified-looking old bookie pick up slips from his runners. Then he'd sit in the passenger seat of his beat-up 1960 Valiant, put on thick glasses, take out the slips, and shakily transcribe them onto the master sheet. One day, while parked in front of a bank, the old man was so engrossed in the transcribing and money-counting that he didn't see Gabarro, dressed in dirty old clothes, walk up and stare right in the open window.

"I'm a police officer, you're under arrest," Gabarro said. Startled, the old man grabbed the slips and put them in his mouth. Gabarro jammed his hand in the man's mouth to retrieve the evidence. The car door was still shut, so the man pushed himself across to the driver's side. Gabarro hung on, not about to let him swallow the evidence, and was dragged part way into the car, his legs left dangling out the window.

People coming out of the bank saw a young man dressed like a bum grappling with a poor elderly gentleman and figured that Gabarro was trying to rob him. Money was flying all over the place, the man's glasses were knocked off, his false teeth had popped out, and an old lady with an umbrella was hitting Gabarro's legs. She yelled, "Call the police."

Gabarro called out, "I am a policeman! Call the police!"

Knowing he only had one thing going for him, the old man joined in with, "Help! I'm being robbed! Police! Police!" Finally, sitting in the front seat next to the old man with one beefy arm wrapped around him, Gabarro managed to show his badge to the crowd surrounding the car.

But then the old man began to breathe hard and clutch at his chest, looking as though he were having a heart attack. He gasped for air; the crowd gasped along with him and started to chant "police brutality." Gabarro looked at the man's slobbery dentures sitting on his lap and hoped he wouldn't have to give him mouth-to-mouth resuscitation. He wondered why the hell he ever wanted to become a cop in the first place.

"I should have stayed in bed," he said, laughing at himself. Everyone laughed with him, and Donovan was ready to go to work.

"Louie, why don't you tell the story of your shooting," Donovan asked. Gabarro's face turned serious as he related how he had been shot with his own gun two years before, after a car chase. It was during the height of the lay-offs, and his partner for the evening was a clerk who hadn't been out on the streets for ten years. When they stopped the car they were chasing, its occupant ran down the street. Gabarro ran after him, caught him, and held his snub-nosed .38 to the man's head.

"Don't shoot, don't shoot," the man begged.

"I'm not going to shoot you," Gabarro said, figuring he was a scared young punk in real trouble for the first time. Gabarro needed both hands to cuff him, and his partner, the clerk, was nowhere to be seen, so he slipped his revolver into his pocket and started to put the cuffs on. The youth, a muscular black about seventeen, swung at Gabarro. At first Gabarro thought he was just trying to get away, but then he grabbed for Gabarro's gun. Gabarro fell, the youth snatched the weapon, then aimed it at the fallen cop.

This time Gabarro begged, "Don't shoot." The first shot entered his left leg, shattered his left hip, deflected through his liver, and settled in the small intestine. The second shot passed through his left shoulder. Shots three and four missed. The punk ran a few steps, stopped, came back, and shot him in the right hip. He pointed the gun at Gabarro's head, but the hammer only clicked — the revolver only held five shots. The youth ran. Somehow Gabarro got to his feet, screaming and stumbling after him. The measurements afterwards would show that Gabarro ran ninety yards.

"I want to ask you a very personal question, and I'm gonna ask it in front of the group because it has to do with feelings," Donovan said. "Would you have preferred to shoot and kill this kid rather than be hurt at all?"

"Then or now?" Gabarro said astutely.

"Now — after all you've been through," Donovan said.

"It's funny, I don't have any animosity towards him. The only person I have animosity towards is my partner."

"He chickened out on you," Martin said. Gabarro talked of the things his partner could have done to assist him when all he did was sit in the cruiser.

"He was so scared he never even radioed for help," Gabarro said.

Gabarro was also angry at the judicial system. His assailant was arrested several months later and tried for the shooting only because he attempted to sell Gabarro's gun, which he had foolishly kept. During the trial, a skillful defence attorney had the jury feeling more pity for the youth than for Gabarro, who by then had been in hospital ten times for a total of 186 days, had had numerous operations, lost a kidney, and still had two of the bullets lodged in him. The attorney argued that the youth came from a welfare family, didn't know his father, and had had nothing but bad breaks. Two white women in the jury cried their eyes out. He was found not guilty of attempted murder. The only thing he was convicted for was stealing the gun. The verdict left Gabarro with a bellyful of bitterness that Donovan was working to neutralize.

In contrast to the extroverted and excitable Gabarro, Ernie Walsh spoke slowly and calmly as he described his flashback experience on the way to the meeting. He seemed embarrassed. He was just a nice, shy old cop, eligible for retirement but working because he liked it, who had gotten shot with his own gun while guarding a grocery store. Walsh and Gabarro shared a common burden: the humiliation of being shot with their own guns.

"How's your sex life?" Donovan asked. Not only was Walsh surprised, but the other newcomers to the group looked puzzled.

"I guess it's okay," Ernie said. Donovan's question wasn't insensitive. Cops who'd been seriously injured had two common reactions: some, mainly the older ones, became impotent; others, their lives almost taken away, went out and, as Donovan put it, "screwed anything that was warm and moved." It seemed, apart from the flashback, that the shooting hadn't affected Walsh very much; he seemed to suffer only the inconvenience of having an injured leg.

Donovan was always cautious in these cases, because a post-traumatic reaction could arise months or years after the shooting, and Walsh's flashback was a danger sign.

Going back to the scene of a traumatic incident was very difficult and had to be done carefully. Donovan had been outraged a few months back by a network television show on violence that took a number of cops back to the scene to re-enact their violent confrontations for the cameras. It was the first time back for most of them, and the psychological consequences could have been serious.

Most cops he knew who had been involved in shootings avoided the scene because of the unpleasant memories. Often, when he felt they were ready, Donovan went with them to the site as part of their recovery process. Even after his own divorce, Donovan couldn't go by his own house, where his family lived, without feeling pain. He would deliberately skirt around it whenever he was forced to go through the neighbourhood.

"Manny, when did you go back to work?" Donovan asked Gomez, a ten-year veteran of a small police department outside Boston.

"Last week."

"You haven't been here for a while, and we remember you as being quite adamant that you'd never go back," Donovan emphasized, pointing his finger at Gomez. "You wanted to go off to Vermont and hide for the rest of your life—never go back to work." Donovan told the group that Gomez had been working the dispatcher's desk in his police station with his back to the main door when a mad man ran in, jumped a railing, and, before Gomez had a chance to turn around, buried a knife blade eight inches into the middle of his back.

"Eight and a half inches," Gomez said.

"Jesus, look at that! Got to brag now," Donovan said. "So talk about it. What's it like going back to work?"

"It sucks." Everyone but Donovan laughed. "Hey, I'd much rather sit home with my family," Gomez said.

"Being with your wife and kids all the time can be pretty boring. You can get sick to death of one another after a while," Donovan said. Gomez explained that he had looked forward to getting back on the job, but his wife was against it, especially when he had to work evenings.

"How long were you off work?" Harrington asked.

"Six months."

"How did you feel putting your uniform back on for the first time?" Donovan asked. Gomez sagged visibly. He said he found it strange, and all his feelings of anger about the injury returned. He compared his feelings to another time in his career when his rage had boiled over.

While patrolling in his cruiser, he saw a Lincoln Continental roar by driven by a little weasely-looking fellow holding a cocktail in his hand. They found out later he had just gotten out of Wapole Prison the day before, had stolen the Continental, and was having a drink to celebrate his freedom.

"My partner is driving, and I'm on the passenger side, and I say, 'Look at the little bastard with the cocktail. He can barely see over the wheel.' We try to pull him over. Wham — before we know it, the chase is on. Over curbs, through fields. He almost ran over a dozen people. He runs the car into a fire hydrant, jumps out with water flying everywhere and starts firing at us with a 9-mm gun. Blam, blam — shots are going everywhere, and the street is full of kids playing stick ball — blam, blam! He keeps going, and we can't get a round off because of the crowd. Finally, we lose him in the backyards." The group chuckled; it was a serious story, but the way Gomez told it, complete with sound effects, made it sound funny.

Gomez went back to headquarters, picked the celebrant out of the mug books and went off with a team of officers to arrest him.

"He's hiding downstairs in his parents' house in a hole behind the furnace. We try to get him out of there, and damned if he doesn't have another gun and tries to blast us away again. We brought in some tear gas and got him out. He was supposed to get ten years in prison, but I get a call a year later to go down to the city hospital to interrogate a stabbing victim. I go in there and blood is pumping out of this guy's chest, doctors working on him, and I have to get information out of him. I take a closer look, and it's the same guy who shot at me. I leaned over and said, 'You motherfucker, I hope you die.'

"This doctor screamed at me, 'Get out of here! Are you crazy?'

"I kept saying, 'Die, you son of a bitch, die.' All I could think of was those shots he took at me, and here he was out of prison already. The minute I saw his kisser I just said, 'Die.' "

"Good thing there weren't any relatives there," Donovan said, "but that is a normal reaction when you're angry."

Martin interjected gruffly with some street advice as to how to handle this kind of anger: "Just think that before he gets out of prison this time, somebody is going to get to him." Gomez smiled, and the others chuckled as Martin went on straight-faced: "So just think of him on his cot in prison, with some lifer slobbering all over him."

"Think of another thing," Donovan interrupted sternly. "Supposing you had him or the guy who stabbed you alone for five minutes, what would you do?" Gomez looked away. He was ambivalent in his anger. When he vented it as he had done in the hospital, he really wanted his assailant dead, but then he felt guilty for thinking such a horrible thought.

Donovan spoke for him: "Your problem is you like to be nice to people, you don't like to be a prick, and you don't like violence. We talked about that upstairs five months ago. Remember the anger you had? You've come a long way since then, but I want to see your smiling face around these meetings a little more regularly. You gonna be here next week?" Gomez nodded. He had no choice in the face of Donovan's high-pressure tactics.

Donovan motioned for Kevin Miller to tell the group the details of his shooting. Nervous and still suspicious, Miller spoke carefully and methodically as did most first-timers, as though they were giving evidence or justifying their actions to a superior officer.

"What kind of support did your department give you?" Martin asked.

"Good, they were really good," Miller said.

"Bullshit!" Donovan blurted. Everyone's head swung toward Donovan, then slowly back to see Miller's reaction. He looked stunned. Donovan didn't want him giving evidence. Donovan wanted the real Miller and the real feelings.

"The chief," Donovan said. Miller hestitated for a second, gulped, took a deep breath, and then let it out.

"He's an asshole," Miller said bitterly, then explained that both he and the chief were on the union negotiating committee and didn't get along. When the chief visited him in the hospital, he asked Miller, who was bandaged to the hilt, attached to pulleys and tubes, and facing possible permanent disability and at least a year's rehabilitation, "When do you think you'll be back at work?"

Donovan quickly got down to the nitty gritty. "Dreams, headaches, flashbacks, nightmares, what have you been having?"

"I've woken up in cold sweats," Miller answered. "I felt ambushed. That's what pissed me off the most. I didn't get a shot off. If he'd been robbing a bank, and we had had a shoot-out, and it was him or me, then it would have been okay."

"Dreams?" Donovan asked.

"I had a dream last week in which the guy who ended up arresting him got shot."

"Whoa!" Donovan said. "You say you dreamt that the officer who arrested the man who shot you, got shot?"

"Yeah," Miller said. The group members exchanged glances signifying 'What the hell does that mean?'

"What do you think that means?" Donovan asked. Miller and some of the others shrugged.

"A little role reversal," Paul Martin said. "Maybe you think you could make the arrest if someone else got shot."

"It's called transference," Donovan said. "Does anyone else see what it is?"

"I think he was going through it again so he could shoot the bastard," Louie Gabarro said. "I think you still want a piece of this guy."

"Guilt," someone else said, as several talked at once.

"Who said that?" Donovan asked. Manny Gomez nodded. "Why is it guilt?"

"He feels it's his fault his partner got shot in the back," Gomez said.

"Right. If he had shot the guy in the driveway, his partner wouldn't have been shot," Donovan clarified. "Now he's feeling so guilty about it, he's even getting his other partners murdered." Miller's subconscious guilt was doing a real number on him: guilt that his partner got shot, guilt that his partner had to save his life, guilt that someone else made the arrest. Now he was dreaming the arresting officer was shot so he, Kevin Miller, could come riding in on his white horse and capture the bad guy.

Miller's eyes widened as things fell in place. He told the group he owed his life to his partner who took a bullet in the back for him. The event was becoming another term paper on stress for him, but this time he was learning from Donovan first-hand, and he was the subject.

Donovan explained to the group that Miller and Creehan each had feelings after the shooting that they weren't telling each other. Miller felt guilty that his partner had to save him and got shot in the process. Creehan felt guilty that he almost botched his attempt to save Miller's life.

The group went through the shooting step by step with Miller. At each critical decision he made, they were quick to point out that he did the right thing at the time. How was he to know the guy was a psychopath? Realizing that the guilt he felt was normal, Miller would have an easier time overcoming it.

"Now that Dennis is healthy and back at work, I feel better," Miller said.

"How do you feel about your own injuries?" Donovan asked.

"Pisses me off," Miller said bitterly, wanting to wring his hands but unable to because of the huge cast that ran from his left shoulder to his wrist. Tears of frustration and rage welled up in his eyes, but he fought them. He leaned slightly forward, stroked his cast with his right hand, hung his head slightly to avoid Donovan's piercing gaze, and stared at the coffee table.

It was no accident that Donovan was sitting directly across the table from him. Donovan bent forward, cocked his head at an angle, intercepted Miller's line of vision, and said in a low whispering tone, "Do you feel angry?" Miller nodded without looking up. Donovan egged him on: "What do you want to do about it?"

"I wanna fucking kill him." Miller's words were coated with acid, the fire in his eyes burned as he looked Donovan right in the eye.

"It's all right," Donovan said, straightening up.

"It's the way I feel," Miller said.

"Don't feel conflict over it; it's a healthy feeling," Donovan said.

"You get very angry and frustrated that somebody attempted to gun you down without knowing anything about you, simply because you were in a uniform and had a badge on," Miller said, explaining his bitterness. "That was this guy's only reason for shooting me. He knew nothing about me or my family." Miller talked about his injuries, how frustrated he was about being dependent on his wife and others. He couldn't go to the bathroom by himself, couldn't take a shower, couldn't drive a car, and he'd be like that for much of the next year.

Donovan heard self-pity in Miller's words, so told him about a cop he knew in Canada who got shot when his partner chickened out on him. He had to wear a truss, and he told Donovan, "Every time I put that thing on and my kids have to look at it, I wanna kill that guy, and I wanna kill my partner."

Donovan pointed at Gabarro. "Look at all the aggravation Louie's had, and he still wants to go back to work, even though he could get full disability. You and him got a lot in common. Donovan encouraged them to get "locked in" with each other, to form a buddy system for support when Donovan or the group wasn't available. He had them exchange phone numbers and suggested a lunch meeting. Donovan's motive wasn't entirely altruistic; this set-up would lessen their dependence on him and give him more time to spend with others.

"How long have you had the beard?" Donovan asked, focussing the group's attention back on Miller.

"Since I was in the hospital."

"Why?" Donovan asked. Miller said it was because of the physical difficulty he had shaving. Donovan asked the question for a good reason: he had seen cases where cops grew beards to hide behind. One cop grew and trimmed his beard exactly like the beard of the man he shot. Donovan had seen protective masks take many forms: rebellious clothing, black humour, reflective sunglasses,womanizing. He even had one cop who shaved his head to make himself ugly and keep people away. Donovan's mask when he was photographing bodies had been a wide-brimmed hat which partially obscured his eyes and a tough-guy cigar hanging from the corner of his mouth. The cigar also had a practical purpose; its smell covered the stench of the bodies he photographed.

"Let me ask you about something you've been avoiding," Donovan said. "You don't want your wife to come here, and we talked about that upstairs, but we insist on talking to every family member 'cause it's a family affair and everyone suffers. How were things before you got shot?"

"Okay, just okay."

"What's happened since the shooting?"

"I've distanced myself."

"Tell me, is there a girlfriend?" Donovan asked. "No."

"Booze?" Martin asked.

"No."

"You've been staying out a few nights," Donovan said.

"Yeah."

"Well if there isn't a girlfriend or booze, what have you been doing?"

"I've been seeing friends."

"What kind of friends?" Martin asked. "Cops."

"Yeah."

"Why don't you wanna go home?" Donovan asked.

"I'm having a tough time considering anyone else's feelings," Miller said.

"Finally," Donovan exclaimed to the group, "some progress, a dent in the armour." Miller shuffled uneasily in his chair, adjusted his cast-encased limbs, then reluctantly said that his wife didn't want him to go back to work, even though he was anxious to return.

"But what I told you upstairs is your wife has feelings, she's in pain," Donovan emphasized.

"What I told you upstairs is, right now, at this stage of the game, I don't have the capacity to deal with somebody else's pain," Miller argued back. "I gotta work things out on my own."

Donovan told the group that since the shooting, Miller's wife wanted to have a baby but explained Miller's fears: if he'd been killed, his child wouldn't have a father.

"You gotta understand where her head is," Martin said. "If it happens again, she wants a piece of you." Miller, overwhelmed, shook his head in frustration.

"Okay, you don't have the capacity to deal with your wife's feelings," Donovan said. "That's fair enough, but you have to realize your wife has feelings."

"I realize that," Miller said proudly.

"Realizing it, and being smart enough to do something about it, are two different things. She's got to get help somewhere from people who understand." Donovan looked Miller in the eye with a "Gee, what can we do about that" look. Miller glanced away, then shrugged his shoulders in defeat, realizing he'd been set up.

"You want me to bring her in?" he asked.

"Naw, she's a big girl, she can get here on her own," Donovan said, grinning.

"You gonna keep coming, Kevin?" Donovan's impish tone was like a lifeguard asking a drowning man he'd saved whether the man was interested in swimming lessons. Miller nodded. Donovan reminded him of the Wednesday night meetings and said to call him any time if there was a problem.

"A lot of things can come out of this," Donovan said. "The biggest one is you can help another person."

Miller wasn't ready yet to hear the second part of the statement. It was the bottom line for any self-help group; it was Selye's philosophy; it was how Donovan kept his sanity. Selye called it "altruistic egotism"; Donovan called it survival: When You're Helping Someone Else, You're Really Helping Yourself.

CHAPTER SEVEN

THE APPOINTMENT

Thursday, 2:00 P.M.

The stress centre was a beehive of activity. The trauma meeting was over, but Louie Gabarro, Paul Martin, and Manny Gomez still talked in the sitting room. Behind them, an older cop who was waiting to see Donovan, Jimmy Connolly sat on the bottom step of the stairway. In one corner of the living room, Millie McCowan, a black detective and program volunteer, quietly counselled a troubled policewoman. In the opposite corner, a young couple nervously awaited a marriage counselling session upstairs with Dr. John Barry.

Dr. John, who had arrived moments before, quickly tidied and rearranged the sparsely furnished room across from Donovan's office for the full schedule of marriage and individual counselling ahead of him. He held sessions here every Thursday afternoon. The smell of his ever-burning pipe wafted into the cramped ILESA office next to Donovan's, where Brian Connor, a volunteer, called potential advertisers for *Police Stress Magazine*.

Donovan smelled the smoke but was oblivious to the activity. His door was closed, and he was hunched over his desk, staring vacantly at the telephone in front of him. His headache and the pain in his side told him he should call for an appointment to see Boston Police Commissioner Mickey Roache and put his career and the stress program on the line. He slowly dialed the number of the commissioner's secretary.

"Hello, this is Eddie Donovan, the director of the stress

program. I'd like to speak to Commissioner Roache, please."

"I'm sorry, but he's in a meeting with the mayor right now. What's this concerning, please?" the secretary asked.

"I'd like to meet with the commissioner early next week."

"I'm afraid that won't be possible for the next two weeks, he's —"

"Excuse me," Donovan interjected, "you tell him Ed Donovan wants some time with him. I don't care if it's in his office, at his home, or anywhere; I want to see him." The secretary paused.

"I'll talk to him when he's free," she said coolly.

Roache was in his mid-forties and had risen quickly through the ranks from acting lieutenant to acting commissioner in just under two years. His promotion to the commissioner's post on a trial basis was a sensitive political appointment made just two months before. He was replacing Joseph Jordon, and the pressure was on him to improve the department's tarnished image. Roache had instituted a senior level housecleaning, many of the old guard were gone. Donovan had waited out four agonizing years to be rid of them. Roache had sent officers to Donovan and the program for help in the past, so Donovan hoped his administration would regard the stress program favourably. But Roache had to perform faultlessly under the scrutiny of the mayor, the media, and the public on a number of sensitive issues or he'd be gone. In the scheme of things, the stress program and Eddie Donovan's problems had to have low priority. The secretary assured Donovan she'd give Roache his message, but she seemed doubtful of his chances of seeing the commissioner soon.

Donovan hung up the phone, slammed his right fist into his left hand in a "go get 'em, Eddie" gesture. He went to his doorway, flung it open, and bellowed downstairs, "Jimmy, you down there?"

"Yeah, Eddie," Jimmy said uncertainly.

"Well, get your ass up here." Donovan was concerned when he saw Jimmy Connolly at last night's stress meeting.

Earlier in the week, his wife phoned telling Donovan about an argument Jimmy had had with his youngest son, a nineteen-year-old, that led to Connolly suffering a serious heart attack. Since leaving hospital four months ago, he had done nothing but sit at home, eating and watching television, fearing he would die. He was bitter toward his wife and his family. No one could help him. Donovan had known the fifty-two-year-old veteran for twenty-six years. He urged him to come to last night's stress meeting, but although Jimmy came, he just sat, saying nothing, his pot-belly spilling out over ill-fitting pants. Donovan was angered by his old friend's appearance and asked Jimmy to see him privately today.

Donovan shook his hand, then seated him in his office, and shut the door.

"Jesus Jimmy, look at yourself," Donovan said, shaking his head. "You're sloppy fat. I remember when you were a strapping young man, working overtime, extra details, working the front lines in the riots, building a house, and now you're trying to eat yourself to death. Your kids are grown, your wife wants to do things, and there you sit, stuffing your mouth and watching TV. She's married to a bloody bore." Jimmy hung his head.

"You're killing yourself and everything around you," Donovan said. "When you gonna smarten up? Do you want to live?"

Jimmy nodded.

"What are you gonna do about things?"

Jimmy shrugged.

"How long since you had sex?"

Jimmy's face turned beet red.

"Jimmy, I'm gonna cross my arms and wait till you tell me." Donovan waited, but Jimmy wasn't going to talk.

"You haven't had sex since before your heart attack, right?" Jimmy nodded. "Jimmy, right now she wants you out of her life. She says you're dragging everyone down. She won't take it anymore. You have all these years invested. Are you going to let them slip away?" Jimmy started to cry. "Jimmy, if the two of you can't work this out, I want to see the both of you in here next week — to see me and to see Dr. John. I'm not going to let you do this to yourself, to your wife, or to your kids."

Donovan heard from Jimmy's wife that the son who had the argument with Jimmy before the heart attack was despondent, feeling he had caused the attack. Donovan wanted to help the son and asked Jimmy where he could reach him. He finished with Connolly and walked him to the top of the stairway. Connolly tried to smile as Donovan shook his hand, but his face was downcast, and his posture stooped.

"Jimmy, you're no old fart, you're even younger than me, and I'm just a pup!" Donovan patted him on the back and sent him on his way.

A couple of hours later, Donovan, still fretting about his futile attempt to gain an interview with Commissioner Roache, cursed at the departmental budget forms he'd been trying to figure out, threw them on the floor, and sulked into the hallway. He saw Dr. John was between counselling appointments, so he walked in and sat down.

"Do you want me to start the timer?" Dr. John dead-panned.

"I just need a break," Donovan said, stretching his legs out, interlocking his fingers, and putting his hands behind his head. Actually, when it came to analyzing Donovan, Dr. John was at a loss to explain how he kept going. Whenever anyone asked him, he just shook his head and said, "Beats me. He's an amazing man. I don't know how he does it."

The BPD had no psychologist, so Dr. John, who was in private practice, was brought in by Donovan for one afternoon a week of counselling, and when he was paid, it was by third party insurance claims. Many cops had no health insurance.

Dr. John had an extensive police practice doing psychological screening and evaluations for a number of police departments in the Boston area. Because of this, he knew police recruits had a naive idea of police work and a "gung ho" attitude that soon gave way to cynicism and pessimism. Problems usually surfaced after five to seven years on the force. Their divorce rate was 73 percent.

Dr. John foresaw the problems growing steadily worse because of the lack of respect for the police, a court system that discouraged their efforts, the increased use of drugs by both the general population and police, increases in violent crime, fear of law suits, and more restrictions and pressures being placed on police officers. The situation cried out for new techniques and approaches, but most police departments were run by old-school officers still ignorant of the problem.

Dr. John brought Donovan up to date on the stress program's request for government research funds. Donovan wanted, with Dr. John's help, to start a research arm of the stress centre, doing psychological, statistical, and medical research on police stress.

When Donovan and Dr. John begged for funds to do research, the common response from the fund-granting bodies was to throw them a pencil and ask to be shown the problem. That was the catch. There hadn't been enough research done to illustrate the problem, and most police departments, including the BPD, wouldn't allow access to their files. Those files would yield valuable information for individual officers, like absentee rates, sick time, medical problems, work problems, traumatic incidents, and a number of other factors that could be tracked and correlated. A few studies, like one done in Detroit, that showed a suicide rate among retired policemen eleven times the national average, were done by illegally scooping city records.

The many problems of alcoholism, burn-out, divorce, suicide and the damaging effects on police officers' families, were things police administrators wanted to ignore. This attitude frustrated Donovan because he knew that a research effort and preventative and maintenance program, could in the long run, save a big department over a million dollars a year.

"Piss on it," Donovan said to Dr. John, "I'm going to disappear for a few hours." He felt he was going to explode if he didn't get away from the building for a break. His phone started ringing and he darted into his office to answer it.

"Stress Program."

"Mr. Donovan."

"Yes."

"This is Commissioner Roache's secretary. He's found a gap in his schedule and you can meet with him here, Tuesday at 2:00 P.M."

"You're a lifesaver," Donovan said giving the desk a firm tap with his fist. "I'll be there."

CHAPTER EIGHT

BARB

Thursday, 7:15 P.M.

"God damn it," Donovan cursed, banging the thermostat in the stress centre's living room with the palm of his hand. It had turned cold out. He'd just returned from supper, the building was freezing, and the wives' meeting was due to start in fifteen minutes.

Because the house was owned and operated by the hospital, a locked, energy-efficent thermostat had been installed. Donovan knew it saved energy all right; it never came on. He gave it one final swat with the palm of his hand, reluctantly admitted defeat, and went to plan B, the old but workable fireplace in the sitting room. There was no wood, so Donovan improvised by rolling newpapers tightly, then straining to twist them into pretzel-shaped logs. He tore into a pile of newspapers next to the fireplace. Knowing the women hated a cold room, he lit the first two logs he'd made, hurrying to roll more. As the first puffs of heat and flame leapt from the fireplace, he boisterously sang an old campfire song but stopped when he heard a noise.

He strained and heard a quiet knock at the side door — not many knocked. Cops and wives who'd been there before just walked right in and made themselves at home, some loudly bellowing to let Donovan know they were there. The only ones who knocked were visitors, like the media, but they knocked heavily, and this was a petite knock telling Donovan it was a wife making her first visit to the stress centre.

"Come on in," Donovan shouted, "it's open." He heard the door slowly open and someone enter the kitchen with light, halting footsteps. "I'm back here," he said, grunting as he twisted another pretzel together. He brushed his hands trying to clean off the newpaper ink, then headed towards the kitchen. A nervous face peered around the corner into the living room just in time to see Donovan with his hair a mess, sleeves rolled up, hands and arms looking like they'd been dipped in soot, coming straight for her.

"Hi, I'm Eddie Donovan," he said thrusting his hand out then jerking it back when he saw the black mess.

"I'm Barb—Barb Miller," she stammered. "My husband Kevin was over to see you earlier today."

"Sure," Donovan said, "glad you could make it." Obviously, the isolated, decrepit stress centre was not the type of facility she expected. Well dressed in a white pantsuit, she looked ready to lounge on a psychologist's plush couch. Donovan showed her where the coffee was, then waved her toward a seat, a metal stacking chair in the chilled sitting room. She perched on the chair, wringing her hands with nervousness and cold, while Donovan manufactured more logs and resumed singing at the top of his lungs.

Some of the regulars started to arrive. Rita DeMarco, a brassy, energetic woman in her mid-fifties, took over the log-making job from Donovan, while he rushed upstairs to answer his phone. Faye, Tommy Branigan's wife, arrived along with two other wives. Mary Rasmussen arrived, said hello to those in the sitting room, and went upstairs to see Donovan. Seconds later she was back downstairs looking angry. She and Eddie had their signals crossed over which of them was to pick up Susan Lindsay who didn't have a ride to the meeting. Donovan, muttering under his breath, breezed down the stairs and through the group, saying his hellos to the new arrivals, then hustled out the back door to get Susan.

Rita built logs and fed them to the fire, while Faye and several others awkwardly tried to make Barb feel at ease. The conversation, pleasant generalities about the weather at first, warmed up along with the room as the topic switched to drinking and the horrors of alcoholism. Barb Miller wrung her hands even more and tapped her toes uncomfortably.

"I'm afraid I don't know much about it," she said. "I haven't known any alcoholics." Rita turned from the fireplace and smiled at Barb.

"I'm an alcoholic, honey, and before I sobered up, I used to do terrible things when I was drunk."

"Really?" Barb gasped.

"I went totally out of control and tried to kill people, particularly my husband." Barb's jaw dropped. Rita added, "Mind you, the son of a bitch deserved to be killed. I should have tried it when I was sober, then maybe I would have succeeded." Rita turned abruptly and threw a finished log on the fire. She seemed to roll and twist each newspaper with glee as if it were really her husband she was stuffing in the fire. As Barb would find out later in the evening, Rita had pretty good cause. She came home from work early one day and caught him in their bed with a woman twenty years younger than herself. Similar incidents happened several more times, and in each case Rita became more violent, drank more, and tried in various unsuccessful ways to kill her husband and his girlfriend. Finally, she went into a treatment centre, dried out, and since then had been faithfully attending AA meetings and the wives' meetings. She was filing for divorce, but her husband was still living at home and openly seeing the other woman, although he had found a more suitable location to meet her.

Donovan returned with Susan Lindsay and started the meeting, fifteen minutes late. Each of the ten women now sitting around the tight circle introduced herself. Donovan felt right at home with them; their openness to talk about feelings made his job much easier, as he'd cajole, castigate, teach, and preach his way through a meeting. Mary's presence made it easier for the group to accept him, and Mary wasn't hesitant when she had a problem with him to lay it on the table. The group loved that. When Donovan was on the road, Mary ran the meeting for him and constantly took calls at home from the wives whenever problems arose.

For the wives at tonight's meeting, the pressures and strains of their husbands' jobs had reached into the home to take a toll on their marriages. Alcoholism was often the common denominator, but the list of problems the group discussed was wide ranging.

Donovan was disappointed with the constant small turn-outs for the wives' group. He felt there should be two or three times the number attending. The need was there. Some wouldn't come because they hated their husband's job, and the stress program represented that job. Louie Gabarro's wife wouldn't come. She told Donovan, "You marry the man and not the job. I like being married to Louie, but I don't like being married to a policeman." Donovan tried to get Charlie Gilham's wife to come to tonight's meeting but she refused. She bluntly told him, "Why should I go to the job to get help, when it was the job that killed my son, Lonnie?" Donovan didn't worry, because he knew she was getting counselling from a competent priest. Charlie had tried the priest before coming to Donovan but didn't feel as comfortable as he did with his fellow cops at the stress centre Tuesday morning.

The main reason wives didn't come was simple. Their husbands wouldn't allow it. Even most husbands who used the program and were helped by it refused to let their wives attend. You could call them male chauvinists or macho men, but Donovan saw their reasons all came down to one word: control.

They didn't want their wives going to those meetings, spilling the family secrets, hearing about bad things other husbands did, then coming home to ask accusing questions like, "Do you do that?" Cops told war stories — that was okay — but wives gossiped, and the police department thrived on rumours. This was their thinking. Only a few enlightened souls encouraged their wives to come.

Donovan quickly glanced around the room to see who he'd start the meeting with. Joyce Lendrum, a jittery, slim woman in her late twenties looked anxiously back at him. Her husband, a motorcycle cop, had a drinking problem. A month ago a hysterical Joyce had called Donovan for help; Frank was drunk, and she'd taken his liquor and poured it down the sink, and now he was threatening to kill her. It was the middle of the night, but Donovan rushed over to their nearby house. Frank was in his pajamas, but with his gunbelt strapped on. Wild-eyed and drunk, he waved his gun at imagined monsters as Donovan and Joyce scurried for cover. Donovan cautiously talked him down and took his gun. Frank also gave up a personal gun he owned. Donovan had a gut feeling that with the proper counselling the career and marriage could be saved. Joyce decided to give it one last try. Donovan took Frank's service revolver to drop off at his sub-station and put the other gun in the safe at the stress centre.

"How's it going between you and Frank?" Donovan asked.

"Well, he's been good for the last four weeks," Joyce said. "He hasn't had a drink and says he loves me and will do anything to keep me, but I just don't trust him anymore. I want to have kids, but I'm afraid to do it and wreck their lives, too. He says he'll kill himself if I leave him, so where does that leave me?" Her tone was despondent.

"Joyce," Donovan said, "you've got to look out for yourself first. If he wants to wreck his life, you can't go down with him. How come he didn't come to the stress meeting last night?"

"He said he doesn't need it. He thinks he has the problem under control, and he'll beat it on his own."

"You know that's bullshit, Joyce. I haven't seen that happen yet. He's going to have to do something or he's going to lose you. Have the two of you started counselling with Dr. John yet?"

"No, he keeps coming up with excuses as to why he can't make the appointments."

"Joyce, I'll give him a call tomorrow and see if I can get him to come in to see me. You shouldn't have to put up with his static any longer. He's going to have to decide how badly he wants you." Donovan knew that no one quit drinking cold turkey and was able to keep it up for long if they didn't have the necessary support systems.

Donovan turned his attention to Faye Branigan. Faye was stout like an Irish washtub, her long face, lined with years of care, topped with striking white hair done up in a bouffant. She had thickened hands and strong arms from years of housework. Her smiling face hid a constitution as strong as steel and as hard as iron. She needed it to tolerate Tommy and his thirty years of alcoholism. They had a love-hate relationship, and Donovan didn't know from week to week what mood Faye would be in.

If nothing else, the meetings really helped her grooming. Three months ago she attended her first few meetings in old, out-of-fashion clothing, her hair a mess, and she wore no make-up. Tonight she wore clean, creased white pants topped by a black blouse, spangled in silver and gold, and a touch of rouge brightening her face.

"Faye, how's it going with you and Tommy?" Donovan asked.

"He's doing okay now that he's shaped up. His only problem is he's paying with health problems caused by the drinking. He's been going through a series of tests that have showed up some problems. But that's great," she said with a twinkle in her eye.

"How's that?" Donovan asked.

"He's afraid of dying. He's afraid of drinking. And he's afraid of me." Laughter filled the room. "If that's not enough to keep him sober, then I don't know what will."

"How's he been treating you?" Donovan pressed, sensing Faye was holding back.

"You'd think he could at least be polite in the morning. Today, I says to him, 'good marnin.' You'd at least think he could say 'good marnin?' The group chuckled at her Boston lilt. She told how Tommy just sat on the porch all day and looked off into space. That morning, the wife of an alcoholic lawyer who lives across the street came over to talk to them.

"Tommy was at one end of the porch, me at the other. She came to me first and said what a miracle it is that Tommy is sober and she wished she could help her husband do the same thing. Then she asked if she could talk to Tommy.

" 'Good luck, he's all yours,' I said!

"She walked over and asked Tommy if he thought it's a good idea about getting her husband to go to AA and her to Al-Anon. 'No,' he snapped at her.

" 'Why?' she said.

" ''Cause you're the whole cause of his problem,' he said.

"Can you imagine him saying such a thing to her, Eddie? The poor woman left in tears," Faye said, gripping the sides of her chair and leaning forward.

"Did he say it in front of you?"

"Yes," she shouted, "right in front of me!"

"That's a zinger," Donovan said, pointing his finger at her. "He knows what buttons to push just to get a rise out of you."

Faye described her years with Tommy. Once, while the kids were at school, Tommy, on a bender, started beating her until she escaped and locked herself in the bathroom. He sat outside the door, in his underwear, with cans of beer all around him and a loaded pistol in his hand. He fired a few shots through the door, as she cowered in the bathtub. After a couple of hours she heard him snoring, opened the door and escaped to call the police. When they came, they reluctantly took him away, but no charges were ever laid.

"They didn't do anything, Eddie. Then he came right back, and it all started again. I can't tell you how many times it happened."

"Why didn't you leave him?" Mary asked bluntly.

"And what could I do? Where could I go? I had children in school, and I had no money. Not like you women today. You didn't just walk out in those days."

"Why don't you leave him now?" Mary asked. Faye hemmed and hawed. She said she didn't have a driver's licence, was too old to get another man, too old to work. Mary's anger with Faye stemmed from her own bitter experience.

"I married a bum who drank and tried to beat me. I took my baby and left even though I couldn't work to support myself." Donovan jumped in to cool things down. Mary and Faye were from different generations with different values.

"You can't talk to a bottle," Faye said. "That's all I ever talked to. There isn't a worse hell on earth than being married to a Boston cop for thirty-five years." Everyone laughed. They knew, for better or worse, Faye would be with him until the end.

Ginny Rios wasn't so sure about staying with her husband. This was the first meeting for the petite, dark-haired woman in her mid-twenties. Her husband, a BPD patrolman for five years, had accelerated from a social drinker to a drunk coming home later and later after his shifts finished.

"I thought it was my fault and blamed myself," Ginny said, fighting back both anger and tears. Recently, in a drunken fit, her husband physically abused her. She called the police. He was arrested, and Donovan quickly had him whisked off to a detox where he'd been for the last two weeks.

"I still love him," she said, "but I hate his guts for what he's done to me." Vicki Bell and several others nodded their heads and smiled; they had experienced the same feeling when their husbands were in a detox.

"I want to leave him, but I'd feel like a shit for abandoning him. I don't know what to do. When I visit him, he tells me how sorry he is and how we should start a family, but I don't think I can ever forgive him."

"If you think your feelings are bitter now, wait 'til he gets home and you find you're married to a stranger," Vicki said. "Their whole personality is different. If he was drinking since you first met him, you won't know him. That's when you'll find out how much you love him."

"Amen," Faye said. She wasn't sure which Tommy she hated the most: the drunken one she knew or the sober one she didn't.

Marilyn Covington, an attractive, smartly dressed black woman in her mid-twenties, joined in. "When my Danny was in the detox I just hated his guts and was going to make life hell for him when he got out. I wanted him to pay for every moment of torture that he put me and the kids through.

"He came back home, and I did just that. I was a bitch, and I had him just where I wanted him, and there was nothing he could do because he loved the kids too much. Four months after he was home and back on the job he got shot in the back by two hoods who jumped him. Now he's partially crippled, and I feel like the lowest scum on earth," she said.

"It's like I personally pulled the trigger. I wanted him to pay. I made him go back to work when he didn't want to. I got my revenge, and it wasn't very nice." She stopped for a moment to collect her emotions. "When he most needed my help, I wasn't there to give it. Thank God he lived, and we're getting it all worked out now. He's really a terrific guy."

Donovan breathed a long sigh of relief. He'd worked hard to help them; first convincing Danny to go to the detox, then helping Marilyn to decide to stick with him, then dealing with the shooting and the wounds it left them with. Marilyn gained solace in the wives' group, and although Danny had missed the morning's trauma meeting because of a doctor's appointment, he regularly attended the trauma and Wednesday stress meetings. As a couple, they saw Dr. John on Thursday afternoons. They were over the worst of it now, and Marilyn saw her main function at the meetings as a helper to newcomers like Ginny Rios and Barb Miller.

Evelyn Biladeau's marriage was long past the point of no return. She needed help for herself. Overweight, fortyish, and plainly dressed, she was an angry woman. Her husband had been a twenty-five year drunk and a twenty-year cop. Eight times in recent years she took out restraining orders to keep him away from the house and their six kids. She received little co-operation from the police in serving the orders or enforcing them. Once, he hid out in the station, and everyone covered up for him.

"One night when he was back at home, he was so drunk he couldn't get to work. He'd wrecked his car, and I wouldn't let him drive mine, so I drove him to work. He crawled out of the car and into the station. Do you know what they did? They gave him a cup of coffee and sent him out by himself in a cruiser to patrol." Donovan just shook his head.

Now he was in the Terraces detox facility, but she held out little hope. He'd dried out several times in the past but always went back to the bottle. She was just relieved he was out of her hair for a few weeks. There was no way she wanted to visit him, or even have any of the kids go up. She had received several calls from him in the evenings, pleading for her and the family to take him back, but it was too late. He had had his chances, and her heart was hardened past the point of any return.

Other concerns angered her. From the psychologists at the detox, the family had received long, complex questionnaires to be filled out. She didn't mind filling hers out, and helping the older kids with theirs, but resented the fact they wanted her to help her five-year-old daughter fill one out, too.

"Don't we have enough problems that we have to involve someone that young?" she pleaded to Donovan and the group. Several wives nodded sympathetically.

"You think she doesn't know what's going on," Donovan said forcefully. "They know. They hurt, and it will affect them for the rest of their lives unless they're helped as soon as possible." Evelyn protested, but Donovan was adamant. "The family is just as much a victim of the disease as the drunk being treated for it.

"Look, the psychologists up there know what they are doing. It's a good hospital, and they're trying to help the whole family," Donovan said.

"What about not visiting him?" she asked.

"That's fine," Donovan said, "Let the son of a bitch come to grips with his problem. He's had enough chances."

"My oldest son is coming back from New York this weekend. He wants to visit him, and I'm afraid he'll try to take him out of there," Evelyn said.

"How old is he?" Donovan asked.

"Twenty." Donovan had been around the track too many times not to know the answer to his next question, but he had to ask it just to be sure.

"Does your son drink with him?"

"Yes, the two of them drank quite heavily together."

"I get it," Donovan said, "He's mad at Momma because he's lost his drinking buddy. Boy, have I seen that often enough. Well, you can't stop him from going up there." Donovan paused to think. "I'll give the hospital a call and see what safeguards they can plan from their side." Donovan still fumed from a case last week in which a young alcoholic officer tried to commit suicide. Donovan convinced him he should go the detox for four weeks to dry out and get counselling. He was only in for three days when his mother drove up and took him out. Donovan knew her. She was an alcoholic and she, too, had lost her drinking buddy.

"Time for a change," Donovan thought. "Let's get away from the booze."

"Susan, how's it going?" Tall, thin, and well-dressed, Susan Lindsay seemed oblivious to the discussion in the room. Her eyes were vacant and seemed to mirror an inner sadness.

"Not too bad," she said quietly. Susan had been suffering

from severe depression for the past six months. She saw a psychiatrist regularly, had the support of her husband and the wives' meeting but Susan wasn't responding. She seemed out of place in the group where others battled alcoholic husbands, drugs, shootings, and other problems that could be easily identified and shared with the fellow group members. Susan was depressed like many other thirty-five-year-old housewives; it had little to do with her husband's line of work, but because she was a police wife, Donovan and the group tried to help with her problems.

"How'd you like to go swimming with me next week?" Rita asked. Susan hesitated. She rarely left her house, but Rita persisted with her offer and the rest of the group encouraged Susan to go. Finally they set a date.

Donovan had watched Barb Miller fidget and sit back for most of the meeting, so he told the group briefly about Kevin's shooting and then turned to her.

"What happened after the shooting?" he asked. Barb hesitated before speaking.

"Well, after about the first day in hospital, when his condition stabilized, he turned into a different man from the one I married. He turned away from me. He was closer to his mother. He was downright mean and bitter toward me." Redfaced and gritting her teeth, Barb appeared shocked at her own bluntness. Donovan leapt in to give her a moment to calm down. He told the group they had only been married a few months prior to the shooting, and of Kevin's bitterness at being shot and how he reluctantly came to his first trauma group meeting this morning.

"What was your relationship with him like before the shooting?" Donovan asked.

"I thought it was good; now, I'm not sure."

"What's bothering you now?"

"I feel betrayed. Kevin got all sorts of help and attention, but no one helps the wife. Now I don't get anything from him, and I feel all alone. My family is out of state, so they're not around to help." She wiped tears from her eyes.

"I was shot too, but no one helped me."

"You're right," Donovan said. It was the truth, but he hadn't heard it put as strongly before. He'd seen many times that a shooting was a family affair, usually affecting the wife and children. Sometimes, they needed as much counselling as the cop. Donovan tried to do what he could, shuddering at what happened elsewhere; most departments didn't have programs for their own cops, let alone their families. Barb needed as much help as Kevin. Donovan wasn't about to pussyfoot around.

"I understand you want to have a baby now," he said softly.

"Yes."

"Why?"

Barb reddened again with anger and embarrassment that Donovan brought up this very personal matter.

"I'm not sure," she said. "Maybe I figure it will bring him closer to me."

"Barb, are you sure that's your reason for wanting the kid?" Donovan asked.

"Whoa, honey," Rita interrupted, "I tried that six times, and it didn't work." Laughter broke the tension. A slight smile even crossed Barb's face. "All you're doing is tying a ball and chain around your neck and giving him another reason to get out of the house. I used it to get the son of a bitch to marry me in the first place," Rita admitted.

"How do you feel about the man who shot Kevin?" Donovan asked.

"I wish I could take a gun and go up to the prison and shoot the bastard. I wouldn't give it a second thought," she said bitterly.

"Me, too," Marilyn said emphatically.

"Oh, oh!" Donovan said to Marilyn. "We've got to work on you a bit more."

"But that's how I feel," Marilyn said. "I'd like a few of those guys to get shot and find out what it feels like." Donovan found the wives were extremely bitter toward the people who shot their husbands, and many needed more help than their husbands in overcoming that anger.

Barb also expressed her bitterness about the friends who never called to offer condolences or help.

"They don't know what to say," Donovan said.

"But all they have to do is call," Barb said. "When I see some people, they look away and don't want to talk about what happened. I'll never forgive them for that."

Carrie Graham was another wife at her first meeting. Her attendance tonight was a well-orchestrated Donovan plot. For nine months Carrie had been coming to him for counselling over the suicide of her nineteen-year-old son, Davie. Her frequent visits chewed away at Donovan's time, and he wanted to get her into the wives' group; it would save him time and probably help her more. She wouldn't come. Her husband, David, was the chief in nearby Braxton, and she didn't want rumours to start. It was really David Graham that Donovan wanted in counselling. Carrie said he felt responsible for the suicide, and the guilt was slowly killing him. She had also told Donovan that he refused to visit Davie's grave.

Davie's death was a classic suicide profile. Their older son, Ken, a popular athlete and scholar, was tragically killed in a car accident when he was nineteen. Davie, then three years younger, had idolized his older brother but wasn't blessed with his many talents. The pressure of trying to follow in Ken's footsteps, much of it self-imposed, became too much for him. He sneaked his father's gun while his parents were asleep, lay on the downstairs chesterfield, put the gun barrel to the side of his head, and pulled the trigger. Both parents were devastated. Carrie knew of the stress program and eventually sought help from Donovan. David Graham refused help, and the overtures Donovan made to him through Carrie couldn't penetrate his pride. The fact he was a policeman had little to do with his son's suicide, but the suicide now had everything to do with his life, both at home and at work.

The next day was to be exactly one year since Davie's suicide. Donovan kept meticulous records on the dates of all suicides and other traumatic events involving the police officers and families he counselled. The anniversary of a child's suicide was a particularly difficult day for parents especially if they still harboured feelings of guilt or resentment. Donovan knew of several cases where fathers had decided to join their sons on that date.

The Grahams' situation, and the fact that David Graham refused help, really worried Donovan, and that's why he had schemed to get Carrie to tonight's meeting.

He had called her the day before and told her about Evelyn Biladeau. Evelyn lived near Braxton, her car was broken down, and she didn't have a ride to tonight's meeting. Donovan easily could have gotten Evelyn to the centre another way, but he relied on Carrie's helping nature to offer to bring her. When Donovan and the group worked on Evelyn's problems, Carrie looked proud she'd helped Evelyn, but she had no idea of what Donovan had in store for her.

"Carrie, how's things going with your situation?" Before the startled Carrie could answer, Donovan quickly explained to the group what had happened.

"I'd say all things considered, pretty good," she said, uncertainly. The pleasant, round-faced woman wore no make-up, but had a natural glow and brightness despite the problems she'd faced.

"Carrie, you know me well enough. If this were a group of men, what would I say to that?"

"Bullshit?"

"Riii . . . ght," Donovan purred.

"Well," she said, "there are some problems." Donovan took her off the hook. He told the group of David Graham's refusal to seek help, and his unwillingness to visit the grave.

"He's spending more and more time isolating himself at home. He's turning himself into a cocoon," Carrie added.

"Is he drinking?" Donovan asked.

"He used to be a heavy drinker," Carrie said, "but it's strange; ever since the suicide he's stopped."

"Do you know why?" Donovan asked. Carrie and the others in the room looked puzzled. "Because he's afraid if he gets drunk, he'll kill himself," he said. Carrie gasped. Donovan knew this thought sobered a number of heavy drinkers. "They're scared shitless they'll do it in a drunken stupor. I went through that myself."

"He's so damned proud and stubborn," Carrie said. "I've been trying to get him to come over here, but he won't — says he doesn't need help." She looked at Donovan. "All you men are stubborn!"

"Oh, you women resent a lot of things about us guys," Donovan said playfully.

"Well, sometimes I wish I had your strength."

"See?" Donovan said.

"No way!" Carrie said. "I'm just talking about the strength to lift things. As far as mentally, you guys will never come up to us women."

"Oh, I agree," Donovan said. "Men are babies."

"Tell me about it," Carrie said.

"The only reason I'm a stronger man today," Donovan said, "is all the pain I've been through and survived. You're all survivors," he said to the group. "It takes guts to come to these meetings. I wish more wives and husbands would do it." Privately, Donovan was pleased about this partial success with Carrie, and he hoped that eventually he'd get to David Graham as well.

CHAPTER NINE
ILESA

Friday, 10:00 A.M.

Friday was usually Donovan's catchup day, the one day when he had no group meetings and very few calls. With the weekend in sight, it seemed as if everyone temporarily put their problems aside, so Donovan prepared to do neglected errands typical of the responsibilities of the director of any one-man operation. First, a trip downtown for toilet paper, a new broom, and some paper cups from supplies; then to headquarters to scrounge a spare typewriter and find someone who could fix his surplus photocopy machine; then track down his missing pay cheque, and, finally, talk some brass into helping a suspended patrolman he'd been counselling get back to work. Donovan was just getting ready to leave when the phone rang.

"Mr. Donovan, I saw you on television last week," a woman said. "You described my son. That's him! That's exactly the way he is right now." Donovan knew she was referring to last week's half-hour Boston area television special on the stress program where Donovan outlined the desperate state people can reach.

"You don't have to die to be dead," he'd said on the show. Donovan had seen many walking wounded every day of his work; walking, talking, breathing human beings, but emotionally and spiritually dead.

"My son's a juvenile social worker in Las Vegas," the woman continued. "He quit his job last week and phoned me and said, 'Ma I'm dead. I can't take it anymore.' He's drinking heavily, and I think he's into drugs, too."

"How do you think I can help?" Donovan asked. Because of the extensive media coverage of the program, Donovan

128

received many calls for help. He calmed the lady down, found out she was from New Hampshire, took her name and number and that of her son in Las Vegas. "Now take it easy. I'll call some people I know out there and see if they can talk to him."

"Mr. Donovan, I want you to get him."

"What?"

"I'll pay you whatever it takes for you to come with me and get some sort of help for him. I'll pay you anything."

"Look," Donovan said firmly, "I'm going to make some phone calls. You phone me back in half an hour." Donovan was already flipping through his Rolex file, looking up numbers of several people in the Las Vegas area. He didn't even bother hanging up the phone, he just pushed the button down and dialed the first Las Vegas number.

The stress program's influence had spread quickly beyond Boston. First, through a mutual aid system, police departments from the dozens of smaller cities around Boston took courses at the Boston Police Academy, so they were exposed to the program from the start. They were also invited to seek help or attend meetings at the stress centre, even though Donovan's budget didn't allow for this. With Donovan's help, some of the cities started their own stress programs, but, even so, about 30 percent of the cops who used the centre were from outside the city. A number of other police agencies within Boston also used the program, such as the transit and the municipal police.

One summer day in 1975, as he was going through the mail, Donovan spotted a brochure from the Massachusetts Criminal Justice Training Council. He showed it to Ravino and said, "This sucks. There are all sorts of courses here for police officers to handle everybody else's problems, but not one course for them to handle their own." So Donovan called Gary Egan, a former state trooper who ran the training council, and told him what he thought. Egan agreed and asked Donovan to develop a course. Donovan developed a one-day stress seminar, later expanded to two, and taught it all over the state.

Donovan then lectured at the FBI Academy and started speaking at police seminars and conventions around the country. The media noticed his pioneering efforts and dogged perseverance which led to statewide then national coverage, with stories in the *Washington Post*, *Los Angeles Times*, *Chicago Tribune*, and other major dailies.

The stress centre began to receive calls from police officials, psychologists, chaplains, and police officers from all over the US and Canada, requesting help. Newspaper, magazine, radio, and television reporters besieged Donovan with requests for interviews. This, combined with his heavy workload of day-to-day counselling and group sessions, ran him ragged; things were happening too quickly.

He retreated from the onslaught for a one-week vacation in 1977 to Newfoundland. The beautiful countryside and slow pace of living helped him collect his thoughts. The mail the program had received from psychologists all asked the same question: "How do I get cops to talk to me?" Police officials wrote begging for information on handling post-trauma and other problems they never knew existed before. Donovan knew some sort of organization was needed to co-ordinate and disseminate the available information, if only to get everyone off his back.

At first he considered a New England organization, but then thought, "Oh, hell, why not a national one." However, he'd received letters from England, Israel, South Africa, Australia, and elsewhere around the world. Every law enforcement agency seemed to have the same problems: alcoholism, divorce, burn-out, and stress-related illnesses. He thought, "Well, let's do it right and make the organization worldwide."

By the time he returned to Boston, Donovan had a plan of action and even a name for his organization: ILESA, the International Law Enforcement Stress Association. He convinced notable people to serve on the board to give it

Holding the first issue of *Police Stress Magazine* are Ed Donovan, President of ILESA; Dr. Hans Selye, President of the International Institute of Stress; and Dr. Paul Rosche, President of the American Institute of Stress in 1979.

Donovan with Dr. Selye in his Montreal office.

In Selye's office just prior to his death in 1982.

2nd International Symposium on the Management of Stress

November 18-22, 1979
Loew's Hotel, Monte-Carlo, Monaco

A Wonderful Thanksgiving Vacation

Sponsored by

International Institute of Stress
Hans Selye foundation
Montreal, Canada

&

International Health Resorts, Inc.
Beverly Hills, California

A PARTIAL LIST OF SCHEDULED SPEAKERS

FULL NAME	TITLE	AFFILIATION	SPECIFIC TOPIC
Hans Seyle, M.D., Ph.D., D.Sc.	President	International Institute of Stress Montreal, Canada	Stress and the Code of Behavior
Linus Pauling, Ph.D. Nobel Prize	Emeritus Professor of Chemistry	Stanford University, California, U.S.A.	Vitamins and Stress
Roger Guillemin, M.D., Ph. D., Nobel Prize	Professor and Chairman	Salk Institute, La Jolla, California, U.S.A.	Brain Hormones & Stress
Sir Hans Krebs, M.D. Nobel Prize	Emeritus Professor Biochemistry	Radcliff Institute, Oxford University, England	Stress Delinquincy Among Children
Ed Donovan	President	International Law Enforcement Stress Association, Mass. U.S.A.	Law Enforcement & Stress

Advertisement for the Monte-Carlo Stress Symposium, 1979.

Donovan speaking in New York, 1983

A television interview.

With Ted Kennedy.

With Hal Linden, "Barney Miller."

With Veronica Hamel of "Hill Street Blues."

With Rodney
Dangerfield.

With Phil Donahue after
the show.

Donovan receives an appreciation award from the union that fought him in the beginning.

Donovan becoming an honorary member of the Massachusetts Association of Afro-American Police.

Recognition and appreciation from the Ontario Provincial Police.

credibility, including Senator Edward Kennedy, who chaired the Senate Health and Scientific Research Committee at the time, author Joseph Wambaugh, and Thomas Hodgson, chief superintendent of Scotland Yard. But the man Donovan wanted most was Dr. Hans Selye. After Donovan made his trip to Montreal and obtained Selye's support, ILESA had worldwide credibility.

Donovan created *Police Stress Magazine* to disseminate material to ILESA members. He wanted a gut-level magazine that would appeal not only to the psychologists, chaplains, and police chiefs, but also to cops on the street and their wives. He asked Dr. Selye, Joseph Wambaugh, Gary Egan, Dr. George Kirkham, Eugene Smith from Harper and Rowe, and Bruce Swanton from the Australian Institute of Criminology to serve on the editorial board.

The first issue came out in the fall of 1978, and 17,000 free copies were circulated to English-speaking police departments around the world. The last paragraph of Donovan's president's message in the magazine summed up what he wanted ILESA to accomplish: "It is the goal of this newly formed organization to exchange ideas, information, counselling techniques, and training methods; to present findings of studies, to identify problems in all areas, and to help others establish stress programs. This will only work if we unite and share these goals."

The feature article, written by Dr. Selye, stated that police work was one of the most stressful occupations in the world, exceeding even the formidable stresses and strains of air traffic control. Subsequent issues lived up to Donovan's goals, as the magazine presented progressive articles on training, research, post-trauma, health, fitness, and many personal stories from cops and their wives.

Although the organization and magazine looked impressive, behind the gloss and the outstanding list of directors there was only one man, Eddie Donovan, working out of a small room next to his office. With the help of a few volunteers, he put together the whole magazine. Donovan wrote stories, reprinted clippings sent to him, and begged, borrowed, and sometimes stole articles for the magazine. He added smart art work, creative layout, and an impressive array of in-depth articles.

But memberships in ILESA and subscriptions to the magazine only dribbled in. The organization and magazine were never as successful as he had envisoned, and he struggled from the start to keep it afloat and print one or two issues of *Police Stress* a year. He couldn't get advertisers for the magazine. Brian Connor, a young recovering alcoholic in the program, volunteered his time daily to call potential advertisers, but the answer was always no. Through Donovan's persistence, another issue, while often late, was always published.

Since 1980, stories on Donovan and the program have appeared in *Time, Newsweek, U.S. News and World Report, Prevention Magazine, Discover Magazine, Police Chief Magazine*, and major newspapers from coast to coast. He's appeared on the "Phil Donahue Show", ABC's "20/20", the "Today Show" with Jane Pauley, "Sunday Morning with Charles Kuralt", an ABC special "The Shattered Badge", Dick Cavett on HBO, and on numerous regional and local television and radio shows. The fear he once had of speaking to his AA groups and his peers at the police academy gave way to a poised, controlled presence. He was an engaging guest, well-spoken with his quick-paced, blunt talk. He showed an ability to think on his feet and handle the most cynical questions on phone-in shows. He shared centre stage with his volunteers and would usually ask one to appear on shows with him. On shows shot at the stress centre, he stayed in the background and let the groups do the talking.

In 1982, "Sixty Minutes" had scheduled an item on the stress program, with Harry Reasoner assigned as the correspondent, but the BPD wouldn't approve it. They also refused Donovan an appearance on the "Phil Donahue Show", but he went anyway. Donovan learned recently that the previous police administration refused most of the interview requests for him that came through regular police channels. Even "20/20" had to shoot outside Boston city limits, because the department didn't want footage connecting BPD policemen with an item highlighting alcoholism in police work.

The brass seemed to resent the publicity Donovan received. There he was, a lowly patrolman, with his face popping up on network television and in articles in prominent magazines and newspapers. Actually, all that publicity probably saved the program. If the program were shut down by the department, the media could raise a furor that would embarrass the department. Donovan was resented mainly because he publicized police dirty laundry. Command staff felt the problems of police officers should be kept quiet and in-house. Most police forces tended to cover up, avoid, ignore, but never fix. Negligent retention law suits are now changing that attitude. Police departments have been successfully sued for using policemen judged not fit for duty, as in this example reported by *Police Stress Magazine* in February 1982:

COP'S WIFE WINS $425,000 FROM CITY

A woman who was shot five times by her policeman husband, who then killed himself, won $425,000 in damages from the city yesterday after she charged that his superiors should have noticed his "strange" behavior.

Virginia Bonsignore, forty-five, of Queens, still has three or four bullets in her from the 1976 shooting, which affects her speech and balance.

Her lawyer, James Sawyer, charged at the five-day trial that the police department's "code of silence" prevented it from weeding out cops who exhibit signs of violence. He noted that between 1973 and 1976, nineteen cops killed themselves, compared with fourteen slain in the line of duty.

The police department countered that Officer Blase Bonsignore had been on the force twenty-three years without a complaint lodged against him.

Mrs. Bonsignore said her husband had been acting

strangely just before his violent outburst and had lost more than thirty pounds. She charged that his superiors ought to have noticed that something was wrong. Her lawyer called a number of doctors and psychologists to the stand to support his client's contention. After deliberating two days, the jury agreed with her.

Since the suits, some departments have panicked and fired problem officers. Now both ends of the spectrum exist: some forces hide the officers, others fire them, but few think or know how to help them.

Cops have come to see Donovan from as far away as California and Canada for help they couldn't receive at home, and over the phone he has handled emergencies from all over the world. From the many who contacted him at the stress centre and from what Donovan saw first hand on his speaking trips around the country, he knew the problem of police stress was everywhere. Every street cop has handled domestic disputes and stopped cars, the two most potentially violent situations, and every cop has cleaned up after accidents and suicides.

Although small police forces don't have the problems and hard core crimes of the cities, they have their own unique problems. In a small community, a cop and his family are known to everyone. When he has to do something unpopular, his wife and kids pay for it. Donovan knew of incidents in Canada where members of the world-renowned Royal Canadian Mounted Police (RCMP) patrolled peaceful, conservative towns, but their wives and kids were spat on simply because their husbands or fathers were Mounties.

The RCMP, respected for their progressive training and impeccable reputation, had done virtually nothing to alleviate stress in the seven years Donovan had observed them. In one recent year, he knew of five officially acknowledged suicides of officers in their force of 13,000. That was a rate almost double the population norm.

The RCMP had publicly stated that their recruits were the cream of the crop, and there is always a long waiting list of Canadians anxious to join the prestigious force. Their training reinforced the image. To Donovan that highlighted the problem. The cream of the crop was not supposed to have problems. Just like in the Marines, the FBI, CIA, or other elite forces, you dare not show weakness.

The RCMP officer shared a common fear with police officers everywhere. If he sought help from the force psychologist, it went on his record. For a cop, that was a death warrant. He felt he'd be blacklisted, and his fears usually were well founded. Often, he was transferred to an undesirable position in order to undermine his morale. This led to his resignation or to a poor performance record that would give stronger grounds for firing. The result was that he told no one and didn't seek help. Often, his problems would explode publicly with brutality on the job, wife beating, or suicide.

The RCMP reaction to its surfacing stress problems was typical; manipulate the statistics, issue impressve looking press releases to skirt the problem, hire more psychologists, and commission a study. Deep down, they prayed like hell the problem would go away somehow. For years, Donovan looked at the RCMP's superficial stress effort and called it "crap." He knew whatever they did wouldn't work as long as the superior, infallible attitude existed.

Today, female officers, who were first admitted into the tradition-bound force in 1974, are quitting in record numbers because of their own discrimination-related problems.

"I got tired of being propositioned by senior officers who thought you were a lesbian if you didn't or a slut if you did," said one female ex-Mountie. "When I complained, I was told I had an attitude problem."

"In the first five years, I became hardened and cynical," said another in an *Edmonton Journal* article of January 20, 1986. "But then I asked myself what the hell was I doing. It was fine for men to come out and pound the wall after hearing a ghastly child abuse case, but a woman who cried was frowned upon."

Donovan had been brought to Canada many times by the Ontario Provincial Police, which was making an honest effort to confront their officers' stress problems. But on other trips to Canada, Donovan saw things that concerned him. Most Canadian police forces followed the military tradition of having drinking clubs for their men. Some major city police forces had up to three bars located right in police headquarters: one for commissioned officers, another for non-commissioned officers, and a third for patrolmen. The Toronto Metro Police had a posh club that would put most nightclubs to shame. Donovan wasn't against the drinking, but the clubs perpetuated the macho image. They encouraged spending more time with those you worked with, telling war stories and bitching, and spending less time at home with families and with activities outside police work.

In the 1981 ABC Television special "The Shattered Badge," which documented the police stress problem, Detroit Police Chief William Hart was asked how stressful a policeman's job is. He said, "A policeman's job is like any other job; whether they work in a factory or anywhere in the corporate structure, it's all big business now, and we're service oriented. Police work is less stressful now than it has been in the past."

The interviewer asked, "If it's not stressful, what accounts for the high suicide rate, high alcoholism, high divorce rate?"

Hart replied, "Well, I think that permeates all society." The interviewer then asked him how he accounted for the six suicides and two attempted suicides in his department that year. Hart's response was, "They don't commit suicide because of a police problem; it's a family problem generally speaking — nothing to do with his job."

Hart's attitude was typical and still is of a majority of police departments. One exception is former New York Police official Tony Bouza, now the innovative Minneapolis Police Chief. At a police stress conference recently, Bouza stated to the group, "I myself was a late and rather reluctant convert to stress programs. I thought they were mostly bullshit, as I thought it was a way for cops to escape their just desserts. I learned the hard way I was wrong. I've seen so many cover-ups, so many evasions, so many attempts to paper over some critical problems, I can tell you it simply doesn't work, so we have to confront the issues. With the transit police [Bouza was Chief of the New York Transit Police] I really made an effort, and we had a very good stress program. Coincidentally, we stole all of Ed Donovan's ideas."

The phone had been ringing continually, keeping Donovan from his errands. First, it was the Danville police chief calling to thank Donovan for his help with Charlie Gilham. Gilham had withdrawn his resignation and was coming back to work. Now, it was Jimmy Connolly on the line, the veteran cop who'd had the heart attack and wallowed at home, afraid he was going to die.

"Eddie, you were right!" Jimmy said. He told Donovan that after he left the stress centre, he had gone home and made love to his wife for the first time since his heart attack, not only once, but twice more later that evening and once again in the morning. He and his wife were going to spend the weekend at the Cape and were planning a Florida vacation at the end of April.

"Instant cured," Donovan called the phenomenon and wished he'd see it more often. One visit to the stress centre and some aggressive counselling was enough to scare some like Jimmy into taking immediate action to rectify their problems. They didn't have to come back. Donovan loved those cases.

Donovan again dialed the phone, this time with a lead on The Meadows, a health facility in Arizona that would take the lady's son from Las Vegas. He made a few more calls to connect the mother with the son and the son with the facility. All he could do now was hope for the best. He had done his part.

CHAPTER TEN
CHIEF

Friday, 2:00 P.M.

The phone call surprised Donovan, and in his line of work, he wasn't easily surprised.

"Mr. Donovan, it's Chief David Graham from Braxton; we haven't met," the stern, official-sounding voice said, "but I believe my wife Carrie has seen you about Davie."

"Yes, she has," Donovan said.

"I want to go to his grave today." Graham's voice cracked slightly.

"Bingo," Donovan thought. His effort to get Carrie to last night's wives' meeting had paid off. What Graham was really saying was, "I want to go, but I can't do it by myself and I need your help." David Graham was one very proud cop who dared not loosen his grip on control by asking for help, but today, the first anniversary of Davie's suicide, would test the limits of his control.

"Would you like me to come with you?" Donovan asked.

"Yes."

Donovan arranged to meet him at three o'clock at the small airport on the outskirts of Braxton, away from police headquarters and its prying eyes. As a result of his frequent media appearances, every police officer in New England knew who Donovan was, but those who didn't understand his work labelled him as the guy who coralled the cuckoo cops. Donovan had to be careful who he was seen with in public. Even cops he helped at the stress centre would sometimes ignore him at the station if there were others around. So Donovan would rendezvous secretly with Chief Graham at the airport and drive him the five miles through the countryside to the cemetery where Graham's sons, Davie and Ken, lay buried side by side.

Braxton was indirectly on Donovan's way home. He'd had his fill of work for the week, and this was his chance to leave early and try to escape the madness for two days. He hurried to shut down the building for the weekend, literally running from room to room closing windows and tidying up. "What a week," he thought. Things seemed to run in cycles — this week it was kids' suicides; last week it was four marriage break-ups; the week before that, three gay cops with problems; and before that, three shootings in two days.

Donovan daydreamed about sailing in the South Pacific, then of skiing down a Colorado mountain as he navigated the beautiful backroads on the way to Braxton. He could have taken the freeway, but he just wasn't in the mood. He relished the chance to relax; the windows were open and the wind blew through his hair.

Donovan drove into the grounds of the small airport and headed for the nearly empty parking lot. The Chief's black Buick was parked at the far side where Graham said it would be. Donovan pulled up next to it. The door opened and out stepped David Graham, a tall, well-built man with military bearing, smartly attired in his uniform, complete with cap and gloves. Donovan, his hair messed by the wind and wearing his customary casual attire, peered out at Graham. The Chief pulled off his right glove, straightened his jacket, adjusted his cap, then opened the passenger door to Donovan's car and slid in.

"Mr. Donovan," he said, reaching across and shaking Donovan's hand. Their eyes met briefly, then Graham looked away, brushed a piece of lint off his sleeve, straightened in the seat, looked down and adjusted the creases on his pant legs, then lifted his head proudly and looked out the front window. Donovan pulled out of the parking lot for the ten-minute trip to the cemetery. Nothing was said, no family talk, no weather, just silence except for music quietly coming from the car radio. When he checked to the right for traffic, Donovan saw the impassive profile of the Chief still looking straight ahead. Twice, he thought he heard him gulp back surfacing emotions, but his ramrod facade never cracked.

The refreshing spring air and the beauty of the countryside were lost on Donovan now. "God, he's got to be hurting," Donovan thought. For him to pick up the phone and call the stress centre must have been an act of desperation. Donovan wondered how close he'd been, or still was, to suicide. The visit to the grave would be a powerful dose of reality, and Donovan worried whether the experience might be too much for him because he hadn't been in counselling to prepare for it.

Donovan had had many dealings with New England police chiefs. In the immediate area just around Boston there were fifty small cities, each with its own small police force, and most had been in contact with Donovan. He helped several set up their own stress programs and most of the others sent their officers to Donovan for counselling, but the chiefs wouldn't come for themselves, and that presented Donovan with a frustrating challenge. When he heard a chief had a problem, he couldn't use his usual aggressive tactics to get him into counselling, and no subordinate officer was going to force him to seek help. A chief coming to even a private counselling session with Donovan risked rumours, his job and his pride. Like Chief Graham, they had to be desperate to call. So those Donovan eventually saw usually had serious problems, often past the point of no return.

Most chiefs were old-school, usually with military training, so they were well entrapped by the macho image. The further they had progressed up the line in their police force, the fewer people they had to confide in. The cops on the street at least had each other.

Chiefs were alone at the top, but their problems and

frustrations in some ways weren't much different from the street cop. They wanted to do good, but were frustrated by the legal system, the political pressures and the general negative attitude of the public. The daughter of an internationally known Canadian police chief told Donovan she had found her father, then retired, crying one day. A newspaper featuring several stories criticizing the police force was crumpled in front of him. He said, "I thought I could help do something, but things are only getting worse." Donovan knew most good cops on the street felt the same way during their low moments.

Donovan frequently lectured at major police chiefs' conventions across the country. Regardless of where he spoke, Donovan's message was blunt. He gave the chiefs hell for not taking proper care of their forces' stress problems . . . and he gave them hell for not doing anything about their own stress. He would say, ". . . Too many of you chiefs think you're the Titanic and unsinkable. But you sink and you take a lot of people with you." Reaching the top of their profession often turned out to be a death warrant for those who succeeded, and Donovan's bulging scrapbooks of newspaper clippings proved it. Some chiefs killed themselves slowly with their drinking, others quickly with their gun; for others, a heart attack rudely intervened.

These deaths were no mystery to Donovan. He knew of over a dozen chiefs in the New England area alone, most in their fifties, who had died in the past few years. To Donovan these deaths provided an argument against those who maintain that if there were better screening much of the police problem would be stopped. Here were men who were judged the best in their own forces and yet even they succumbed to the job and to the image.

As the countryside rolled by, Donovan looked over at Chief Graham. The Chief sat motionless, eyes forward, both gloves rolled together neatly and held in his hands on his lap. There was no hint of emotion on his face. Donovan wanted to shout at him, "For Christ's sake cry, let it out, you've got nothing to be ashamed of." But Graham had to do it his way; Donovan just hoped he'd do it before he had another clipping to add to his collection.

Donovan pulled through the front gates of the cemetery and looked to Graham for instructions.

"Stop the car here . . . I'll walk over by myself," he said calmly. Donovan watched him get out of the car and walk briskly towards the far side of the grounds. Donovan felt helpless. There was nothing he could do but wait. Donovan watched him reach the graves, stop, and stare at the immutable marble testament in front of him.

Donovan had more experience with death, wakes and cemeteries than he would have liked. He worked hard in groups and in individual counselling to help cops and their families come to terms with the grief, guilt and resentment felt over the death of someone close. Often, it took a visit to the cemetery which might not happen until weeks, months, or years after the death before the person could accept the finality and unburden their guilt.

Donovan had his own personal experience. For years after his father died, Donovan carried resentment toward him for abandoning the family and not giving him the love he wanted. Donovan grew to understand his father's failings, and five years ago had visited his grave for the first time and said his piece over it. He said the angry things that had been on his mind for years and talked until he felt that if his dad were alive the two of them could have worked it out. Frequently, when working with alcoholics whose parents were also alcoholics, Donovan had them visit their parents' graves to express the feelings which had been numbed for so many years. The visit was a key to recovery for many alcoholics.

Like the visit with Graham today, Donovan had accompanied dozens of cops to cemeteries and saw each one handle it differently. Therefore, he understood Graham's silence.

For a few, the visit to the grave was an instant cure; for most, it took time. Donovan also saw an extreme where some cops became prisoners of the grave by visiting it daily. One officer maintained an eternal flame on his son's grave, refusing to let him go. Donovan quite bluntly told a chief he was counselling, "What the hell are you doing to yourself? You think one day you're going to reach in there and he'll reach up and shake your hand and say, 'It's okay, Dad. I forgive you, it's not your fault?' "

Donovan looked across the cemetery at Graham standing rigid with his hands behind his back. "Come on and cry, break down, get down on your knees and talk to him," Donovan silently urged. Graham stood for about five minutes, then turned and started back to the car. Suddenly he stopped, looked at Donovan, looked down at his gloves which were folded and held tightly in his clenched fists, looked back toward Donovan, pivoted and headed back to the grave. This time he walked quickly, almost breaking into a run; there was no military bearing or pace to it. He moved with his heart now. Reaching Davie's grave he knelt on it, dropped his hat and gloves to the side, and leaned forward with his fingers, caressing the grass as one might run their fingers through a child's hair.

Donovan couldn't get a clear look at his face, but he appeared to be crying and talking. Graham spent five minutes on the ground, then stood, brushed the grass clippings off the knees of his trousers, and collected his hat and gloves. Then he took a deep breath and slowly let it out. As he did, the official bearing and composure returned to his face, posture and walk as he turned and headed toward the car. His head was up, but looking past Donovan, a faraway look in his eyes.

He opened the car door, nodded that he was finished, and took his seat. Neither said anything. Donovan drove him back to the airport and his car. The two men shook hands and David Graham got out. His eyes seemed a little red and moist; the only tell-tale signs of the outing were some faint grass stains on his trouser knees and some bits of grass on the back of one sleeve.

Donovan watched him drive off, then broke down and cried. He cried for the Grahams, he cried for his own kids and he cried for the heartbreak suicides cause, he cried as a release from the exhaustion and emotional roller coaster he'd been on this week. It was only a few minutes, but it was a good cry, and he left the parking lot, ready to enjoy the weekend and do something for Eddie Donovan. Dr. Selye had given him some advice about priorities which helped account for his sanity as a counsellor. "Eddie," he said, "think of yourself first, your family second and your counselling as number three, or you'll burn yourself out."

Donovan was in no hurry to head to the insanity of the Friday freeway, so he stayed on the backroads to crisscross his way home. He felt like doing something impulsive. It was a powerful feeling and to him it was exciting and relaxing. Once, after working thirty-six hours straight on a trauma team case, Donovan found himself at home but unable to sleep because his system was too charged up. He'd read several days previously that scientists found keeping fish to be relaxing. Donovan went to the nearest pet store, bought their largest aquarium and a selection of fish, went home and spent eight hours assembling the aquarium and then ceremoniously baptized his new pets Huey, Duey, and Louey. Donovan had a cat called "Birdie" and a bird called "Kitty," and carried on loud discussions with parrots in pet stores; for him the names were perfectly normal.

Right now was really the first time he had had all week to miss Suzanne. He needed something to touch, something to talk to, the special no-strings-attached love a dog gave. When Suzanne had gotten sick, he vowed he wouldn't get another dog. He had said "no way" to Mary when she suggested that he get a new dog. Now, with his compulsive nature, he found himself driving down Main Street in Braxton searching for the animal shelter, singing at the top of his lungs, ". . . where, oh where can my little dog be . . . oh where, oh where can she be."

It didn't take long for Donovan to find her. He walked directly down the first row of cages at the shelter until he spied a jet black, nine-month-old Labrador with white paws and chest, who had been reluctantly given up by her owners when they moved to a no-pets-allowed apartment building. "Magic . . . great name," Donovan thought as he paid the forty-five dollars to claim the dog. "Mary's right. She'll be good for Anne Marie and she'll be great for me." The dog was well trained and full of life and fun as she licked and jumped on her new master. Donovan put Suzanne's old leash on her and put her in the front seat of the LTD for the trip home.

As he headed the car toward Plymouth, he serenaded the bewildered dog with a rollicking version of . . . "How much is that doggie in the window?"

"Forty-five dollars, pilgrim," he said in his John Wayne voice.

CHAPTER ELEVEN

THE WEEKEND

Saturday 9:00 A.M.

Donovan had a full day of weekend tasks ahead of him, but he had something important to do first. He finished breakfast, left Anne Marie and Mary at the dining room table, and charged downstairs into his workshop to get some white paint and a brush, then headed out to the backyard. He stopped for a moment and looked back at the house, an expression of wonder on his face.

This house was a luxury he never expected to have. Since his divorce, he had lived in a succession of apartments in the immediate Boston area, and then with Mary in her apartment in Braintree just south of Boston. He and Mary had bought the house several months ago when they decided to marry. Although it was a long drive to the stress centre, thirty-seven miles, he usually travelled at non-rush times, and the trip gave him time to be alone with his thoughts.

They bought the cottage-style bungalow in a lightly populated area southwest of Plymouth because the cost of comparable houses in the Boston area was prohibitive. Only minutes from the town of Plymouth and the famous harbour where the Pilgrims landed, the home was picturesquely set in a wooded area with several ponds nearby.

The house looked small from the front, but it was built on the side of a low hill, so the finished lower level opened at the back to a ground level patio. On the main level, a screened porch overlooking the backyard had been extended out from the living room. Wooden beams and the high ceilings gave the kitchen, dining, and living rooms a feeling of openness. The house was filled with tasteful furniture, lamps, and ornaments that Donovan had accumulated in ten years of judicious shopping at yard sales, flea markets, and used furniture shops. He boasted proudly of his bargains.

Donovan loved the sense of history that came with living in Plymouth, with its many historic points. "Look, this is where it all started," he'd say to Mary. The Pilgrims landed on Plymouth rock in 1620, and by 1630 the Boston Police Department was formed. Donovan joked, "It only took the Pilgrims ten years to find sin." The shoulder patch of the BPD uniforms was proudly emblazened with, "Boston Police AD 1630."

Donovan's yard backed onto a densely wooded area. A large rock about two feet in diameter sat between his lawn and the trees. Carrying the paint and brush, Donovan walked toward the rock and knelt on the damp grass in front of it. He opened the can of white paint and stirred it, shooing the curious Magic away at the same time.

"What the heck is he doing?" Anne Marie asked her mother as they both peered out the screened porch.

"I don't know," Mary said, "but it's probably something crazy."

Donovan dipped the narrow brush into the can and carefully began to paint numbers on the side of the rock: 1 . . . 6 . . . 2 . . . 0. He stepped back to look at his handiwork, "1620." He shouted at Magic before she could foul his newly painted rock, put down his paint brush, stepped up on the rock, and slowly turned to face the house. With his hand shielding his eyes from the sun, he surveyed the neighbouring woods, the backyard, and his new home. It was the first chance he'd had to really believe this was his.

While Mary and Anne Marie, both puzzled, looked out the porch screen at him and the dog frolicked at his feet, Donovan took deep breaths of the clean air as he balanced on the rock. He smiled as he stepped down, picked up the paint and brush, and walked back to the workshop.

"Anne Marie," he yelled. "C'mon! We're going for a bike ride." After chasing Magic into the house, Donovan pulled the tarp off his motorcycle, handed Anne Marie a helmet, and with a puff of blue smoke followed by the roar of the engine, they were off down the country lanes.

Eddie Donovan had learned how to relax, and he pursued recreation with the same vigour and creativity as he did his work. Relaxation for him wasn't curling up with a book or spending the day on the sundeck. Although he liked to read good books, or watch a selected television documentary or movie, he usually reserved those for the late evenings on weekdays.

During the working day, when his frantic pace became intolerable, he took ten-minute naps wherever he could. He'd pull his car to the side of a busy freeway, go into the back room at the stress centre, or, when travelling, find a bench in an airport waiting room, then lie down and nod off. Sometimes, at the office or home, he'd take off his clothes and even his watch to shed his identity completely. Initially, he used meditation and visualization techniques to fall asleep, but now, from practice, he only had to close his eyes and he was asleep. He'd wake up ten minutes later, refreshed and ready to continue.

On weekends, relaxing to Donovan was detaching thoroughly, going at a project at full speed plus an extra notch. He'd undertake projects on his boat or in the house and build, wire, paint, repair, or improvise in whirlwind fashion, usually whistling or singing while he worked.

Dr. Selye taught him he was the racehorse type that needed almost constant stimulation in order to survive. "You'd go crazy lying on a beach for three hours, Eddie," Selye said to him. Donovan loved speed, anything fast, daring, or adventurous. He'd mount his motorcyle and race along the backroads to the Cape. He'd run his boat full throttle, whenever he could get it to work. Even as he pedalled his bicycle, hunched over with his cap on backwards and his shirt blowing in the wind, he looked like he was in a race.

He liked to escape to the outdoors. His home, with the ocean and trails nearby, was the perfect setting for him. He knew good physical conditioning was essential in handling stress, so he also lifted weights, walked at a whirlwind pace, and climbed stairs rather than take elevators.

Donovan's favourite relaxation, but also his main source of aggravation, was his boat, a thirty-two-foot wooden Luhr's motor cruiser that was twenty-five years old and in constant need of repair. But the boat had sentimental meaning. Previously, it had belonged to Bill Norton, once the editor of *Police Chronicle*, the magazine of the International Brotherhood of Police Officers. During the tough times with the program, both in starting it and in maintaining it through the lay-offs, Norton was Donovan's ear and support system. When Donovan was depressed and thought of quitting, Norton would tell him, "Fuck them. They need you. They won't put you out of business." Before Norton died in 1983, knowing of Donovan's love for boating, he had sold Donovan the weatherbeaten craft for a bargain amount. The cost of maintaining and mooring the twin-engined cruiser drained Donovan's bank book, but his feelings for Norton wouldn't let him get rid of it.

Norton was one of three influential figures in Donovan's life: Norton, Hans Selye, and Jerry Penney. Penney was a long-time Alcoholics Anonymous worker and Donovan's sponsor in AA through his early years of sobriety. Penney helped Donovan keep a check on his ego by telling him, "Everything has a price tag — always check your motives."

After Donovan's first apprehensive meeting with the legendary Selye, the two developed a relationship as colleagues, with Selye even suggesting they write a book together. Selye told him, "You remind me of me thirty years ago," and joked that Donovan had an Irish heart and a German brain.

"He made me feel important in the right areas," Donovan said later. It wasn't until Selye died that Donovan realized the extent of the man's influence on him. All three men had died within the last few years. He mourned each one of them; they had given him the guidance his own father never had. Wiping the tears from his eyes at Penney's wake, Donovan had said, "I guess I'm on my own now."

Another influential figure in Donovan's life was Mique

(pronounced "Mike") Burkette, a brilliant, well-educated woman who had been an alcoholic, then a counsellor of alcoholics for seventeen years. But the people she helped put her on a pedestal, and over the years she felt she couldn't break out of her own image.

She told Donovan, "Remember, Eddie, when you're counselling people, some you help will later turn on you. Someday, some will want your job, or others will use you and use you. They're like vampires. They'll suck you dry and leave you nothing. I got to that point, and I didn't tell anybody, and I started to drink again and had to go away to dry out."

Some people Donovan has helped have tried to take over the program, others have criticized him behind his back. Even though he'd been warned, it hurt him. He needed to be liked but soon found out that if he was to run a successful program, there would always be a few jealous and spiteful people who'd try to destroy him. Burkette's advice helped Donovan to be tough with those he counselled, and if they didn't meet him half-way, he'd cut them loose like he did Vinny the vampire. There were others who used him. Psychologists, chaplains, and police forces contacted him for ideas and materials, but afterward took his ideas as their own. Some said, "He's just a cop trying to do a professional's job." But Donovan was used to it, and while it still hurt, he continued to help anyone who asked.

Donovan treasured his days at home. He knew everybody needs space away from his job, especially a cop, but most police department regulations made cops be cops twenty-four hours a day. New York police officers were once required to have their guns with them off-duty. Some departments still require it. In Boston, they are to have their handcuffs and badge with them at all times, and in all police forces police officers are encouraged, often as part of their oath, to be always on the look-out for trouble. If, off-duty, a cop was at the scene of a crime or disturbance and didn't take action to stop it, he'd be liable to charges in many police departments.

"It's no wonder so many cops are paranoid," Donovan said. "If they see a kid running down the road in front of their house, they don't see him as jogging or having fun. Instinctively they look to see what he's running from. They trust no one. It's one of the things that drives their wives nuts. A kid comes to the door selling chocolates for the church summer camp, and the husband interrogates the kid thinking he's Al Capone come to rip off the world."

On duty, Donovan breaks regulations by not carrying a gun. He isn't flouting orders. Because he's counselling in so many volatile situations, he doesn't want his gun used on him. Donovan knows that people who keep guns in their homes for protection often end up having the guns used on them, either by intruders or in domestic disputes. Police are no different. Off-duty cops get drunk together, and one friend shoots another. Donovan has the clippings to prove it. He believes it should be mandatory for cops to check their guns at the station before going off duty. In fact, he quips that a sign should be hung by all locker room exits: "Please leave your macho images at work."

Donovan returned with Anne Marie on the motorcycle, then went straight to his household tasks. He tidied the basement, went shopping with Mary, then after working in the yard, he started to train Magic. With his chores done, he and Anne Marie frolicked with the dog in the backyard. His headache was gone, and he barely noticed the pain in his side. His biggest pain hung on his belt — the beeper. He could get away from the job, but with the beeper at his side twenty-four hours a day, it was impossible to relax completely. Mercifully, it had been silent so far today, and Donovan relished every precious second of peace.

He sat for a quiet moment with Mary on the porch, watching Anne Marie playing ball with Magic in the yard. Mary smiled as she watched Anne Marie delight in the dog. She was worried about her daughter's adjustment to the move, to leaving her friends behind, to attending a new school, and living in a neighbourhood without kids her age. Because of her own difficult, handicapped childhood, Mary wanted everything perfect for Anne Marie.

Donovan reached over and squeezed Mary's hand. He'd met her at a Parents Without Partners dance five years before and became friends with her first while they were dating others. Their interest in each other developed gradually, they dated, became serious, and eventually he moved in with her. Ironically, Mary came from a police family. Her grandfather had been a cop, and her uncle was a retired detective, whom, coincidentally, Donovan had known years before, so Mary had some exposure to what life with a policeman was like.

Donovan's nine-year relationship with the woman he left his wife for was destroyed by the pressures he went through while establishing the stress centre. The constant demands on his time and the calls in the middle of the night left her resenting his job as if it were another woman. Donovan almost left the job for her, and both suffered serious health problems because of the conflict. Finally, after a number of agonizing years, they split up.

Mary was fairly understanding about the unpredictable hours. When she did get upset, Donovan would say, "Mary, you knew that when you met me. It comes with the turf; it's my life." But she saw the job slowly killing him, and she urged him to quit if the department didn't give him help soon. His upcoming meeting with the commissioner worried her. She'd seen him get his hopes up many times before, only to have them quashed by lies, politics, or the system. She knew he had to have full-time people at the stress centre if only to have someone else carry the cursed beeper so he could have some time when he could forget about the job entirely. One year, Thanksgiving dinner had to be put back in the oven for three hours while Donovan talked down a cop who was threatening suicide.

Their lifestyle prevented an active social life. Work took so much time, and with the constant threat of interruption, he and Mary were content to savour their quiet time together. Mary occasionally accompanied Donovan on his speaking trips. It was often their only chance to escape from the pressure for a while.

Anne Marie initially had resented Donovan's presence, but he put effort into becoming a real father to her. Donovan had also worked hard in recent years re-establishing a good rapport with his own children. When he had lived at home with them, despite his boozing and long work hours, he had always found time to spend with them. Often, he took them on details with him to Boston Gardens or Fenway Park. Off-duty, he'd play ball with the older ones or put them all in the car and take them to a drive-in movie. When he left home, the two oldest, Susan and Michael, sixteen and fifteen respectively, took it the hardest. They felt abandoned. The others were young enough to adapt more easily. Donovan worked hard to patch things up with Susan and Michael, and lately his efforts were improving the relationships.

Donovan's boys had their dad's bug to be an entertainer, and all four were trying to make it in show business. Michael was a successful comedian in the New England area. Patrick and Dennis were in California pursuing musical careers, and the youngest, Ed, Jr., lived in Boston, working in a warehouse by day and playing in a band at night. Susan, a single mother, had lived in New York for a number of years and was back in Boston with her ten-year-old son, working for an advertising agency. Linda was married with two children and also lived in Boston. Donovan's ex-wife has not remarried and he still pays child support for Mary, a poised and beautiful sixteen-year-old, the only child still at home. At various times in recent years, most of the boys have lived with him, and he has seen all the children as often as possible, although usually individually.

Tomorrow afternoon would be different. He had an important family gathering planned, and four of his children, including Susan and Michael, and his mother and brother, would be coming to the house. This was a rare chance for Donovan to see the kids together, for them to see their ailing grandmother, and for Donovan to show off the house which no one had seen yet. For the first time in fifteen years, Donovan was having a family gathering in his own home, and he was really excited about it.

Donovan told a recent class, "At one time I wanted to die. Now I want to live, and I'm afraid of dying because there are so many things I want to make up for and do for my kids."

Mary, Anne Marie, and even Donovan were exhausted after the hectic day and in no mood to cook supper, so they headed into Plymouth for a quick dinner at an Italian restaurant. When they returned, Anne Marie went straight to bed, and Donovan and Mary settled together into a large, comfortable easy chair and watched a movie he had taped earlier in the week. The day's work and shopping left them tired but relaxed. They were in bed by midnight and quickly asleep.

Buoyed by the session on Tuesday with other cops who'd lost kids through suicide, Charlie Gilham went back to work at 10:00 P.M. Saturday evening, his first shift since Lonnie's death. Five minutes later, he responded to an emergency call in a middle-class neighbourhood. The hysterical parents led him to an attached garage where, dangling from a rope suspended over a beam, the body of their fifteen-year-old daughter hung limply. Her date for the community dance had stood her up. Gilham managed to cut down the girl's body, calm her parents, and do the preliminary paperwork, but he wasn't able to make it back to the station. At 1:00 A.M. he called Donovan from a phone booth.

Gilham was sobbing and trembling so badly Donovan couldn't understand him. After he heard the story, he told Gilham not to move. Donovan feared that with his gun at his side, Gilham could impulsively commit suicide. Donovan told him to take off his gun, lock it in the trunk of his cruiser, and stay put in the car. Then Donovan called the station to explain Gilham's absence. Donovan was too far away to get to Gilham quickly, so he called Joe Lenthome from the suicide group who lived near Danville. Donovan paced in the living room until he heard back from Lenthome that he was with Gilham and was calming him down.

At three in the morning Donovan's beeper went off again. It was Barb Miller. Kevin had come home in a drunken rage and was swinging his crutches around the house destroying furniture and threatening her. She'd called the police, and they were there now trying to settle Kevin down.

"Well, there's not much I can do now," Donovan said. "Have them take him somewhere where he can sleep it off. He's got a lot of anger pent up in him, and these things are going to happen. If there's a problem when he sobers up, give me a call. Otherwise, I'll see the both of you next week in the meetings, and I'd like the two of you to see Dr. John on Thursday."

The setbacks in both cases were normal. With Donovan's perseverance and the invaluable help of his volunteers and groups, most situations got back on track. Donovan read for an hour from a favourite book, *When Bad Things Happen To Good People,* then fell once again into a deep sleep.

CHAPTER TWELVE
THE SOURCE

Sunday, 9:00 A.M.

God, grant me the Serenity
to accept the things I cannot change;
Courage to change the things I can
and the Wisdom to know the difference.

As you enter Donovan's house, the first thing you see hanging on the entrance-way wall is the Serenity Prayer, stylishly lettered, nicely framed, and positioned at eye level. It isn't there to impress or to preach, but for Eddie Donovan to see and be reminded of its philosophy every day. One hangs prominently on a wall in the main meeting room in the stress centre and another in Donovan's office. To most recovered alcoholics, and to thousands of other people around the world, whether they are religious or not, the prayer is at the very core of their ability to handle life.

Donovan glanced at the entrance-way copy as he hurriedly put on his windbreaker and stepped outside into the fresh New England morning. To anyone in the neighbourhood up early enough to see, Donovan looked like he was heading off to church. Every Sunday he arose early while Mary and Anne Marie slept, downed a quick cup of coffee, then jumped into his car and headed for a church in suburban Braintree, not for the service, but for his regular Alcoholics Anonymous meeting held in the basement. Most of the congregation upstairs had no idea what happened downstairs. Like most outsiders, they didn't realize there was just as much faith below them at the AA meeting. To understand that was to understand Eddie Donovan and know what made him tick. Donovan had been dry for fifteen years but still went to his meeting every Sunday, no matter what his mood.

This Sunday was a bright, early spring day, and Donovan whistled happily as he drove through the back country towards Plymouth and the freeway for the thirty-five mile trip into Braintree. He dreamed idly of getting his boat out of drydock in two months and heading to the beauty and freedom of Cape Cod Bay. The freeway was clear of traffic, making it easy for him to relax and think of the good things in his life and the important get-together with his family in the afternoon.

The blare of his beeper shattered the morning peace. In seconds, through the crackling static, the dispatcher gave him a name, Gary Rowan, with a number to call. Rowan, a sub-division sergeant, was a Donovan birddog. He had come to Donovan for help several years ago after threatening to kill his wife. The program helped him overcome his problems and saved his marriage, and he now called Donovan whenever he spotted a troubled officer.

Donovan cursed that he didn't have a radio or phone in his car. He'd have to pull off at the next exit on the freeway and call Rowan from a payphone. Donovan slowed as he approached the exit and pulled off into a service station. When he called, Rowan told him that a policeman, off-duty and drunk but in uniform, had crashed his car into a tree in front of a Catholic church just as mass ended. He resisted arrest and had to be taken forcibly to the cells at Rowan's sub-station.

"Well, I'm not going to miss my meeting," Donovan said. "He'll be too drunk to talk to me now anyway. Go through it all the way," he told Rowan. "Book him, treat him like any other drunk. You do your job, and I'll do mine. Let him sit in the cell and feel sorry for himself. I'll be there around noon."

"Damn," Donovan swore as he jumped back in his car, "there goes the family gathering. First time in seventeen years my mother is going to come to my house, and I could miss it." Donovan tried to think of volunteers who could cover the situation for him, but even if there were any, he didn't want to ruin their Sunday, too. He was angry now. Not at the cop or the situation, but at the system which made him a one-man program. He was glad he had the meeting with Commissioner Roache on Tuesday. He stopped whistling and gripped the wheel more tightly as he headed back onto the freeway towards Braintree.

This AA meeting was a big one, with several hundred people crowding into the large hall. Latecomers searched out their friends and found a seat at their favourite table. In this crowd, socio-economic and age barriers were dissolved: teenagers, golden agers, white collar, blue collar workers were there. Doctors sat next to longshoremen and ex-hookers next to housewives. They all had one thing in common. They were victims of the disease of alcoholism. More than a failing of willpower, alcoholism is a symptom of inner problems, a sickness that the word "dis-ease" refers to. An alcoholic is not necessarily classified by how much he drinks, but why or how he drinks. He could be a light drinker, or even a weekend drinker, but if his compulsion to drink controls him, then he could be an alcoholic. Conversely, it is possible that someone who is a heavy drinker isn't necessarily an alcoholic if he's able to control his habit.

Hollywood has dispensed an image of the alcoholic as a falling down drunk, with AA meetings as a last chance for the desperate, but in fact the vast majority of alcoholics are employed, socially responsible people. Statistically, the more affluent and prestigious a person's position, the higher the occurrence of alcoholism. The recent openness of people like Betty Ford, Joan Kennedy, Mary Tyler Moore, and others illustrates that the disease respects no rank and that a person could carry on a high level of activity with no one noticing. The derelict, skid row stereotype of drunks accounts for only 10 percent of alcoholics.

Not only does alcoholism not respect social class, but it

is called the biggest problem in society, either side of the Iron Curtain. Russia has acknowledged it as their major problem, and the annual cost in the United States and Canada in time lost from work and from other costs is estimated at over one hundred and fifty billion dollars.

As Donovan moved toward his favourite seat in the back corner, he passed the many cops he knew there. He nodded at some, ignored others, and quickly spoke to a few, but he wouldn't sit with them. This was his meeting. He was there as Eddie Donovan, private citizen, and he was happiest when people didn't know what he did for a living. Many alcoholics don't like cops. Most have had bad experiences with them, and it seems someone is always telling stories of cops beating and roughing up drunks.

"Everyone looks at you as if to say, 'Did you do that?'" Donovan says. "Every so often someone will become rowdy at a meeting, and they look at me as a cop to get them out. I say, 'Wait a minute, I'm here as an alcoholic trying to get help. Either we all take him out, or call the police.' They don't let you stop being a cop."

Donovan also steers clear of other AA meetings that are composed mainly of police men and women. "They talk too much about the job, or they ask about my counselling or a television show I did. I don't want that. I just want to be myself."

He sat at the back with his friend, Billy, a trucker, and talked to him while the formalities took place in front of the group. In smaller groups, the format for the meetings usually consisted of choosing a topic and having members share their thoughts and feelings about it. That wasn't practical in large meetings like this one, so, here, two or three people were selected to tell the story of their decline into alcoholism and how they gained and maintained their sobriety. Some listened attentively to the speakers as their stories unfolded, laughing at the funny parts, and nodding their heads at the parts they related to. Others were more interested in talking quietly with their friends, either about their own problems or just keeping up with small talk. There was a constant stream of people over to the coffee urn and the donuts at the side of the room.

Donovan was content sitting at the back with Billy and a few other friends who'd joined them at their table. They half listened to the speakers but seemed more content talking about the Celtics and the Bruins, and Donovan was eager to tell them about the family gathering this afternoon.

Donovan's friends and associates in and out of the program, the many reporters who watched him work, and even Dr. Selye had wondered how he kept from burning out. Only other alcoholics knew. The answer was in this room. Donovan had learned not only how to stop drinking and accept life here, but also how to become a solid citizen and help others. He provided the heart and brains; AA gave him the soul to do it.

A reporter from Los Angeles recently asked him how he managed to keep from burning out and Donovan answered: "With me, it's the twelve steps of AA. I couldn't do it without the AA program." The reporter didn't include that in his story because he didn't understand—most people don't. Most think the meetings are a crutch, a place for the alcoholic to go instead of drinking. The company of those who share the problem and the peer counselling are helpful, but they aren't the key to the program. The key is a twelve step program the alcoholic has to learn. It might take him months or years to work through, and, when he finishes, the twelve steps have to be maintained daily.

The program and steps are based on the idea that the disease of alcoholism is three-fold: physical, emotional and spiritual. To keep sober, the alcoholic has to deal with all three, and the twelve steps are the blueprint for doing it. The physical is to stop drinking. However, if an alcoholic stops through the use of willpower or other means and doesn't address his emotional and spiritual concerns, those concerns will eventually cause his downfall.

The emotional aspect is based on the premise that an

alcoholic's drinking is often a symptom of deeper psychological problems. It might be a poor self-image, hatred for a dead parent, anger, resentment, self-pity, self-centredness, guilt, a need to be punished. The twelve steps work to clear out the debris of the past and equip the person to live for today. A key to recovery for many alcoholics is in making amends with parents, children, or old enemies; to cease the hatred, guilt, or jealousy that dominates and controls their lives. That's why so many visit the graves of dead parents, like Donovan had, to make their peace.

The spiritual component of the program is often the toughest step for many alcoholics to accept. It calls for a belief in a higher power and the complete surrender to it. Many people confuse this part of AA with religion, but the step says, "God as you understand him." That means there is no religious doctrine to follow, no dogma, and the higher power, for some, is a power they find within themselves. The step states that only God or the power, and not the person, can control alcoholism. A belief that everything happens for a reason, nothing is a mistake, allows an alcoholic to forgive himself and his enemies and to gain a freedom from past constraints. He develops a philosophy for accepting the good and bad things which happen in his life.

Because Donovan knew that all he'd been able to accomplish came from another source, he couldn't take credit for it. He could let the world give him credit as long as he knew what the source of his success was. "What you're doing is God's will — everything happens for a reason. But you don't sit back and wait for it to happen," Donovan says. "God leaves the leg work up to you.

"I've been to AA for fifteen years now, and the program won't let me become a phony, won't let me be a big shot. It reminds me of where I came from. I accept life and enjoy life, and I'm always grateful. It might not sound like it at times, but I forgive my enemies. If I get angry, I don't let it destroy me. If I do something good, I share credit with the higher power. It keeps me humble."

By maintaining his sobriety, by dealing with his emotions through nurturing spiritual strength, Donovan has developed a proper perspective on life through his successes and setbacks. But he knows the components are like the legs on a three-legged stool, if one isn't working, the stool overturns. He works his program every day, and that is the reason the Serenity Prayer is everywhere, to remind him.

For an alcoholic, the program is like learning to fly when he has never been in an airplane before. At first, he has to be convinced the plane can fly, then there is ground school and many basics to learn, then tentative flight with the help of an instructor, and finally, when ready, the joy of solo flight. When an alcoholic reaches the twelfth step, he's free and flying like a bird, free of the restrictions that held him down for years. But if he forgets the basics, he crashes. The sober alcoholic is only one drink away from failure. The steps, used daily, provide checks on character defects and a means for improving relations with others.

The final step of the AA program, the twelfth, is to step out into the community and not only be a good citizen, but help others, thereby dovetailing with Selye's philosophy of altruistic egotism: "When you're helping others, you're really helping yourself."

Donovan grumbled to Billy about today's speakers spending too much time trying to outdo each other with the horrors of their bad days, rather than describing how they handle their sobriety. Some poorly run groups let their people get on the "pity pot"; they wail out their hard luck stories but don't offer construcrtive help. This attracts the professional gripers who only want audiences and drive away those with sincere intentions. The successful groups follow the program, giving each meeting a topic or theme, often on one of the twelve steps, then limit speakers' time and caution those who stray off course.

Donovan wanted to stand up and yell "Bullshit!" to the speaker who was now talking about drinking his urine in a drunken stupor, but he reminded himself that this wasn't an appropriate action for a man who wanted to be off duty. "Bullshit," he whispered to Billy.

The AA success rate with alcoholics is about 75 percent. Upon coming into AA, 50 percent achieve sobriety immediately, and another 25 percent find permanent sobriety after several relapses. The success rate of medical science is less than 5 percent. Obviously, the twelve-step program works, but AA also encourages their members to use, in addition to the program, outside resources, such as the medical profession, government programs, or the clergy.

Similar groups, motivated by AA's success, work on the same basis and even use AA literature. The physical problem differs, but the emotional and spiritual causes are the same, so they use the twelve-step program to overcome their compulsions. Overeaters Anonymous, Narcotics Anonymous, Emotions Anonymous, Gamblers Anonymous have been quietly helping others for years.

Donovan always tells alcoholics, "You're lucky. At least you have a group you can go to. It's too bad they don't have groups for others. There should be Grouches Anonymous, or Bullies Anonymous, or Naggers Anonymous. People pack the luggage of guilt, hate, or a poor self-image around for their entire lives and don't realize it. But alcoholics, because of their disease, get a chance to unpack and unburden themselves." Donovan has been exposed to the best positive thinking and personal development courses, but he has found no better plan for day-to-day living than the twelve steps.

The Los Angeles reporter asked Donovan, "You're a very hyper guy, you have a lot of stress. Aren't you afraid you'll have a heart attack if you continue like this?"

"If I die tomorrow or the next day, don't feel sorry for me," Donovan told him. "I've *lived* the last fifteen years of my life. I have my sex life, my reading, my little naps. I have a family that loves me now that I'm not an alcoholic father any longer. I have people that love me, and I love an awful lot of people. I enjoy the work I do. I have people that can check my ego, rip me apart, say anything they want (including my own kids), and get away with it without fear of repercussion. I don't have to go around hiding my feelings or playing the superior role, and you know what? I owe it all to Alcoholics Anonymous." The puzzled reporter didn't include that in his story either.

When Donovan hurried out of the room at the end of the meeting, he was refreshed. There was no communion like in the service upstairs, but it was as if he had had a bite of something all powerful and a drink of a cleansing spirit.

The fact he is an alcoholic is almost irrelevant now. It is the program, the humility and strength it gives him, that makes Eddie Donovan run. He told the Los Angeles reporter: "If there's one thing on this earth that you're made to do, it's to give to other people." The reporter used that.

CHAPTER THIRTEEN·
SHAKY

Sunday, 11:00 A.M.
Donovan hurried in through the back door of the district sub-station. About a dozen policemen, working at their desks or talking in small cliques around the large squad room, saw him come in and head for the centre of the room. Conversations and work stopped. There was deadly silence. Most knew and liked Donovan and usually talked freely with him, but this morning was different. Locked up in the cellblock just a few feet behind them, with the petty thieves and winos, was a patrolman from their own station. No one liked locking up a brother officer, and many knew it could just as easily be them in the cell.

"Where is he?" Donovan growled, still upset that his Sunday morning had been ruined.

"Third one back on the left," the duty clerk answered.

Donovan turned and wheeled into the cell block that intersected the middle of the squad room. He was welcomed by the ugly stench of urine and vomit as he entered the dimly lit, narrow corridor lined with a dozen dingy cells on each side. Little wonder it was called the "tombs." Each cell was like a dirty little time capsule containing the wasted life of the occupant.

Donovan stopped and peered into the third cell. It was darker than the rest and looked empty. He blinked his eyes, trying to adjust from the outside brightness to the darkness of this hellhole.

Suddenly, through the bars in the dark of the cell, he saw glittering brightly in a solitary beam of light the silver metallic lettering, BPD, the shirt collar insignia of the Boston Police. Gradually, the outline of a man's shoulder appeared, and, as his eyes adjusted more, Donovan made out the hunched body of a fully uniformed officer, sitting on the edge of the bunk. His face was buried in his hands, and his elbows rested on his knees. Slowly and unsteadily, aware someone was staring at him, he raised his head. Donovan grabbed a bar for support and squatted down to talk to him at eye level.

"Hi, brother," he said in a low, serious tone. "I'm Eddie Donovan from the Boston Police Stress Program. How're you doing?" Stupid question, Donovan thought, but how else could you start a conversation like this one?

The prisoner mumbled incoherently, as he swayed forward to search out the voice. The beam of light that illuminated his BPD insignia, now shone on his face, giving Donovan a good look at the man's battered features. His eyes, bloodshot and beaten, squinted out at Donovan. His nose was crusted with blood, his hair a mess, and his face dirty and unshaven.

"Do you know who I am?" Donovan said.

"Yeah," the voice said, "I saw you on television last week."

Donovan heard from many who saw him on the Boston area special on the stress program. "I guess there's good news and bad news with this guy," Donovan thought. "The good is he watched the show, the bad is he didn't get anything out of it."

The prisoner's head drooped forward. "What's your first name?" Donovan asked.

"Max," he said. He belched, and the strong smell of alcohol wafted out of the cell.

"Max, do you know why you're here?" Donovan knew these questions would be a waste of time while Max still had a tank-full. When you talked to a drunk, all that talked back was the empty bottle.

"I shouldn't be here. It's all a big mistake," Max said. "I just swerved to miss a truck. I wanna go home."

"You're hurt, Max. You hit your head on the steering wheel when you hit the tree."

"No, I didn't. They grabbed me; they beat me," Max whined.

"Who did, Max?" Donovan's headache had returned, and his temples were beginning to pound.

"The cops—this whole thing's a set-up. I wanna lawyer. I wanna go home," he blubbered.

"Bullshit, Max. You were drunk and hit a tree." Donovan paused and looked him sternly in the eye. "Were you drinking on the job?"

"Naw. Look, I just had a few social drinks after work." Max sounded like a broken record. "I had to swerve to miss a truck." Donovan wished he'd kept a file of everything drunken cops told him they swerved to miss. He'd heard them all: little kids, dogs, deer, rabbits, chickens, cyclists, and even one extra-terrestrial being. His patience had worn thin.

"Cut the crap, Max. You're in a jackpot. You've been arrested for drunk driving, and your job is on the line."

There were only six other prisoners in the cellblock beside Max, but all were grouped together in the seven cells closest to the squad room. They pressed their faces against the bars, like monkeys at the zoo, as they tuned in to this unique drama. It wasn't every day you had a pig in the slammer with you.

Donovan knew it was humiliating for Max to be bunched in with them, rather than in a vacant cell at the far end of the corridor, but he was put there for a good reason. Here it would be easier to keep an eye on him, to lessen the chance of suicide, a strong possibility, given the circumstances and the antiquated cells.

Donovan was getting more frustrated in his futile attempts to communicate with Max. He knew the answer to his next question would be no, but he felt obliged to ask anyway. "Max, do you want to sit in a private room with me for a few minutes to talk about this?"

"No, I don't have to. This is a mistake. I was set up. I just wanna go home and forget it," Max pleaded.

"Max, I'll talk to you later." Donovan abruptly headed back to the squad room. As he entered, the officers looked down, pretending to work, but just like the prisoners, when Donovan wasn't looking, their eyes and ears followed every turn of the plot.

"Who was the arresting officer?" Donovan asked the duty clerk.

He responded hesitantly, "Jerry Leonard."

"Christ," Donovan blurted aloud. He suddenly had a problem he hadn't bargained for. Three months ago, Donovan had come to see Jerry Leonard, locked up in this very jail. Twenty-nine years old, an alcoholic for ten years, Jerry was arrested for busting up a lounge and then crashing his car. Donovan got him into a detox hospital where he dried out. Since then, Jerry had been sober, took counselling from Donovan, participated in the Monday night police AA meetings, and was back on the job doing well. It hadn't been an easy battle for Jerry, and having to arrest a brother officer might cause a set-back. There is an unwritten code that you look after your brother officers and cover for them when they are in trouble. You don't arrest a fellow cop.

Donovan looked around the squad room and saw Jerry sitting on a bench in the corner of the squad room with his back to everyone. Donovan walked over, sat down next to him, and put a hand firmly on his shoulder.

"How ya doin', brother?" Donovan asked.

"I'm okay, Eddie," he said, then shrugged his shoulders, and shook his head in disbelief. Donovan gave him a couple of pats on the shoulder and glanced back at everyone in the squad room. He caught most of them staring, but they quickly looked down at the work they weren't doing.

"Jerry, come on where we can talk privately," Donovan said sarcastically for the benefit of the big ears in the room. He and Jerry walked into the cell block, past Max, and down the corridor to the area at the back by the empty cells.

"What happened, Jerry?" Donovan asked. He wasn't much

interested in the facts but wanted Jerry to talk about the arrest, to unload some of his concerns. Slowly and nervously, Jerry described the incident.

"I was parked at the Doughboy having coffee around nine this morning, and a car comes by and stops, and the driver says one of your brother officers just wrapped his car around a tree in front of the Catholic church. My partner and I drove over. There was a big crowd around the car because mass had just ended. Shaky was still sitting in the car, and he was trying to get it going," Jerry said.

"Who's Shaky?" Donovan asked.

"That's Max. His last name is Shakura. Everybody calls him Shaky," Jerry said, shrugging his shoulders.

"Very appropriate, I guess," Donovan said, smiling impishly.

"He said he wanted to go home and that there wasn't any problem," Jerry continued. "I started to reach in to get the keys away from him. He was in full uniform, and then I saw he was wearing his gun." Jerry's face reddened and his jaw clenched.

"I backed off a bit and tried to talk him down. I wanted to get the keys, get him out of there, and get his gun away from him." Donovan frowned and nodded his head in empathy.

"He was being belligerent, and nothing seemed to work. We had to radio for help; then the sergeant came down." Jerry's hurt and frustration boiled to the surface.

"Boy," Donovan said, "you must have thought you were talking to yourself. That was you three months ago."

"You're damned right," Jerry said. His face reddened further at the irony of the situation. "It took five of us to get him into a squad car and back to the station. He wouldn't co-operate. I really wanted to let him go, but I couldn't. There were so many witnesses. I had to do it," Jerry said. "We ran a check on his car and found it hasn't been registered for three years. He didn't even have a valid driver's licence."

"Jerry, you did the right thing," Donovan said. "He didn't give you any choice. Look, you probably saved his life by bringing him in." Donovan tried hard to reassure him. This was an especially critical time in Jerry's recovery. For an alcoholic, the first few months of day-to-day living after drying out are the toughest.

"Best thing that can happen now is if they keep him in here until he goes to court tomorrow," Donovan said. "Let him sober up and have plenty of time to feel sorry for himself. I'll never forget the day I spent in a cell. It was the best lesson I ever had."

Donovan worried that the police union rep would come over and bail Max out. He's seen it happen many times. The reps figure they're helping, but they just allow a cop to get into a bigger jackpot. No matter what, Donovan knew he'd be in court tomorrow morning to help Max, even though it meant cancelling his long-awaited ultra-sound test. Right now, his priority was Jerry Leonard.

"Jerry, it's not your fault. He made you do it. You gave him every chance," Donovan said. "Do you know if he's a boozer, or had previous problems?" If Shaky had a history of trouble, Jerry could accept arresting him more easily.

"I haven't heard of any problems," Jerry said. "He always worked the 5:30 P.M. to 1:00 A.M. shift. Someone told me he goes to a lodge he's a member at to drink after work."

"How does it feel to be in the other shoes?" Donovan grinned, patting Jerry on the back.

"Jesus, it blew my mind. I looked in the car and thought, that was me. Now here I am three months later arresting a guy for the same thing."

"You couldn't mess with him, you had to do it. If you had let him go and he killed someone, then your neck would be on the block," Donovan said, trying to pull Jerry out of his funk. He was glad the regular AA cops group was meeting tomorrow night where Jerry could get more help. He told Jerry to call if he had any problems.

Donovan headed out of the cellblock, through the squad

room, to the office of Lieutenant Dick Scofield, the officer in charge of the sub-station. For Jerry's sake, he wanted the lowdown on Max "Shaky" Shakura. He poked his head in the door and saw a tired and drained Scofield sitting at his desk.

"Come on in, Eddie. Shut the door. What a morning this has been." Scofield knew the incident wouldn't reflect well on him.

"Dick, from what I've been able to find out so far, the man doesn't have a drinking problem." Donovan looked intently at Scofield as he sat down opposite him. Scofield took a long, hard, deep breath and slowly snorted it out through his nose.

"Look Ed, the man's worked for me for fifteen years, and he's a heavy drinker," the lieutenant said, defeatedly.

"Good," Donovan said loudly, "I've finally got someone who will admit it. What other problems have there been?"

"There's been a few, Eddie. One of them involved a gun incident."

"Jesus, you've been covering for him for fifteen years. You haven't been helping him, you've been slowly killing him," Donovan said. Scofield outranked Donovan by many levels but took his scolding shamed-faced like a rookie cop being chewed out by his sergeant.

"When is everyone going to smarten up. You think you're doing the guy a favour, and you're helping him dig his grave. And look at the legal consequences. If he kills someone, the department can get their ass sued off and then you're really screwed." He hated "enablers." That's what AA calls the supposed helpers of drunks. Their wives, the unions, their bosses, their friends, all think they're doing alcoholics a favour by covering up for them, yet all they're really doing is making the problem worse. The alcoholic never has to deal with the consequences of his drinking.

"Look, Dick," Donovan said, composing himself, "the best thing for him is if he stays in jail and gets a chance to sober up and wallow in self-pity for a while. He doesn't want my help now, but tomorrow he'll be a lot easier to talk to. Is the union going to try to bail him out?"

"I don't know," Scofield shrugged, "they usually won't touch it if it's off-duty."

"Keep him here till court tomorrow. Get him some clothes and get him out of that uniform, but for God's sake keep him here. It's his only hope," Donovan said. "If the court sees he's gone into the stress program and is willing to go to a detox, then they might give him a break. Right now, I'm more worried about Jerry Leonard. He's taking it pretty hard. I'm going back out to tell him this guy's been a problem for fifteen years," Donovan said jumping to his feet.

He burst into the squad room to look for Jerry. Without prompting, half the cops in the room raised their heads, looked at Donovan, and then simultaneously pointed to the outer lobby where Jerry was sitting.

CHAPTER FOURTEEN
FAMILY

Sunday, 4:00 P.M.

Donovan paced up and down his front lawn, anxiously awaiting his mother's arrival. She lived with Donovan's older brother, George, who was driving her to the family gathering, and they were already an hour late. It was their first visit to Donovan's house, and it wasn't easy to find in the maze of quaint, ambling backcountry roads with confusing names like Federal Furnace Road and Kings' Pond Plain Road. In the driveway behind Donovan, Linda's husband and children, Susan's boy, and Donovan's sixteen-year-old daughter, Mary, played a spirited game of basketball. In the house, Linda and Susan talked in the living room, while Mary worked up a traditional Irish meal of corned beef and cabbage in the kitchen. Michael had worked late the night before at a comedy club north of Boston and would arrive with his girlfriend after supper. Eddie, Jr. was working and couldn't come.

The phone rang. Mary yelled out to Donovan that it was George, and he was lost. Donovan cursed and ran in to take the call.

"God damn you, Sonny! Can't you do anything right," Donovan shouted into the phone. The brothers still referred to each other by their childhood nicknames. Donovan held the receiver away from his ear as George yelled profanities at him, part of the nature of their relationship, something Donovan claimed went back to their youth when George stepped on his head in the water at the beach, almost drowning him. They finally calmed down, and Donovan gave him a new set of directions.

George finally pulled into the driveway at dusk. On one

side of the car, Donovan's daughters ran out to greet their grandmother whom they hadn't seen for months. On the other side, the brothers resumed their bickering; Donovan at "Sonny" because he was late, and George retorting that "Buster" had given him bum directions. George lived alone with his mother. He'd been in the service and now drove a truck and, like his brother, had fought a long battle with alcoholism.

Susan, Linda, and Mary helped Eddie's mother transfer from the car to her wheelchair and then pushed her to the front door. She was in her eighties and hadn't been well in recent years. She had diabetes, was crippled with arthritis, and had a pacemaker, as well as a myriad of other medical problems. Donovan would say, "She's too stubborn to give in." Once inside, and before she had time to recover from the onslaught of grandchildren and great grandchildren, Donovan swooped behind her chair, and started wheeling his reluctant mother on a tour around the main level.

"Buster, Buster—my heart—take it easy," she protested. Donovan finished the tour and wheeled her back to the living room where she could gripe about her ailments comfortably to anyone near her.

"That's what keeps her going," Donovan chuckled to Susan.

"Sonny, Sonny," she called out. She told George she was tired and wanted to rest, but Donovan stepped in and told her to be more sociable. That roused her fighting spirit and she demanded to see the rest of the house. In a family effort, Donovan, George, and the girls managed to move her, wheelchair and all, down the steep basement steps to see the lower level. She had a bumpy trip out to the backyard to see the rock, then they finally pushed and pulled her wheelchair up the steep incline to the front of the house and back into the living room. While Donovan and George sprawled on the chesterfield, gasping in exhaustion, their mother snapped at them with renewed vigour.

"What's the matter, you two! You'd think you were old or something."

After dinner, Donovan looked at his daughters chatting happily and thought of his upcoming wedding to Mary in the summer and of Dennis and Patrick coming from California for the ceremony. His family would be together for the first time in years. A sense of family was important to him, and while old age and pain had dampened his mother's enthusiasm, she had ingrained the spirit in him.

When he came home from the navy for the first time, his mother cooked a Christmas dinner with all the trimmings for him and the family but it was three months after Christmas. She taught him that the holiday feeling can occur anytime. "I don't believe you should have those few special days and then be a hypocrite the rest of the year," Donovan said recently. "I think Christmas should be all year long. I'm not talking about giving presents either. I'm talking about giving of self, that's the best gift you can give someone."

Michael and his girlfriend arrived around eight, and while Mary quickly reheated the leftovers, Donovan gave Michael the tour. Donovan felt a special warmth for his oldest son tonight. Linda told him earlier of something Michael and Eddie, Jr. had been doing on Christmas eve for the last ten years, but Donovan had never known anything about it. Michael and Eddie bought large supplies of cigarettes and cigars and took them to the Pine Street Inn, a shelter for alcoholic, indigent men. They gave the men the smokes, then sang and entertained them. "It's a God-given gift for helping others," Donovan said proudly to Mary later. "The whole family's got it." Donovan hugged everyone warmly when they left. He even surprised George when he asked him to be best man at his wedding.

The success of the gathering and the anticipation of good family times ahead put the incident with Shaky and the upcoming meeting with the commissioner far from Donovan's mind.

CHAPTER FIFTEEN
COURT

Monday, 9:50 A.M.
About a hundred people jostled for position and space in the crowded lobby of the Dorchester Courthouse as they waited for the 10:00 A.M. opening of Courtroom B. Monday morning court in this predominantly black South Boston ghetto area was always a zoo.

Cops and robbers, drunks and victims, the vice and sin of the weekend accumulated, ready to face the music. Only the uniforms singled out the good guys from the bad. Detectives in plain clothes, distinguishable only by their mandatory ties, looked like they had been dressed at the nearest Goodwill centre, as did many of their quarry. One young detective had a posh navy and red striped tie but was wearing a crumpled pink shirt, check pants, a beaten raincoat, and brown running shoes with blue stripes. The faces all looked the same. The cops were just as weatherbeaten, wrinkled, and hung over as the "bad guys."

Today, Max Shakura was a bad guy. Eddie Donovan elbowed his way through the waiting throng in search of him. Donovan was boiling. As he feared, the union rep had come along Sunday afternoon to bail Shaky out of trouble. "They think they're doing the guy a favour, and all they're doing is taking him off the hook," Donovan muttered to himself. "If they had let him rot there for a day and let him really think about the mess he's in, then maybe I could get through to him." Donovan spotted Max standing alone in a far corner of the lobby.

He was tall and skinny and looked terrible. His swollen eyes had turned purple, and his large nose was an ugly red where it had hit the steering wheel. His clothing, although a clean change, was rumpled and his shirt-tail hung out the back. His coarse dark hair was messy and matted.

"Max, it's Eddie Donovan. Do you remember me from yesterday?"

"Yeah, you're the stress guy," Max grunted, looking down. His right hand shook as he tried to cradle a cigarette in his long fingers, yellowed and burnt from holding endless cigarettes for one drag too many.

"Max, do you remember the accident?" Donovan asked, trying to look into Max's bloodshot eyes to see if there was any flicker of reason.

"Look, this whole thing's being blown out of proportion. I just had a little accident. I had to swerve to miss a car that was coming right at me."

"Yeah, you swerved all right," Donovan thought, "but it was to miss a pink elephant." He motioned Max to sit on a wooden bench in the corridor by the bailiff's office and then sat down beside him.

"Max," Donovan said firmly, "cut out the bullshit. What are you going to do?"

"I just had a few beer. I'd been up all night. Maybe I just fell asleep," Max said.

"Quit being so defensive. You go like that into court, and they'll eat your ass. They're doubly tough on cops. Your only hope is if you seek help," Donovan said. "Look, let me get you into a detox hospital. If the court sees that you're trying to do something about your problem, they'll be lenient, otherwise they'll throw the book at you."

"I don't have a problem. This is the first time anything like this has happened to me," Max said. Donovan tensed with anger.

"God, what liars they are. They suck in the psychologists, the lawyers, their friends, but you can't fool someone who's been there," Donovan thought. By now, two elderly black ladies sitting next to them and four punk teenagers on the bench opposite had quit discussing their own problems and were listening, bug-eyed, as Donovan's voice rose along with his frustration. He called it his Irish whisper.

"Max, you're a bloody liar," Donovan shouted. "You come to the stress centre at 7:00 P.M. this evening for our regular alcoholics meeting. You'll see twenty other guys there who have the same problem. You're not alone. As long as you seek help, there's hope. If you don't, you just might kill someone the next time."

Max, a full six inches taller than Donovan, hunched forward and looked down at his feet just like a little kid being scolded by his father. The lobby was nearly empty now, as the assembled throng paraded into Courtroom B. Donovan saw the police union lawyer on the other side of the lobby and leaped up to talk to him, leaving Max twiddling his thumbs. In a few minutes, he returned and stood, hands on hips, in front of Max.

"Look, . . . the union lawyer will try to get your court date put back. He won't want to deal with the judge until he can show you're doing something about your problem. You can start by coming to the meeting tonight." Max looked reluctant.

"If you don't, you're done for. You don't stand a chance." Donovan started to leave, but stopped and turned quickly to face Max. "I'll see you at seven tonight," he said pointedly.

Max started to protest. He stumbled to his feet, gathering his long legs under him, and, half-running, tried to catch Donovan, who was charging out the main door.

"I'll see you at seven," Donovan said, turning to shake his clenched fist and pointing finger in Max's face. Donovan sprinted down the front steps, leaving Max sputtering at the front door.

CHAPTER SIXTEEN
MR. X

Monday, 11:00 A.M.

The phone was ringing as Donovan unlocked the door to his office. He raced in, then reached across the front of his desk to flick off the answering machine and grab the phone.

"Stress Program."

"Yeah, can I speak to Ed Donovan?"

"This is Ed Donovan."

"Look, uh, I know, uh — I worked with you years ago. You'd know me if you saw me, but I can't tell you who I am." Donovan sighed as he listened to the husky but hesitant voice on the other end. He received a lot of these calls. A cop in trouble, but unable to drop the image enough to risk that final step of identifying himself. This type of phone call was trying and time consuming.

"What's your problem?" he asked.

"You know, I've had it, I've really had it with my wife and kids. I can't take it anymore. I'm gonna blow them away, and I'm gonna blow myself away." The man paused for a few seconds. Donovan was silent. "I don't know what the hell is going on. I don't even know why the hell I'm calling you. I don't even know what you can do." Donovan knew he couldn't do anything if the man wouldn't identify himself. He had to keep him on the line and chip away at him, using every trick he'd learned, fair or dirty. Almost all gave their names before they hung up, but if they didn't, Donovan had usually extracted enough information to figure out who they were. He kept the man talking, managed to find out he worked days, was a uniform, probably working in the south end.

"Well, the first thing I can do is get you in here to sit

179

down, or if you want, I'll come over and meet you somewhere right now, " Donovan said. There was no response on the other end. "Let's start talking about it and see what hope there is for you. Let's first find out what the problem is." Donovan found putting the caller on the spot worked best. Most cops will respond to a challenge, but it wasn't working with this guy.

Donovan couldn't get much out of him, other than bits and pieces, except that he was upset, depressed, and wanted to kill his family. From his voice, Donovan assumed the caller was white, and if he had worked with Donovan, that meant he'd been on the job for at least fifteen years. Donovan had a hunch he was on duty right now.

Then the man abruptly hung up. Donovan had only a few clues to go on, but he'd found needles in bigger haystacks than this one. "Okay," he said to himself, "let's see what we got." White, at least fifteen years' service, patrolman, probably working out of a sub-station on the south side. Donovan wished for a computer at times like this to help in his search. What he did have were some old personnel records that listed officers by sub-station. All 2,000 cops in Boston knew of Donovan; he probably knew six hundred and maybe worked with two hundred. He grabbed the lists and methodically went through them. After thirty minutes, he came up with the names of twenty officers who fit the bill. Eight of them he knew well enough to recognize their voices and would know if one was the mystery caller. That left twelve possibles, and Donovan only knew two things to do, and he did both of them. First, he phoned friends of the program in each of the sub-stations and asked if they had any idea who the person might be. No one did.

"To hell with confidentiality," Donovan thought. "The guy never gave his name anyway, and there are other lives to save besides his." Next, Donovan started through the twelve names, phoning those he could reach and using his razor sharp senses to either recognize the voice or spot a suspicious response.

"Hi, George. It's Eddie Donovan over at the stress program. How's it going?"

"Fine."

"That's good. By the way, did you phone me an hour ago?

"No."

"Oh, that's great, glad to hear it, keep up the good work." The confused voice on the other end said, "Thanks" and wondered what the hell was going on. Before he could ask, Donovan was already dialing the next name, Rod Callaghan, on the list.

"Hi Rod, it's Eddie Donovan over at the stress program. How's it going?"

"Fine." Donovan listened carefully to the answer. He thought he had his man.

"That's good. By the way, did you phone me an hour ago?"

"No."

"Bullshit," Donovan said. "Look Rod, you called me for help and that's just what I'm going to give you." Callaghan weakly said he hadn't called, but Donovan's tone stopped him in a hurry. Finally, Callaghan admitted he made the call but didn't need the help any more.

"Bullshit," Donovan said. "You get your ass over here right now, or I'll call your captain." He could tell by the silence on the other end that the threat had worked. "I'll see you here in fifteen minutes," Donovan said and then hung up.

Ten minutes later, Donovan heard a car pull up to the stress centre's side door. He waited and listened for the car door to open. Nothing. He walked out of his office and into Dr. John's small counselling room, peeked out the window, and saw a cruiser parked almost on top of the side steps. A cop sat in the driver's seat, both hands gripping the steering wheel, his arms ramrod straight.

Donovan ran down the stairs, out the door, and peered into the car. Rod Callaghan stared straight ahead, his hands tightly squeezing the steering wheel. He was trembling. "I think I'm cracking up, I think I'm cracking up," he muttered.

"Take it easy," Donovan said, then slowly walked to the other side of the car, opened the door, and slid in beside Callaghan. Donovan reached over, loosened his belt, and took off his holster. "I'll give it back to you later," he said to the rigid officer. "I'm just gonna take it upstairs and put it in the closet." Just then, a call came over the radio. Donovan reached over, shut off the engine and radio, and took the car keys. Callaghan's hands were still frozen on the wheel. Donovan eased out the passenger side and walked back to the driver's door.

"Rod, I'll be right back." He ran inside, threw the gun and holster into the fridge on the way through the kitchen, and raced to the phone in the sitting room to catch the dispatcher before he could send squad cars to look for the missing officer.

"Rod's here in my office right now," Donovan said to the dispatcher. He can't respond to any calls, and he's off the air for the rest of the day."

"Who's authorizing that?" the dispatcher asked.

"I am. I take the responsibility." Donovan hung up and raced back outside. Callaghan hadn't moved.

"Rod, come on inside."

"I can't. I can't let go." Despite the cool temperature, sweat ran from Callaghan's face. Donovan reached in and started to peel his fingers, one at a time, off the wheel. With his hands free, Callaghan went limp and couldn't move, so Donovan had to slide, haul, drag, and carry the portly officer out of the car into the stress centre. He rolled him onto the couch in the sitting room.

"Hang on, Rod, I'll be right back." Donovan dashed into the kitchen, grabbed the gun and holster from the fridge, ran outside, and slipped it under a hole in the back porch. In potentially volatile situations like this, Donovan usually called a volunteer to assist him, but there just wasn't time now. Donovan stopped in the kitchen, poured a coffee for Callaghan, then returned to the sitting room where Callaghan had raised himself to a sitting position and seemed to be looking better. Donovan started to talk to him, and Callaghan answered but in a superficial way. He played down the threats he made and the state he was in.

"I'm okay now, Eddie. Just get me my gun, and I'll get back to work."

"Rod, I can't do that," Donovan said.

"No, I'm really fine," Callaghan said, standing and looking around for his gun belt.

"Rod, in fairness to yourself, your family, the union, and the department, I can't let you go back to work."

"Why not?"

"Federal law won't allow it. You've told me you're going to commit murder and suicide."

"You traitor," Callaghan said, jumping to his feet and moving toward Donovan. Donovan crossed his arms and stared at him, knowing he was faced with the choice of subduing him and forcibly committing him to a hospital or convincing him to commit himself. Donovan wasn't a fighter, and besides Callaghan outweighed him by fifty pounds. He just hoped like hell Callaghan wouldn't charge like an enraged bull. Donovan had been in these situations before. Once, an officer he was driving to a detox pulled out a hidden gun and pressed it to Donovan's head. Donovan simply said, "Go ahead and pull the trigger and see if that solves your problems." The officer thought for a moment, then handed the gun to Donovan.

"Fuck you," Callaghan said, turning to storm out to his squad car.

"Okay, I will," Donovan yelled after him. Donovan climbed the stairs, ducked into the washroom to slip Callaghan's car keys into the toilet tank, then walked into his office, sat down, and swung his feet up on the desk.

He heard the cruiser door open and close several times. Finally, a door opened, and he heard Callaghan stomp through the main floor and then puff and pant as he climbed the stairs to Donovan's office. He walked in, sat down, and looked disgustedly at Donovan.

Donovan looked back at him.

"Okay, okay," Callaghan finally said. "What do I have to do?" Donovan talked to him for half an hour about his problem and getting help by admitting himself to a hospital, but Callaghan wasn't buying.

"I can't let you go back to work, and I'm going to have to inform your superior officers," Donovan said, hoping to jar him into some action one way or the other.

"Hey, wait a minute!" Callaghan yelled at him. "I came here confidentially," Donovan settled him down, finally convincing him to agree to enter hospital on several conditions. Callaghan wanted to save face by driving back to the station on his own and explain things to his captain before leaving for the hospital. Donovan agreed, but told Callaghan he was going to phone the captain to let him know what was happening. He would give Callaghan's gun to the captain, who'd keep it until Callaghan had a letter from a doctor saying he was fit to go back to work.

Callaghan grunted his agreement. Donovan told him where to fish for his car keys, and Callaghan returned to his station. On his way back, Callaghan had a change of heart. He stormed into the captain's office and said Donovan bullied him and there was no way he needed to go to a hospital. He was going right down to the union to complain. The captain immediately phoned Donovan, because the union wielded a lot of power.

"That's okay," Donovan said calmly, "While he was on his way to see you, I called a union official, told him what was going down and not to be surprised if Callaghan landed on his doorstep." At first the official wanted to protect Callaghan until Donovan said, "I've informed you of what he told me, and if you don't help relieve him of his duty and he goes out and kills someone, I'm not liable, you are." When Callaghan arrived at the union office there was a reception committee waiting to help him with his trip to the hospital. Not only did Donovan have to do good, but he also had to be good. Good at covering his ass.

Donovan with Joseph Wambaugh.

Ed Donovan, George Leehan and Millie McCowan.

The stress centre.

Donovan lecturing at Georgia Police Academy in 1979.

Paul Martin, head volunteer of the trauma team.

Martin and Donovan in a trauma meeting in the sitting room of the stress centre.

Dr. Michael Scott, a cardiologist studying stress for the police in Belfast, Northern Ireland, visited the Boston Police Stress Program.

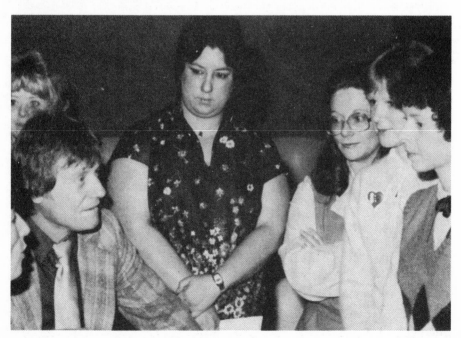

Donovan counselling police wives in Chicago.

Donovan and Commissioner Mickey Roache.

Roache presenting Mary with a plaque for the help she gave Donovan at the stress centre during the lay-offs.

With Magic in Donovan's livingroom.

With Suzanne.

Donovan, Anne Marie
and Mary.

Donovan and Mary at
their wedding in 1985.

CHAPTER SEVENTEEN
THE ENCOUNTER

Monday, 4:30 P.M.

George Leehan came by and Donovan related the story of Shaky and his concern for Jerry Leonard. They talked about a variety of things, and the friendly diversion relaxed Donovan, but he was emotionally and mentally drained. He talked about training Magic, and George, a police dog handler, offered some suggestions. Suddenly, George interrupted himself in mid-sentence.

"Eddie, what happens if both Shaky and Jerry show up at the meeting tonight?"

Donovan hadn't thought of that awkward possibility. He paused for a long moment, then colour and life returned to light up his face. A coy smile spread from ear to ear.

"Well, that's show business."

The possible confrontation at the meeting between Max "Shaky" Shakura and Jerry Leonard started his adrenalin flowing. A few cops met their arresting officers weeks or months later in the meetings when both were under treatment and sober, but this was the first time two would meet the day after, with one of them still a drunk. "That'll liven up the meeting," Donovan chuckled to himself.

At 6:30 P.M., Brian Connor climbed the stairs to Donovan's office. He was thirty minutes early for the AA meeting and had a worried look on his face. "Eddie, I've got to talk to you. Have you got a few minutes before the meeting?"

"Sure, come on in, Brian." Donovan had been concerned about Brian's tendency to depression and the fact he had been battling a cold for several weeks, a sure sign of stress coming to the surface. Brian plopped his husky, 200-pound frame on the chair opposite Donovan's desk and with his round baby face looked uneasily at his mentor. Ten months ago, drunk and desperate, he had threatened to throw Donovan out the office window. Only George Leehan's presence had stopped him. Then George and Donovan verbally worked him over for three hours until Brian broke down and cried like a baby. They admitted him to a detox hospital that evening. Now, after a month in a detox, and nine months of sobriety, he was like a helpless puppy dog as he sat in front of Donovan.

"I'm really down, Eddie. It's like I'm going through a long tunnel, and I don't see any light at the end. I'm sick. I'm shaking and trembling all the time. There's nothing to do. I'm depressed, and I just don't see much reason for carrying on," he said.

"Wasn't it your birthday on the weekend?" Donovan asked. "Did you have a party?"

"Yeah, it was all right."

"How old are you now, Brian?"

"Thirty," Brian said, as his large, brown hound-dog eyes looked sorrowfully at Donovan.

"Does that bother you?"

"No."

"Bullshit, Brian. You're feeling sorry for yourself. No one said it was going to be easy. Where would you be if you hadn't sobered up?"

"Probably dead," came the reply. Donovan knew he had to be firm. The worst thing he could do was feed Brian sympathy. He had to toughen him up — cut the strings — so Brian wouldn't become too dependent on him, so he could handle his own problems.

The noise of the downstairs door opening and closing signaled the early arrival of others. Once drunks attracted to drink, these sober men now grabbed for the life-line the meetings offered. This meeting, for many, was the only thing they had. Drink had cost some of them their marriages, their kids, and their possessions. Sobriety had cost them their drinking buddies. Now, they had nothing, except the program. They'd pour a coffee and take their spot in the large circle of chairs in the main meeting room and comfortably wait for the others to arrive, secure in the feeling they were among friends who understood. The casual, joking banter they used to greet each other hid the deeper feelings and tragedy below.

"How are things with you?" one cop asked another.

"The same, nothing's new."

"What does that mean?"

"Life sucks; then you die." Both men smiled and sat down.

A black cop joined two other blacks sitting together at the other end of the room. "How you doin', brothers?" he said with a wink.

The atmosphere at the Monday night AA meetings is much looser and freer than Wednesday's stress sessions. At the Wednesday meetings, cops usually come only when they have a problem. They might come for two or three meetings, some for a few months, but the group is always in transition. At the Monday AA meetings, there is a stronger common bond and more long-time attendees. To stay sober, most, like Donovan, keep going to their meetings, no matter how long they've been dry.

Donovan, upstairs in his office with Brian, felt like a circus ringmaster. The phones were ringing continually: guys needing rides, wives checking up on husbands, excuses from those who couldn't come. Donovan fielded the calls, counselled Brian, and thought of his meeting with the commissioner without missing a beat. The sound of feet climbing the stairs drew his attention to his half-open door. Jerry Leonard peered around the corner, his face flushed with embarrassment, his eyes filled with panic.

"Shaky, he just came in. He's downstairs right now," Jerry said in an excited whisper.

"Take it easy, Jerry. He's got a problem, and he's here to

deal with it. It's no reflection on you." The wheels whirled in Donovan's mind at this interesting turn of events. "I'll be down in a few minutes."

Jerry hesitated for a second, then left. Donovan listened to his footsteps, treading slowly down the stairs at first, stopping for a moment near the bottom, finally fading out as he returned to the meeting room. Donovan went right back to dealing with his phone calls and Brian.

Downstairs, Shaky presented a logistical problem. He sat nervously, chain-smoking cigarettes at the side of the main meeting room by the kitchen door where everyone entered. With his lanky frame, he looked like an uncomfortable octopus draped around the small folding chair. One long arm extended almost to the floor as he continually flicked ashes with his yellowed fingers into the ashtray on the floor beside him. Around him, on his side of the room, were a dozen empty chairs.

All who entered had puzzled looks on their faces as they wandered over to the far side of the room where about nine other men were sitting. Some knew about Shaky and immediately recognized the sticky problem of him and Jerry Leonard being there. Those who didn't know looked around, puzzled, realizing something was up, not understanding what. They were quietly filled in when they went out to the kitchen to pour their coffee. Shaky was treated like he had the plague. No one talked to him, no one sat with him. For years, he'd been a loner without friends on the police force, and now he'd caused a suffering brother officer unnecessary grief.

Gradually, the room filled, but the chairs around Shaky were the last to be taken. In the corner near the stairway, Brian was talking to several senior group members about his depression. They had a quick solution for his problem.

"Brian, you'd better lead the meeting tonight," Dick Winter said. Brian was put on the spot, and he knew he couldn't say no. In Donovan's groups, they didn't let you hide.

Brian took a chair at the head of the circle where the AA

literature was spread on a coffee table in front of him. Donovan escaped from his phone calls to join the group, taking a seat with the troops on the opposite side of the room facing Shaky. Brian called the meeting to order, and the laughing and talking stopped immediately. Everyone turned to look at Brian, serious looks replacing the smiles and grins.

Brian read the creed of Alcoholics Anonymous, and then everyone quickly introduced himself:

"Jack, alcoholic."

"George, alcoholic."

"Jerry, alcoholic."

"Steve, alcoholic and drug addict." Around it went, with the same terse statement of name and disease coming from each. Only four were left to identify themselves.

"Dick, alcoholic."

"Carl, alcoholic." All eyes turned to the next seat, Shaky's seat. The men held their breath and waited.

"Max," he hesitated, "I'm not sure." There was a loud explosion of laughter. Shaky grinned sheepishly, the tension broken for now.

When the introductions finished, Brian, in the normal fashion of an AA meeting, told the story of his decline into alcoholism and his battle to overcome it.

Brian always wanted to be a cop, so when he finished school, he became a paramedic because it was good preparation for police work. He liked the exciting work, the fast life, the fast women, and the hard drinking. Brian spoke cautiously, pausing to look at the faces around the room, and although they made him nervous, their interest gave him a feeling of comfort and strength.

"I found I could deal with the stress by going out with the guys and drinking it away," he said, interlocking his thick fingers to keep from fidgeting. "A couple of incidents stand out in my mind."

He was at a Christmas party for doctors, nurses, and paramedics attended by all the medical bigwigs in Boston.

A friend of his wanted to line him up with a certain nurse. He was telling her what a nice guy Brian was and really building him up.

"I came stumbling through the crowd, my jacket turned inside out, tie pulled around my neck, and my fly open. He introduced me, and I grabbed her by the arm and peed down her leg," Brian said.

Some members of the group laughed, but most just cringed at Brian's actions. "Did you get the date?" a voice from the far side of the circle said.

"I was in a blackout and didn't know what I was doing. Everyone thought it was funny," Brian said pitifully. "I passed out and woke up the next day, freezing, with a tight feeling around my big toe, wondering where the hell I was. I pulled the sheet off that was covering my head, and there I was, toe-tagged and lying on a table in the Southern Mortuary. My buddies put me there when I passed out."

The group members shook their heads, not in disbelief, but in empathy for Brian. Everyone had experienced something just as bad himself.

Contrary to the stereotype of alcoholics, Brian was a weekend binge drinker. He didn't need to drink every day, but when he drank, he lost control. The drinking controlled him, and that, by definition, made him an alcoholic, no matter how much or how little he drank, or how long between binges.

Brian told them about other chaotic incidents, his decline into hopeless alcoholism and, finally, his arrest for drunkenness and assault and battery a year ago. A friend took him to a couple of meetings at the stress centre, but he still thought he could handle the odd drink. One evening, after drinking alone in his room, he pulled out his shotgun, loaded it, put the barrel in his mouth, and was about to pull the trigger with his toe.

"When I worked in the ambulance, I'd seen four cops who did it this way. But I couldn't do it. I was afraid," Brian said emotionally. "The sick feelings you have — you think death is preferable to living your life this way. You don't know there's another life out there. Then something dawned on me — I'm sure it was God. I called up Eddie. I caught him at the office just as he was leaving for the day.

"He said, 'Brian, yeah, I remember you. You're the heavy set guy who sat in the corner at the meetings and didn't say anything. Have you been drinking?'

"I said, 'Yeah, I've had a few.' He knew bloody well I was blasted.

"Then he said, 'Are you alone?'

" 'Yeah.'

" 'Do you have a gun?'

" 'Yeah.'

"'Brian, how'd you like to come over to the stress centre and meet with me right now?'"

Everyone laughed at Donovan. They knew how he worked. He was like a salesman sizing up a client. "Drunk, alone, gun — hmmm," he would think. "Sounds like he needs the number one hard sell. Better meet with him right away."

Brian continued. "So I floated over. The hardest thing in the world for me to do was walk through these doors. But I was defeated. My family had rejected me, my department didn't want anything to do with me, my productivity was gone. Everything I lived for was gone."

When Brian went up to Donovan's office, George Leehan was there. Donovan always tried to have someone with him in volatile situations, for safety, for legal reasons, and for teamwork.

"They sat me down upstairs and started to work on me," Brian said. "George was the good guy and Eddie the bad guy. He scared the shit out of me the two meetings I went to, because he looked right through me. I saw him lookin' at me that way again, so I said, 'I'm fine now, and I think I'll leave.' Eddie said, 'The hell with you, you're fine.'"

Brian told how he had threatened to throw Donovan out the window, and how George had stopped him. Then how they had worked on him for three hours to break his defences down, finally convincing him to go to a detox. He talked about his difficulties in the detox, about coping with the stigma of being an alcoholic, and explained his current depressed feelings to the group.

Brian was now facing the realities and frustrations of sobriety: the debts, bills, and family problems that used to be ignored. He lived with his mother and, up until a month ago, a drug addict brother and his family. The brother brought nothing but grief to Brian and his mother. He had to take legal action to evict his brother and family from the house. Doing it tore Brian apart.

"You think when you're an alcoholic, once you sober up, all the worst is behind you," Donovan explained. "Instead, you find harsh realities you previously ignored that now you have to deal with." An alcoholic's maturity level often stagnates from the age he starts to drink. When he sobers up, you find a fifty-year-old man with the maturity of a teenager. He faces the grim reality of having to do a lot of growing up in a short time, and trying to do it sober.

Carl, who was both an alcoholic and addict, said, "Boy! I used to tell the IRS to stuff it. Now that I'm clean, I see they won't do that. They want their money, and they want it now." Everybody laughed, nodding their heads.

"I hate paying for things I don't have anymore," Bobby added. "I'm paying for a wife and house I no longer have. Two cars which I cracked up when I was drunk, and a pile of charge accounts. Not only that, but I have liver damage, diabetes, and the chronic shakes, all as a result of my drinking. And yet everyone says, 'Isn't it great to be sober; isn't it great to be alive?' Sometimes I don't know about that. I don't feel very good right now."

Donovan felt it was time to be aggressive. He knew they were frustrated, and that Brian, Carl, and Bobby were on the bubble, that critical period when, now sober, they had to deal with the damage of their drinking and drug addiction.

"Did you think it was going to be easy?" Donovan questioned the trio. "When I first sobered up, after alimony and car payments for two cars I didn't have, I was taking home thirty dollars a week, and that was in the early seventies. It wasn't easy living on that. I felt just like you guys now, but do you know why I made it?" Donovan looked each one of them in the eye. "Do you know why I made it? Because I wanted to live, and there were a bunch of people in the AA meetings that I went to every night who wanted to help me live, help me control the disease and get the monkey off my back."

"Brian, how many meetings have you been going to a week?" Donovan asked, knowing the answer. Brian hesitated, shuffled his feet, and looked down.

"I know, I know I should be going to more," he said. Dick Winter wasn't going to let him squirm out of this one.

"How many meetings, Brian? How many meetings have you been going to a week this month?" Dick said.

"One a week, this one."

"Brian, I've been sober for five years, and I go to three meetings a week," Dick said. "Look at Tommy over there. He goes to nine or ten a week. You've got to put the effort into it."

"I know you're right. It's just that I keep wondering, what have I got to be thankful for? I don't have a wife, kids, or girlfriend. When I sobered up, I lost my social circle and most of my friends. I turned thirty on the weekend. What have I done with my life?" Brian asked.

"Have you come to grips with your father's death?" Donovan probed, knowing there was more to Brian's anguish. His father had been an alcoholic who died a victim of his disease several years ago. Brian had been deeply scarred. He loved his father but hated him for the disease and what it had done to the family. Brian saw himself in the clutches of the same devil and feared he was destined to die in the same way.

"I'm trying, Eddie, but it's really hard. Like you suggested, I went out to the grave to try to make peace with him. I feel a bit better, but it's just going to take time."

George Leehan, acting as the good guy again, wanted to draw out the positives in Brian's life.

"Brian, what have you to be thankful for?" he asked. Brian thought deeply, then blushed.

"Well, I got laid yesterday." Laughter filled the room, and Brian breathed a welcome sigh of relief.

"I rest my case," George said proudly. Brian had received his needed boost.

The focus now shifted to others in the group. Obviously, Donovan was going to leave the encounter with Shaky until the meeting was well along, so Shaky could see how the others bared their souls and feelings.

George Leehan became the target. Although George was a senior member of the group and one of Donovan's most able volunteer counsellors, he was not immune to the honest probing of the group.

"Have you got a sponsor yet, George?" Carl asked.

Everyone, no matter how long they've attended AA, has to have a sponsor. A sponsor is like a big brother, someone you can talk to if you have a problem. A sponsor usually introduces you to AA and holds your hand during the early meetings. Later in your recovery, he's a friend who is there if you need him. This provides a system of checks and balances that is an integral part of the Alcoholics Anonymous program. Donovan still had a sponsor, and so did everyone in the room who was a treated alcoholic. George's sponsor had moved away from Boston three months previously.

"I haven't got one yet, but I'll get one soon." George replied defensively.

"George, you've been telling us that for the past three weeks." The group didn't buy George's feeble excuses. As a leader in the group, he had to practise what he preached.

It was now time for the main event of the evening. Usually,

Donovan let the meetings run themselves, but this issue was too important to leave to chance. Donovan took the lead.

"Jerry, you were involved in an interesting situation yesterday. Could you tell the group about it?"

Jerry rolled his shoulders in discomfort, the embarrassment and tension colouring his face a crimson red. Just three months before, he had been a drunk being forced to attend his first meeting. Now he'd been sober for two months and a regular contributor to the Monday meetings, both as a participant and volunteering to help with some of the chores. Tonight, he was uncomfortable in his new role as arresting officer.

He glanced at Shaky who looked away uneasily.

Jerry carefully told the story of getting the call and how he was forced to arrest Shaky. His face reddened further as he agonized over arresting a brother officer.

"I'm not worried about the other officers in the station. They know I was forced into doing what I did. I did everything possible to let him off, but he wouldn't let me. I'm worried others who don't know the circumstances will say, 'What kind of prick is he for arresting a brother officer?'"

Several officers in the meeting jumped in to defend Jerry.

"Hey, you did what you had to."

"If you had let him go, and he killed someone on the way home, your ass would be in a sling. You were doing him a favour."

They all looked at Shaky to see how he was reacting. He slowly lifted his head, his face filled with shame. He looked at Jerry.

"Look, I don't hold anything against you. You were just doing your job," Shaky said, "so don't worry about it. I don't want to cause you any trouble. I'm just a big dummy who had a few too many drinks."

Everyone sighed with relief. Shaky's comments would ease Jerry's conscience, and it was a first step for Shaky to admit he had a problem.

"Jerry, just look at the number of guys in the room who've

been arrested," Donovan said, "Brian over there was arrested by Tommy when Tommy was still a drunk. It was a drunk arresting another drunk." Tommy Branigan looked drawn. This morning he'd finished the last of his medical tests that he told the Wednesday stress group about. His thirty years of alcoholism had done its damage, and he was now waiting for a hospital bed for stomach surgery.

Tommy described his encounter with Brian. "I tried to give him every break in the world to sleep it off, but he fought us." It took six officers to finally bring Brian in.

"Brian, how did you feel about Tommy?" Donovan asked.

"At the time, I hated his guts, but when I dried out I realized he probably saved my life," Brian said. Ironically, five months after arresting Brian, Tommy was himself arrested and forced to dry out. He had started coming to the Monday AA meetings and, two months ago, he and Brian met each other sober for the first time. They shook hands, and then hugged, both finally understanding the disease that almost destroyed their lives.

Several others in the group talked about their own arrests. Dave didn't deny the rap he was picked up for just six weeks ago. He crashed his car into a tree and was so drunk he'd blown 2.9 on the breathalyzer. Short and stocky, with arms crossed arrogantly, Dave bitterly recalled being put into the cells with the other drunks and crooks.

"Why couldn't they put me in a private room, or in a cell away from the others? It was humiliating being in there in uniform," he said.

Donovan silently thought, "We've sure got a lot of work to do with him."

"You got to look out for your brothers," said Peter, a transit cop who was sitting beside Shaky, "because when they get into court, the judge eats their ass. It isn't fair. We arrest someone for murder, larceny, drugs, and the goddamned court always lets them off or goes light. A cop goes to court for being drunk, and it's like you were a murderer."

"They make an example out of you," another agreed.

Bobby, a close friend of Jerry, jumped in to boost Jerry's cause. "It's not his fault that some son of a bitch — I'm sorry that gentleman over there," he said, momentarily forgetting Shaky's presence, "got drunk and acted like an ass. Jerry was just doing his job like any of you would."

"You've got to show professional courtesy," said one of the black officers. "Jerry did what he had to. Shaky didn't give him a choice. But you've got to bend over backwards to help your brother." Feeling a bit more comfortable with the discussion's new direction, Shaky told of several incidents where he let drunk officers off or went out of his way to drive them home. Donovan didn't like this switch in the conversation. Shaky was painting himself as a good guy and was avoiding his problem.

"Max, you tell us what happened with you," Donovan said firmly.

"Well, I just had a few social drinks at my lodge after work, and one thing I learned here tonight I hadn't heard before was about blackouts," Shaky said. "I must have had a blackout, because I can't remember hitting the tree. I don't remember anything until hours later in the cell." His hands shook as he lit another cigarette.

"Max, were you drinking on the job?" Donovan demanded.

"No. I never drink on the job."

"And do you have a drinking problem?"

"No, I'm just a social drinker. I must have had a few too many on Sunday."

"Max, who are you trying to fool? What are you doing here if you don't have a drinking problem?" Donovan said angrily, shifting and twisting his upper body to ease the discomfort in his side. "What other trouble have you been in because of your drinking?" Donovan knew of four other incidents, including one where Shaky discharged a shotgun in his backyard.

"Oh no, there's been nothing else," Shaky answered assuredly. Alcoholics are accomplished liars who easily fool strangers, friends, and often doctors, but there is an unofficial slogan in AA. "You can't shit a shitter." No one in this particular room was fooled by Shaky.

Another black officer, looking right at Shaky, said, "Before I sobered up four months ago, I used to drink and do drugs and think I was really bad. But when I saw you at the station, I used to say to myself, 'Now that guy is really blasted, I hope I don't get as bad as him.' So don't bullshit us about not drinking on the job. You were at least half in the wrapper any time I saw you." Shaky fidgeted and ground another cigarette butt into the filled ashtray at his feet.

Donovan resumed his attack. "Shaky, your job is on the line. It's up to you to figure out you've got a problem and you need help. How many of you guys didn't think you had a problem when you first came here?" Most put up a hand.

"Hell, Brian was going to throw me out the window," Donovan said.

Shaky offered some feeble excuses, maintaining he didn't have a problem. He admitted he'd had a blackout or two, a convenient way to avoid responsibility for his actions. Donovan knew that Shaky wasn't going to be a one night miracle, seeing the error of his ways and his salvation on the same night. But, then again, there weren't very many of those. Most cases took time, agony, and hard work. Shaky would be no different.

Donovan nodded to Brian that it was time to adjourn the meeting, but George Leehan interrupted for the last important piece of business: the awarding of sobriety pins. They were given for every three months of sobriety, during an alcoholic's first "dry" year, and the inexpensive little pins meant a tremendous amount to the recipients.

George presented Brian with his nine-month pin. Moved to tears by the group's hearty applause, Brian thanked everyone for the help and support they'd given him, then four others received their pins. After Brian adjourned the meeting, everyone clustered in twos and threes around the room for a few minutes of relaxed conversation before hitting the icy roads home.

Donovan tried to corner Shaky but saw him quickly heading out the back door. He hurried through the crowd and out the door after him but was too late. Shaky was already backing his car out of the parking area. Donovan smiled and shook his head as he watched him roar off down the icy road and hoped Shaky wasn't heading straight for his lodge.

The ice-cold, early-spring wind chilled Donovan as he stood on the steps for a moment, wondering if Shaky would return for other meetings. He took a deep breath of the fresh, crisp air and thanked God that he, Eddie Donovan, was alive and sober.

CHAPTER EIGHTEEN

MEETING DAY

Tuesday, 9:45 A.M.

Donovan unlocked the side door, stepped into the stress centre's kitchen, and began cleaning and filling the coffee urn for the day ahead. He had a couple coming from Canada for counselling at ten, a special trauma group meeting at eleven, which the Canadian cop would join, and then he'd have to hurry downtown for his two o'clock meeting with the commissioner.

Donovan had tossed and turned all night, the meeting with Commissioner Roache weighing heavily on his mind. Should he threaten Roache with quitting if he didn't get what he needed? Donovan liked Roache and thought he had a good chance, but he'd been burned so many times in the past: broken promises, knives in the back, the old song and dance. Previously, Roache had sent troubled officers to the program, but even if he were sympathetic, the tenous nature of his position as acting commissioner might prevent him from helping. Sometimes, the superintendent-in-chief wielded more day-to-day power than the commissioner. Budgets were always tight, and whatever money was available was usually put towards appeasing the public with tangible priorities, such as buying more squad cars and putting more men on patrol. The priority of helping a cop with his mental well-being was last on the list. "They spend money fixing squad cars with worn brakes," Donovan once cursed, "but they won't fix a burned out policeman."

If he put his job on the line, could he quit if he didn't get what he wanted? Donovan didn't know, and the indecision tore at him. If he did quit, what would he do? He'd receive an adequate pension for his twenty-eight years of service, and he had had offers to start programs elsewhere, or he could turn to full-time speaking and teaching combined with consulting work. He'd seen George Kirkham and ex-commissioner De Grazia become professional expert witnesses, usually testifying in cases against policemen. This growing, lucrative field offered six-figure incomes, but Donovan would have no part of testifying against his brother officers. "I'd be a whore if I stooped to that," he said when he was offered the chance.

Buying the house had stretched his financial resources to the limit, and he needed money, but not at the cost of his fellow cops. He only earned a basic patrolman's salary, received no overtime for all the extra hours worked, and got no management stipend for being director of the program. He did make money from some of his speaking, consulting, and teaching engagements, but most paid no more than expenses.

Donovan plugged in the urn and slowly walked through to the main meeting room and looked around at the empty chairs. He sat down, closed his eyes, took a deep breath to ease his tension, then savoured a flood of memories from the hundreds of meetings held in this room.

Suddenly, with a snort, he started laughing. He was thinking of an officer he counselled over a long period of time who couldn't get along with his fellow cops. Sometimes, officers like him would transfer to motorcycle patrol or to the horseback squad where they could work alone. This officer decided, with Donovan's encouragement, to switch to the horse unit.

In the first phase of his training, the officer worked to overcome his fear of horses, and Donovan heard he'd made good progress. But at a Wednesday stress meeting a week later, the officer appeared to be depressed, so Donovan asked him to tell the group what was bothering him. He explained he'd overcome his fear and was working on the next phase of training, developing a rapport with his horse. Suddenly, he blubbered, "The stupid horse don't like me.

He won't do what I tell him." There was dead silence among the officers. They dared not look at each other for fear of bursting out laughing. Some looked down, others covered their eyes, a few bit their lips.

"The horse don't give a shit for me," the officer wailed. Even Donovan strained not to laugh. What could he say to the guy? He'd dealt with rejection from wives, children, parents, friends, and society, but this was the first cop he knew of who'd been rejected by a horse.

One special moment in this room stood out for Donovan. When he thought of it, the laughter left his face and tears filled his eyes. Bert Gee, infamous for the shooting of his dishwasher two and a half years previously, had become a regular attendee at the Monday night AA meetings after drying out from twenty years of drinking. His seventeen-year-old son was especially proud of his dad for recovering from alcoholism, and the two had become very close.

Three weeks ago, the son was killed in an early morning motorcycle accident. That night, Bert came to the AA meeting. Donovan and the group knew nothing of the tragedy. Bert waited patiently until it came his turn to share at the meeting, and then he talked about his son's death. Everyone was stunned. Yet Bert talked eloquently and lovingly of his loss and his feelings. He thanked the group and the AA program for the strength to face this crisis.

Three days later at the wake, while Donovan and others from the stress centre looked on, Bert took his AA medallion, given to him for his second anniversay in AA, and pressed it into his dead son's hand. "Thank God, I was given two years of sobriety to give to him," Bert said.

Donovan stood as he wiped the tears from his eyes and walked into the sitting room. Just one incident like that made it worthwhile. The program had grown and helped many people, but so much more could be done with the proper manpower and resources. He wanted to fix up the building and have a small budget for supplies and training material. Most critically, he needed two full-time counsellors, and he'd been grooming them for the past two years. George Leehan presented a low key, gentle contrast to Donovan's dynamic, hard-hitting approach. Millie McCowan, a black detective who'd also been a police wife, was gregarious and enthusiastic with some rough edges, but Donovan saw her potential and wanted to refine her abilities. She would attract more policewomen to the stress centre, and she could take over the wives' group.

With George and Millie on hand, the program could take more preventive measures to reach cops before their problems became serious. Donovan would be free to implement dozens of plans and pet ideas he'd had for a long time. For instance, he'd seen the difficulty people had accepting the death of a loved one, and he wanted to start a grief group to help cops and their families handle their losses.

Donovan sighed as he took a broom from the hall closet and started sweeping and rearranging the sitting room for the couple who were to arrive any minute. He paused for a moment to look at the battered room with its soiled furniture, peeling paint, cracks, and grime. He took a deep breath, closed his eyes, and visualized the room cleaned, painted, and outfitted with some decent furniture. "Not bad at all," he thought.

CHAPTER NINETEEN
NORMAN

Tuesday, 11:00 A.M.

Norman Gibbs seemed to be in a daze. Around him in the stress centre's sitting room sat a trauma team that Donovan and Paul Martin had assembled especially for him. Four years ago, Gibbs had killed in the line of duty; now a victim of post-traumatic shock, he suffered from physical, mental, work, and marital problems.

Most newcomers sat rigid and cross-armed in a posture of defiance, but Gibbs' six-foot, 170 pound frame was limp and slightly stooped, his body apparently without bones. He was only 35, but his face was lined beyond his years. He was like an injured football player who'd been blindsided. He knew something had hit him; he just didn't know what. Gibbs looked apprehensively at the faces around him, not knowing yet that except for Donovan and Martin, they had all gone through the same experience. Freddie Washington, a black Boston cop, Dan Flaherty from the Boston Transit Police, and Frank Schroder from suburban Braxton, all had killed in the line of duty.

Based on superficial evidence, most cops might envy them. Each had faced death in situations police men and women are trained for but rarely experience. Each had shot and killed, in self-defence, a man who was threatening the lives of others. In Gibbs' case, a knife-wielding husband had attacked him in a domestic dispute.

In their early days on the police force, cops dream of becoming heroes in situations like this, receiving the front page headlines, citations, and the admiration of their peers. They expect that when you shoot someone, you just blow the smoke from the end of the barrel and go home to dinner or on to the next case as in the cowboy movies. Gibbs' shooting had happened four years ago, and his gun was still smoking.

Like Flaherty, Schroder, Washington, and many other police officers who've killed, Gibbs found that there is a curse that goes with the shooting. Not only is it hard for the public and other police officers who haven't experienced it to understand, but even the bewildered Gibbs sitting in the group at this very moment didn't understand. Donovan understood all too well.

He knew that police who made the conscious decision to pull the trigger often regretted the decision, no matter how justified. Even Washington and Schroder, who had killed as soldiers in war, found killing as a policeman to be different. In war, the enemy is nameless, often faceless, and generally one has a strong sense of cause and the support of others. In police work, one usually shoots at close range and afterwards finds out all about the person and his family. One may get crucified in the media, investigated by his own force, and possibly sued. The policeman and not the criminal is put on trial.

Most police departments don't understand what their men go through when they kill and consequently give them little or no help. A seemingly minor but recurrent problem that Donovan encountered was that some cops were afraid to use their guns again after taking a life. Donovan would take those cops to the BPD shooting range when no one else was around and help them overcome their fear. One day, an instructor at the range walked by as Donovan was working with an officer.

"Getting ready to kill someone else?" the instructor said, smiling.

Donovan had cops who came from as far away as California for the help they couldn't get at home. Gibbs wasn't from the Boston area. He was a Canadian from a small east-coast city, and it hadn't been his idea to make the four-hundred-mile trip to Boston to see Donovan and participate in a group. His wife had seen Donovan and learned about post-traumatic shock on the CBS Sunday Morning show with Charles Kuralt. She had written Donovan to see if he could help her husband. Donovan phoned her, and now she and her husband were at the stress centre, she waiting upstairs in Donovan's office and he sitting nervously downstairs, waiting to tell his story to the group.

Donovan asked Gibbs to describe what had happened to him.

It was late in the evening one day in April, 1981. Gibbs, who'd just come on duty, was driving his one-man cruiser slowly down a narrow street in a poor, black part of the city. Suddenly, he heard a yell, looked in his rear-view mirror, and saw a teenage black girl, wearing a nightie, running after the cruiser. He slammed on the brakes.

"Help, help, my dad is killing my mother," she screamed. Gibbs saw blood coming from her nose and mouth, staining her torn nightie. Before he could get her address, she turned and ran towards some houses across the street. Gibbs quickly radioed for a back-up and bolted from his cruiser, trying to follow the girl as she ran through the yards of two adjacent houses, cut through to an alley, and raced towards the back entrance of a decrepit three-storey apartment block.

For Gibbs, the run should have been easy. He was a runner who trained daily and had four marathons to his credit. But as he charged up the three flights of stairs, his heart pounded, adrenalin shot through his system and his legs felt weak. He thought of the wall runners have to conquer late in a marathon, but decided it was nothing like the wall a police officer must cross into the unknown explosiveness of a domestic dispute. Panting heavily, he reached the third floor landing, unsnapped his holster, and ran down the dimly lit hallway toward the yelling and screaming coming from an open doorway at the far end. Sliding to a stop short of the doorway, he sneaked a quick look into the apartment before entering. What he saw sickened him: a woman, bloodied and beaten, lay moaning on the floor of the living room, pleading for help, while over her stood a man who repeatedly kicked her in the face and stomach. A small boy in pajamas about ten years old, with blood on his face, was trying to pull the man away.

In one motion Gibbs knocked, said "Police," and stepped into the apartment. The man jumped back, pulled a butcher knife from a nearby table, and grabbed the sobbing boy as his shield.

"Jesus Christ," Gibbs muttered, recognizing the man. He was well known by the city police. He had a long rap sheet and a reputation for violence and knife work. He glared at Gibbs, his eyes a dancing inferno of hatred and rage.

Gibbs felt for the security of his gun but didn't bring it out. "Let the boy go," he said. Surprisingly, the man threw the boy to the floor, ran into a bedroom, and shut the door. Gibbs breathed a sigh of relief, grabbed the boy, and shooed him out into the hallway where his sister peered around the corner.

She screamed, "My little sister's in the bedroom." Gibbs' heart sank. He had only seconds to make a critical decision. Dozens of questions, the result of years of training and experience, raced through his mind in that instant: wait for his back-up to arrive; call in the SWAT team; drag the moaning and battered wife from the living room; try and talk to the man through the closed door? But one emotion was stronger than any other. Gibbs had a little girl of his own whom he loved dearly. He pulled his gun, then kicked in the bedroom door with one well-placed kick. In a corner of the room was the little girl. She was as cute as a button, about six years old, wearing a white nightie with a large Mickey Mouse head on the front. The man was in the corner, too. He reached out cruelly with a muscular arm and yanked her in front of him.

"Come on and hit me, you son of a bitch," Gibbs raged. He hated wife- and child-beaters. To him hitting women and children was the ultimate cowardly act. He knew he should have said something like, "Could you please release the child?" or "Why don't you and I sit down for a few minutes and chat about this calmly?" Real-life dramas didn't always work that way. The man reached with his free arm and pulled out a sawed-off shotgun from behind a dresser. He jammed the muzzle into the little girl's side.

"Drop your gun, or I'll shoot the kid," he shouted. Gibbs relaxed his gun arm and reluctantly pointed his weapon down to the floor but held his gaze into the man's eyes. Gibbs realized his life was on the line. If the man had his way, they both were going to be dead. The man shoved the little girl away, tossed the shotgun onto the bed, and pulled a long, curving switchblade from his back pocket, snapping the blade open. Its well-honed edge glinted in the dim light. The man grinned dementedly, then charged at Gibbs, the knife held out to the side but its point aimed at Gibbs' pounding heart. All policemen dread being stabbed. They can face guns and other dangers, but stabbing is messy and personal.

"Stop or I'll shoot," Gibbs shouted, as he raised his gun to shoulder height. But he knew from the look on the man's face and the knife raised to the side in the killing position that he wasn't going to stop. It would take only two seconds for him to cross the small cluttered room, but Gibbs' mind ran through his short list of options: turn and run and get it in the back; backpedal and fall; try to disarm him and miss; try to wing him and miss; shoot to kill.

Gibbs pointed the gun at his chest and yelled a frantic, final "Stop."

"Bang, bang, bang." Three lethal shots thudded into the charging man's chest. He crumpled and fell at Gibbs' feet. Blood spurted from the holes in his chest as he rolled on his back for his final few gasps. His eyes, overflowing with hate, shot back at the cop. Gibbs was in shock. The gun shots sounded like cannons going off, temporarily deafening him; the smoke from his gun burnt his nostrils.

The little girl leapt onto the mortally wounded man crying "daddy, daddy." Her nightie turned crimson red as the blood soaked through. Gibbs didn't know what to do. They didn't teach you this at the police academy. The man no longer threatened anyone's safety; he'd be dead in seconds. Should he pull the girl off? The sight of the blood on her made him physically ill. He tried not to vomit. The rest of the family hurried to the room. The boy spit on Gibbs, and the older daughter, who had begged for his help, struck at him with her fists. The mother crawled to the bedroom doorway swearing and screaming obscenities at the stunned cop.

Gibbs was oblivious to them. He just stared at the little girl. She realized her father was dead, turned, and stared helplessly at Gibbs with her large brown eyes. He looked away.

The sound of sirens converging on the apartment shook him back to reality. He quickly regained his composure and pushed his way past the family. There was plenty to do. Fellow officers were amazed at Gibbs' calmness as he made his statements and filled out the necessary reports. One said quietly to another, "Christ, what a cold son of a bitch. You'd think killing someone would bother him."

Norman Gibbs looked frustrated and helpless as he finished his story. "The papers said I wouldn't have shot him if he were a white guy instead of a black. The chief was quoted right in the paper as saying he read my report and really didn't know if it was the right thing to do."

The trauma group sitting around Gibbs wouldn't judge his killing the way an internal investigation would. The purpose of Donovan's groups was to give the officer the emotional support he needed to face the consequences, whether his shooting was right or wrong.

"What support did you get?" Donovan asked. "Did anyone suggest you see a doctor?" Gibbs shook his head sadly. While a few departments have procedures for officers involved in such serious situations, most, particularly the smaller departments, have nothing. Gibbs was with a small force of one hundred officers, and this was the first killing in its history. Departments that have post-shooting procedures immediately give the man from one to two weeks off to come down from the adrenalin high, to minimize the number of times he has to tell the story, and to give him some time with his loved ones.

Paul Martin knew how dangerous it was to go back to work too soon after a shooting. Impatient after several days at home after his shooting, he had returned to work, not realizing he was still pumped up. His first day back, he was called to quell a disturbance at a tough bar. Later he said, "I walked into the bar like I was Clint Eastwood, come to kick ass. Nothing was gonna hurt me. I was careless and lucky I wasn't killed." When he came down from the high, he crashed and had to fight off the depression and doubts that crept in.

Norm Gibbs had been working a 9:00 P.M. to 5:00 A.M. shift the night of his shooting and because of a shift change was due back at work at 1:00 P.M. that afternoon, but with all the confusion and trauma he was five minutes late for work. The department made him fill out a late report.

Donovan asked some key questions, "Are you bitter?"

"I'm more mad at the chief for not standing up for me," Gibbs said.

"Norm, are you second guessing yourself?" Donovan asked.

"Naw, I never had no doubts with the guy, he didn't bother me. I couldn't even tell you what he looked like, but the kid. . ."

"Why is the kid bothering you?"

" 'Cause I got a little girl, the same age, the same size."

"You deprived her of a father, is that what you feel?" Donovan asked. Gibbs nodded. During sessions like these Donovan was like a skillful boxer. He would jab home a point concerning the realities of what the person had to face. The group would listen compassionately to the person, then try to rebuild his confidence. Donovan would then jab home another point.

"Do you think the father wanted to commit suicide?" Martin asked. Gibbs nodded again.

"It's not uncommon for a man, angry and suicidal, to take a cop with him," Donovan said. "It's a way of saying 'screw you' to society, killing the ultimate authority figure. He's a martyr."

"Everything he did made you more aggressive," Martin said, reassuring Gibbs.

"What's the family doing now?" Donovan asked.

"I still have to pass them on the street. They yell, 'Scum bag, scum bag, you're gonna die.' The wife's been arrested for hold-ups since then."

"How's it affecting you?" Donovan asked. "I just got a little smattering from your wife that you ended up having a girlfriend for a few months, drinking. How's your life changed since the shooting?" Gibbs looked puzzled and confused. Donovan and the group were smoothly and effectively taking him somewhere he didn't want to go. They seemed to know more about him than he did himself.

"I thought things were good after the shooting. Everything went okay until a year ago. It was just last April, exactly three years since the shooting." Gibbs had been working alone again and driving down a street at four in the morning. He saw a man on the street pull a gun and point it in another man's face. Gibbs jumped out of his car and fired a warning shot in the air. The startled gun toter turned and ran, then, when Gibbs fired another shot in the air, threw down his gun and surrendered. Gibbs wrote in his report that he had fired two warning shots to scare the man, but the department had just come out with a new set of guidelines for using firearms. Unknowingly, Gibbs had violated one of them. The chief called Gibbs in and suspended him for a week, saying, "We don't use warning shots."

"They found out the gun the guy had was a toy one. How am I supposed to know that from thirty feet away?" Gibbs pleaded. Donovan steered him back to the issue at hand.

"I asked you before, how did the first shooting change you?"

"I don't think right away it did," Gibbs said.

"How were you sleeping the first few weeks afterwards?" Donovan persisted.

"First few days I was nervous a bit; my stomach was jumping."

"Nightmares?" Donovan asked.

"No, never — well, I dreamt about it; I kept seeing the kid's face."

"You don't think that's a nightmare," Martin said firmly.

"You kept seeing the kid's face, the blood on her nightie," Donovan said.

"Yeah," Gibbs answered weakly.

"That's a nightmare," Donovan said. "You don't need screaming monsters. Seeing that child's face over and over is a constant reminder to you of the shooting."

"Yeah, now I even see the face when I'm driving around."

Martin was lucky when he had his shooting that he'd already been to the stress centre and knew what to watch out for. Like Gibbs' vision of the little girl's face, most cops had recurring flashes from their experiences, usually of the wounded victim. The man Martin shot was badly wounded in the chest and had lain on his stomach pleading for help, but Martin wouldn't turn him over until reinforcements came to do it. Even then, he didn't look. If he had seen the wound, it would become an image etched forever in his memory, the source of vivid flashbacks and nightmares.

Cops often suffer insomnia after shootings; they don't want to relive the event in their dreams. Cops who've been shot suffer insomnia for another reason; closing their eyes and falling asleep is too much like dying. Many are afraid to receive anaesthesia for operations, because they fear they might never wake up.

Donovan continued his probing. "Headaches?"

"Yeah, headaches. I was in the hospital; they thought I was having a heart attack, couldn't breathe."

"What's happened with your drinking?"

"Well, I drink beer, but, naw, there's no problem with it."

"When did you get the girlfriend?" Donovan asked.

"Just last April, just after they suspended me for firing the warning shots."

"Pissed off they suspended you?" Donovan said.

"Yeah, course I was."

"Feeling sorry for yourself?" Martin added.

"Yeah, probably."

"Needed a little extra attention?" Martin continued. Gibbs hesitated, embarrassed. He was on the ropes, so Donovan changed his approach.

"How do you feel about your own little girl now? Have you changed toward her at all?"

"I feel good; I don't think I've changed. She's about the same age as the other girl, maybe a few months older, she's ten now. My wife says I've changed; she says I don't spend as much time with the kid."

"Why don't you listen to your wife?" Donovan said. "Maybe you feel guilty when you look at your own child that you deprived that other girl of her father." Gibbs struggled to absorb this.

"How would you have felt if he'd killed the girl," Martin said. "You saved her life."

George Leehan came into the room to pick up some books Donovan wanted him to read. Donovan went out to chat with him briefly to give Gibbs a breather. Donovan found that if he left the room, it defused the atmosphere and left the other group members freer to talk. These meetings were intense and could overwhelm a newcomer. When Donovan first began to run the trauma groups, he mixed cops who'd been shot with those who killed but ran into an unexpected conflict. Those who killed were filled with "I wish I hadn't done it" feelings, while those who were injured were filled with feelings of "I wish I'd blown the bastard away." Now Donovan kept the two apart and held separate meetings.

Donovan changed tactics when he returned. "I wonder how you've changed as a cop?" Donovan asked Gibbs. "Were you an ordinary cop before, or were you very aggressive, or did you lay back a lot? What are you doing differently?"

"I think I'm basically the same kind of cop." Gibbs dodged the essence of the question but by doing so confirmed Donovan's and the group's suspicions.

"Were you aggressive?" Martin asked.

"Yeah."

"You haven't laid back at all," Donovan said. "What else came out of the shooting?"

"His wife sued me for $300,000."

"Don't worry, we all go through that," Frank Schroder said, speaking for the first time.

"Actually, Frank went through a situation very similar to yours, Norm," Donovan said. Frank Schroder was also called to a domestic dispute where it appeared the man wanted to die. The husband, an unemployed Viet Nam vet, went berserk and turned his abuse from his family to Schroder when the cop entered the house. He shot first, narrowly missing Schroder, who fired back and killed him. The shooting disturbed Schroder, who was a Viet Nam veteran himself and identified with the man. He was haunted by the anguish in the family's faces. He wanted to talk to the wife, tell her how sorry he was, but she was suing Schroder and had become a media celebrity on talk shows where she described the police as monsters, her husband as an angel. Invited to tell his side of the shooting on one show, Schroder was set to appear, but a last-minute order from his department nixed it. Schroder was angry. No one would hear his side of the story or learn how sorry he felt for the family.

"You have to remember, when you got a family fight where the old man's kicking the shit out of the old lady and you go in to break it up, you've got trouble," Paul Martin said. "The old man gives you some trouble so you knuckle him. Then you got mamma on your back who called you in the first place. It happens all the time. What you've got to remember is they've been fighting like cats and dogs, he probably abused her and the kids, but when he's dead he means something to them." Martin paused and looked at Gibbs. "He means dollars. Unfortunately, you become the victim now because it's all going to be taken out on you. And all you've been doing is your job — and you save people's lives by doing it."

"Lousy fuckin' job though, isn't it," Schroder said bitterly.

"Norm, have you changed at all?" Donovan pressured. "What brought you to the point that your wife is calling me for help?"

"Well, we got a new chief, and he's a nice guy," Gibbs said. The new chief sent him to a psychiatrist and said it was regrettable he hadn't been sent for help immediately after the incident. "Now this doc he sent me to has got me on all sorts of crazy pills." Gibbs' statement set off alarm bells in the group. Everyone jumped in trying to speak at the same time. Donovan tried to get control of the chaos but couldn't be heard. Finally, he put his fingers in the corner of his mouth and let loose a deafening whistle, then nodded to Paul Martin.

"There's something I want to say about psychiatrists," Martin said. "I'm having a great deal of difficulty understanding how they deal with cops. Did you tell him about the shooting before he put you on the pills?"

"I touched on it, but he said, 'That ain't your problem, you were out screwing around on your wife and you've got marital problems.' "

"This is the problem I have with psychiatrists," Paul Martin said, "they treat us like everyone else, but we're different. They don't know what a shooting does to us." Suddenly, Martin stopped mid-thought, interrupting himself, "Excuse me," he said. "When did you say the chief sent you to the shrink?"

"April."

"Wow!" Martin exclaimed. "Just hang on for a minute.

April seems to be a very important month for you. New chief, psychiatrist, drugs, girlfriend, another shooting, suspension."

"All on your anniversary in April," Donovan said, admiring Paul's insight.

"Boy, I'll tell you it all came together in April," Martin said. "And then you crashed."

"My wife mentioned the other night that I started going out with that girl three years to the day I shot the guy," Gibbs said. A chorus of oohs and ahhs came from the group.

"Need to be punished, need to hurt yourself," Donovan said.

"Let me ask you a question," Martin said softly. "How long have you been married?"

"Nine years."

"Ever mess around before?"

"No, well, not really, a few one-night stands, but never a girlfriend."

"It's a form of punishment," Paul Martin said. "You're doing something you really don't want to do. Going out and getting laid on a one-night stand is one thing, getting a hugger is heavy-duty stuff. How'd you get caught?" Gibbs hesitated, bewildered by what was happening. "Did you do something stupid?"

"Oh, yeah," Gibbs said sheepishly.

"Good man, Paul," Donovan said. Everyone but Gibbs chuckled as the pieces of the puzzle started to fit together.

"Your subconscious set you up to be punished," Martin said.

"The cop in *The Onion Field* did it with shoplifting, you did it with sex," Donovan added.

"Specially if you did something stupid to get yourself caught, because if we don't want to get caught, we don't get caught," Martin said. "What did you do that was so stupid?"

"Well, I'm pretty good with numbers," Gibbs said slowly.

"But I left the girl's name, phone number, and address on a piece of paper on my bureau in the bedroom."

"Right there for your wife to see," Martin said. "Boy, and you don't think you set yourself up."

"You mean I got myself caught?"

"That's right, that's what we're telling you." Donovan said. "You had a need to be punished; you were crying out for help. But there's a reason you did that. You wanted to be punished for screwing around on your wife. You wanted to be punished for taking that little girl's father away."

Gibbs was dumbfounded. It all made sense, but he couldn't believe it was happening. His hands shook as he reached inside his jacket for his cigarettes, slowly extracted one, then awkwardly lit it. He drew deeply on the smoke, hoping it would slow everything down. Donovan excused himself for a minute to allow Gibbs to regain his composure. He'd seen many cases like Gibbs' where the post-traumatic problems showed up years later often causing the officer to be permanently disabled. Police departments, not understanding the forces which cause an officer to suffer years later, don't recognize disabilities that aren't directly attributable to a recent event. As a result deserving officers were being refused disability pensions. Donovan had been contacted by police officers, unions and lawyers from New York to Los Angeles for help with this problem. When Donovan returned, the group was trying to bolster Gibbs' flagging spirits.

"The bastard committed suicide," Martin said. "You didn't kill him, he committed suicide."

"It's like Eddie said with my case," Frank said. "That vet committed suicide, I was just his instrument."

"Your problem," Donovan said to Frank, "was the wife; you keep seeing her face."

"One of these days I'll go see her, I want to tell her how bad I feel," Schroder said.

"Frank, you're looking for absolution, and she's not going

to give it to you," Martin said. "She's going to call you a murderer, and you're going to walk away feeling even worse." Schroder didn't know that Donovan was already planning to talk to the wife for him. Donovan was accustomed to people telling him where to go.

"Okay, Norm," Donovan said, ready to jab again. "You bared your soul to your wife, you admitted everything. Right? What's the next step?" Gibbs looked shamefacedly at Donovan. "You started having trouble on the job? Your wife told me on the phone, 'I think he wants the job to fire him and me to get rid of him.'"

"Ooh, double punishment," Martin said, using a child-like voice. "Ooh, you bad boy."

"I like my job," Gibbs protested. Donovan came at him like a machine gun.

"Taking a lot of sick time?"

"Naw."

"Drinking on the job?"

"Naw, well, once I did. I got suspended for that."

"Ever thought of suicide?"

"What?"

"Anyone else in this room ever think of suicide?" Everyone nodded.

"Well, I've thought of it but never really considered killing myself," Gibbs said.

"Suicide is killing oneself," Donovan said impatiently. "Now you said you thought about it, but not for yourself. Which is it?"

"Well I've thought about it, but . . ."

"That's enough," Donovan said. "Ninety percent of the guys out in cruisers right now have thought about it. How'd you handle Christmas after the shooting? Did you have any problems thinking about those kids who had no father?" Gibbs shook his head unconvincingly.

"Did you buy things for them?" Donovan had seen cops do this anonymously to ease a heavy conscience. Gibbs shook his head.

"Did you buy more toys than usual for your own little girl?" Again Gibbs indicated no.

"When you're shopping or something and see a little black girl, does it bother you?" Donovan asked.

"Well, some do, some don't."

"Norm, you had one kid at the time of the shooting," Donovan said. "That was four years ago. Did the shooting affect your desire to have kids?"

"Naw. We had decided before the shooting we only wanted one," Gibbs said, this time convincingly.

"What are those pills doing to you?" Martin asked.

"I don't know, it's really strange; it seems they make things worse, and the worse they make it, the more pills he gives me." Gibbs told Martin he was on Tofranil, an anti-depressant, Mellaril, another anti-depressant, and Xanax, an anti-anxiety pill.

"You know what you're doing by taking those pills?" Donovan asked. "You're suppressing your feelings. You gotta get those feelings out sooner or later. Does this guy think you're depressed?"

"I don't know."

"Do you think you're depressed?"

"Yeah, I think so." Because of his training and experience, Donovan was probably more qualified than most doctors in the area of psycho-pharmacology, especially dual addictions. He knew a drug could occasionally help a person over a tough spot, but because of his own addiction, it bothered him that some doctors ignored the real source of a problem and simply prescribed drugs that caused the patient more harm than what he was going through in the first place.

"My advice to you is get another psychiatrist. Always get a second opinion," Donovan said. "Try to find a shrink who's dealt with cops, death, or trauma."

"Why did your new chief send you to the psychiatrist?" Schroder asked.

"He called me in and said, 'I think you've changed since that shooting.'"

"Good for him," Donovan said. "He's not burying his head in the sand. Maybe he didn't send you to the best shrink, but at least he was trying. How are you and the chief getting along now?"

"Oh, good."

"Besides looking out for you he's covering his ass, too," Donovan said. "He's got it on record now that he's sent you for help."

For the first time Gibbs volunteered some information: "After the last shooting in April, the department came down on me hard. They said I'd been involved in three incidents where I used my gun and that I'd better be careful." He explained that just three weeks ago he had come across a car parked suspiciously on a side street. As he pulled up, he saw two heads duck down in the back seat. He told his partner to cover him and went to the driver's side of the car, even though he knew he should have been more careful. He didn't pull his gun out, he just walked right up to the car door and poked his head in. A .45 stared him in the face. At first he froze, then said, "Drop your gun and get out of the car." The man kept pointing the gun in his face. Gibbs said, "if you don't throw that gun down, I'm gonna yank this door open and pull you out of there." The man threw down the gun and surrendered.

When he got back to the squad car, Gibbs was shaking uncontrollably. His partner, who had watched the whole thing in stunned horror, screamed at him for being so stupid and jeopardizing both their lives.

The headlines in the paper the next day said, 'Hero Cop Stares Down Gunman.'

"Here I was: I panicked and I froze and I get made out to be a hero," Gibbs said.

Donovan looked Gibbs straight in the eye and then said, "You wanted him to blow your head off, didn't you? You were trying to commit suicide." Flabbergasted, Gibbs said nothing, he'd never thought of it that way. Donovan had done it himself, by going out with no bullets in his gun, and he knew of many others who had done the same thing. He put a canine officer into counselling when he learned the officer was leaving the dog in the car and charging into dangerous situations on his own.

Donovan was worried about Gibbs' situation for another reason. Critics would look at it and say, "See, you don't have to use your gun to disarm people." This attitude, combined with the fear of law suits, trial boards, and negative publicity, could cause a cop to hesitate in a split-second kill or be killed situation. One mistake, and a cop is dead—not a very forgiving line of work.

"Do you want to stay married to your wife?" Martin asked Gibbs.

"Oh yeah — sure."

"You don't sound very convincing," Donovan said. "A lot of guys don't. What about you: do you or don't you want to stay married?"

"I do."

"Freddie over there isn't sure what he wants," Donovan said, laughing, "The girlfriend or the girlfriend." Freddie Washington, the young black cop, had been involved in a domestic shooting six months ago.

"Prior to the shooting, I didn't want to get close to anyone," Washington said. "I was very selfish and self-centred. One night stands were fine, but no relationships."

"That's the Wyatt Earp syndrome," Martin interjected. After the shooting, Washington changed and formed relationships with two women who were pressuring him to get married. The shooting trauma, followed by his women troubles, caused him to break down.

"After the shooting, I tried to make it by myself," Washington said. "I thought it didn't bother me, and to prove it I went after the women. But I couldn't tell them about my doubts and fears from the shooting. I was embarrassed to say to anyone that I needed help. I held it in but found I was crying frequently. Eddie kept bugging me to come here. Finally I did."

Dan Flaherty spoke: "I've been doing something the last month that's comparable to your situation, Norm. I've been married eleven years and I've never screwed around. I used to wear my wedding band all the time. I killed a guy last May, and for a long time afterward I was high, bitter, and angry." Flaherty was a Boston Transit Policeman. In his incident, he was being badly beaten by a gang of five youths, but semi-conscious and bleeding, he was able to get his gun out and shoot one of his assailants.

"I noticed two or three months ago that I wasn't feeling the anger and hate anymore, but I started feeling weak and came down with psoriasis all over my head; my hair started falling out and, of all things, I developed a rash all around my rear end. At the time, I didn't see what an itchy asshole had to do with the shooting," Flaherty said. "Even my doctor didn't know."

"Pain in the ass," Donovan said. "I've known many people who've gone completely bald because they're going through a divorce or some other heavy shit. When it was over, they grew it all back."

"I felt old and tired," Flaherty said. "Last month, I started leaving my wedding band in the drawer, not that I am going to screw around, but it makes me feel younger and freer."

"Danny, you're setting yourself up. There's gonna be a hugger walk right into your life if you're not careful," Martin said.

"I was becoming so low, I was trying to develop an image that's not me," Flaherty said.

"Then start wearing your ring," Donovan urged. "Hang in there." He turned his attention to Gibbs. "Norm, you're aware of what you're doing wrong, so try to undo it. Start giving your daughter more attention than you ever gave her before in your life. Hold her, hug her, kiss her, tell her how much you love her. If your wife says she sees a difference in you, listen to her. We don't see the changes in ourselves, someone else does." Donovan knew from Gibbs' wife that he had been avoiding his daughter more and more since the shooting.

"Do you and your daughter ever do anything alone?" Martin asked. "Just you and her?"

"Yeah, I take her places. Every year I take her on vacation."

"How about daily?" Donovan asked.

"Oh yeah, I play with her all the time."

Donovan had had enough of Gibbs' avoidance. "Do you ever talk to her about the shooting?"

"No," Gibbs said, quickly avoiding Donovan's glance.

"She ever ask you questions about it?"

"Yeah, one time she did."

"Are you honest with her?" Flaherty asked.

"Not really."

Flaherty hesitated to say what he thought but saw the nod of encouragement from Donovan.

"I think you're making a mistake. You have to be honest with them, because they're going to hear from someone sometime. Your kids are the first ones who'll figure out you're full of it."

"Better she hears it from Daddy," Donovan said. "Kids are cruel. She's going to hear it from them, so better you explain it first. Not gory details, just what Daddy had to do to a man who was being bad."

Paul Martin spoke: "We've all been out on the street and had a kid come up to us and put his hand on the gun and ask us, 'Have you ever used your gun?'"

"Yeah, it drives you nuts," Gibbs said.

Martin went on: "Especially if you've used the gun, it causes you a problem 'cause you don't like lying, and you're caught in one of those rock and a hard spot things. If you say you shot someone, you open up a Pandora's box of questions from the kid. If you say you use it for cracking walnuts, you're not being honest."

"The day of my shooting I went home," Flaherty said. "My wife kept my kids home from school. I sat them down at the kitchen table and told them what my job sometimes makes me do and what others might say. They understood, and when they went to school and kids said, 'Your dad's a prick, he killed a man,' they at least knew what it was about."

Donovan continued: "Norm, in your particular case, you tell the kid point blank that the man wanted to be killed. You tell her you had no choice, or she wouldn't have had a father." Donovan looked closely at Gibbs again. "Think about your child, think about how you touch her, handle her, and kiss her. Are you doing it the same now as before the shooting? Why is your wife saying you're different? Can you look at her and touch her or kiss her without feeling apprehensive? What's different?"

"Well, she says I don't spend as much time with her, but I don't think there's much difference."

Paul Martin jumped in: "How's the communication between you and your wife since the shooting?"

"Good, well, it hasn't been too good the last few months. But I never mention the shooting to my wife.

"You just let her handle it by herself?" Martin said.

"Well, I told her the night it happened, but I don't think I ever mentioned it again."

"What we're trying to say," Martin emphasized," is you get so wrapped up in your own problem, you're not thinking about your wife, and it's her problem, too. Just the fact that your life was in jeopardy, really on the line, has taken a piece out of her, too."

"Since I've been taking the pills, I've really been irritable; I fly off the handle at everyone. I've had constant chest pains," Gibbs said. Donovan knew the chest pains were caused by improper breathing which was constricting his arteries and that a frequent side effect of the use of tranquilizers and anti-anxiety pills was irritability.

Gibbs started to talk more freely. "You know how I told you I got suspended in April and when I was drinking that time it was April? Well, I started smoking in April."

"Your subconscious is really something," Martin said. "It's doing a real number on you. How old are you, Norm?"

"Thirty-five."

"That's a tough age for a lot of people. When did you turn thirty-five?"

"April."

"If I were you," Martin said, "I'd start taking vacations every April. Month-long vacations." Everyone laughed. "Seriously, you should at least look at taking a week off over the shooting date and take Momma and the kid and go somewhere nice where there's a lot of distractions to keep you busy. Just get away, stroke yourself. Do it for yourself and your family, and you're going to get good vibes to help you carry on and outweigh those negative vibes." Donovan nodded his head in agreement. Recent research had shown that of cops who kill, 90 percent won't work on the anniversary date of their killing. They take a holiday or book off sick.

"You're lucky," Schroder said. "All your problems are coming down at a predictable time. A lot of guys I know don't know when it's going to hit. Donovan slipped out of the room to go up and talk to Gibbs' wife. With Donovan gone, Paul Martin had an issue he wanted to deal with.

"Do you ever cry on her shoulder?" Martin said.

"Naw, never, I won't do that."

"Even when you're really hurting? What, you think it's unmanly?"

"Probably."

"Believe me, it's not," Martin said. "When things get so bad and you're hurting, who better to turn to than your wife? We don't show our emotions to every Tom, Dick, and Harry that comes down the pipe. You've got to realize that you're human. With that badge, they make us feel like supermen, that we can walk on fire, but, baby, we get hurt."

Donovan returned to the room with a surprise for the group. "You know, I think it would be nice to bring Norm's wife down here to join the group. We haven't done that for a while." Everyone, including Martin, was shocked. Gibbs squirmed in his seat, and some of the others started making noises like they had to go, but Donovan had them trapped.

"Hilary," Donovan yelled upstairs, "come on down and join us." The trim, long-haired brunette stepped nervously down the stairs and into the sitting room, taking a seat next to her fidgety husband. Donovan wrung his hands in glee, and a coy grin spread from ear to ear — he loved doing the unexpected.

"Gentlemen," Donovan said loudly, "this is Hilary. We've been talking about issues relating to a shooting tragedy and how hard it is for the wife when she's left to deal with it on her own. All the attention is centred around the officer. Did you find it that way?"

"Yes, pretty much."

"And you made the statement to me upstairs that you didn't think he thought you cared." Hilary explained how they'd failed to communicate for most of their nine years together. Each thought the other didn't care, and they never shared their feelings. But in the eight months since she found out about the affair, all their feelings, good and bad, had spilled into the open. The psychiatrist frustrated her because he didn't seem to understand what was happening to them.

"I felt he was missing the root of it, and before he'd find anything out, he'd kill Norm with the pills," she said.

Norm interjected: "The only thing he seemed concerned about was who's going to pay? Every time we went he said, 'Who's paying?' He'd take up half of his hundred-dollar hour getting that clear."

Hilary continued: "The last visit, when I asked him about all the pills and Norm's explosive behaviour, he suggested putting him on Librium."

"What explosive behaviour?" Martin asked.

"Especially in the doctor's office, the psychiatrist would get into some really sensitive issues and Norm would explode. Then the hour would be over and he'd send us home to deal with it."

"That's no way to leave the office of a doctor," Donovan said bitterly. "Hilary, the group brought out the fact that the girlfriend represented a need to be punished, a cry for help. Norm left evidence around so you would find out about it." She confirmed the fact that he had been very obvious about it. Donovan wanted to find out from Hilary what happened the night of the shooting. "We know what the cop goes through after the shooting, the headaches, the nightmares. What about the wife, what happened to you?"

"Norm called me around midnight and told me he shot a guy. His partner brought him home around 5:00 A.M. and poured him into the house. That I resent deeply, that their answer seemed to be to get him loaded, then bring him home and dump him on me. He didn't say much, then passed out."

"I want to hear about you," Donovan said. "Who was meeting your needs?"

"I don't think it was bothering me at the time. Three years ago, the word was out that some relative of the guy Norm had to kill was flying up from Detroit to kill him. That bothered the both of us." Donovan wanted to know if either of them were carrying guns or keeping an extra one around the house, but both said no. Dan Flaherty explained that after he killed one of a gang, he feared the others would seek revenge on him or his family, so he carried guns everywhere: mowing the lawn, going to church, taking a shower, under the pillow, under the car seat. He even made his wife carry a gun.

"April's been a very bad month for Norm," Martin said.

"Not all bad," Hilary said. "He met me in April." Everyone laughed at that. "We figure it's his month for women, too, because he met the both of us in April. He met her on a Thursday night, three years to the day of the shooting, and by Sunday he was in hospital with a suspected heart attack."

"Are you two still seeing that psychiatrist?" Martin asked.

"No," they answered in unison. Hilary had told the psychiatrist about coming to see Donovan and he had said, "I don't think that will be the answer." She had told him, "I don't like your way of handling it, only dealing out drugs."

"Look, you can't knock a whole profession," Donovan said. "There's a lot of psychiatrists, psychologists, and social workers who are sharp enough. If you go to them and give them their fifty dollars, they'll send you to group counselling programs like ours. If a guy's got a drinking problem, a good shrink will do what he can but send the guy to an AA group as well."

"Norm's been drinking more lately to get through the day, and I've really been worried because that's dangerous with all the pills he's been taking. I asked the psychiatrist about it, and he said, 'Well, you'll just have to get him to cut back on his drinking.'" Donovan had reached the saturation point. He excused himself for a few moments and shot upstairs to his office. He phoned Dr. John Sawatsky, the head psychologist of the Ontario Provincial Police in Toronto. Gibbs' city wasn't in Ontario, but Donovan hoped that Sawatsky could recommend a good psychologist or psychiatrist in Gibbs' area. Sawatsky had invited Donovan to Canada many times to help him with the Ontario police. He was one psychologist who saw the value of Donovan's work. Quite happy to return a favour, he gave Donovan two names to pass along to Gibbs. Donovan hustled back downstairs to the group and gave the names to an amazed Hilary and Norman Gibbs.

Donovan handed something else over to Hilary Gibbs as they were about to leave. It was a set of relaxation tapes and a biofeedback program given to Donovan by the company who marketed it. "Here, take this, it's a gift from me. It's relaxation tapes for Norm to help him improve his breathing and get rid of his chest pains. Make sure he uses them."

"Norm," Donovan said, shaking Gibbs' hand firmly and winking at Hilary, "Norm, listen to your wife."

CHAPTER TWENTY

THE MEETING

Tuesday, 1:00 P.M.

Donovan waved goodbye to Norman and Hilary Gibbs at the side entrance as they left the parking lot for their long drive home. He returned to the sitting room and distractedly straightened chairs, emptied ash trays, and collected paper cups. Donovan had put Gibbs through hell today, but now it was his turn in the hot seat as he faced his meeting with the commissioner. He tried to run strategies and options for the meeting through his mind, but he couldn't think clearly.

"Relax, I gotta relax," he said to himself. "A quick nap to get my head straight." He locked the back door, went up to his office, and flicked on the phone machine, then stepped into the back room where he kept an old army cot. As he lay down, he visualized his boat in Cape Cod Bay and took his usual deep breaths, but sleep wouldn't come. For fifteen minutes, he visualized in succession mountain scenery, a tropical beach, sensuous women, then unbridled sexual ecstasy, but nothing worked. The meeting wouldn't leave his mind.

"The hell with it," he said finally. "It's showtime."

Driving downtown to headquarters, Donovan thought of Selye, Bill Norton, and Jerry Penney, and his apprehension gave way to quiet determination. Before leaving his parked car, he bowed his head and silently prayed for the program and for guidance in the meeting. By the time he walked through the door of police headquarters and into the lobby, where he had once broken down and cried for help, he felt confident.

He nodded to the security guard, took the elevator to the sixth floor, passed through more security, then walked down

229

the hallway and into the commissioner's reception area. He checked in with the secretary and took a seat. Within minutes, Commissioner Roache emerged from his office. The dark-haired, intense man, a runner who regularly ran the Boston marathon, strode nimbly across the room to greet Donovan.

"Eddie, is it okay if I have a couple of assistants join us for the meeting?"

"No," Donovan heard himself say, "I'd rather talk to you alone, Mickey." Donovan surprised himself at his answer, but Roache only nodded and escorted Donovan into the spacious wood-panelled office, shutting the door behind him. Roache motioned Donovan to sit next to him at his conference table.

"Can I still call you Mickey?" Donovan asked, "We are friends, but you're the commissioner."

"Of course, Eddie. What can I do for you?"

"The last administration tried to put me out of business, but I've hung in here for four years. I've been waiting for a new commissioner to see if there would be a change in attitude," Donovan said. His hands were clasped in front of him, and his right foot tapped nervously, but his voice stayed calm and firm.

"I've fought to keep this program alive, but I can't go on any longer the way things are. I need staff, and I need a budget. If I don't get co-operation, I've got to quit. I can't take it any longer. I've been in hospital several times from the strain of trying to keep it going, and I've lost relationships because of it." Roache nodded his head slightly. Donovan tried to gauge his reaction.

"Either I get what I need, or for the sake of my physical and mental health, I'll have to leave the stress program."

"Oh, no, we don't want to lose you," Roache said. "You've done a good job, Eddie. Everyone knows that. What do you need?" Donovan breathed more easily.

"Additional personnel, the building cleaned and fixed up, and a small budget so we could do other things. We want to spend more time with recruits, go to roll calls so we can talk to the cops on the street, and we want to talk to command staff."

"You really want to talk to command staff?" Roache questioned.

"I look forward to it," Donovan said. "They'll find out what the program really is. Some just think I'm a drunk working with alcoholics and drug addicts. Some think cops hide in the program. I'll take anybody, anyway, but they don't hide there. The group will kick them out. If they don't, I will. The problem is when we kick someone out and send them back to the supervisors, they don't do their jobs."

"Will you tell them that?" Roache asked.

"You bet your ass."

"Specifically, what do you want, Eddie?" Roache said, leaning forward.

"I want George Leehan."

"You got him."

"I want Millie McCowan."

"It might take a while longer, but you'll get her."

"Fix the building," Donovan said.

"We'll fix the building up. It will take time because we don't have a budget for it," Roache answered, "but we'll do it piece by piece."

"I need a decent police car so I don't have to use my own."

"You'll get a car," Roache said.

"I need a small budget for some decent equipment that works, like a Xerox and a good typewriter."

"I'll try for you Eddie, but I can't promise. You know what our budget constraints are like." Now Roache asked him a question.

"Eddie, what can we do for the families?" Roache spent another fifteen minutes expressing his concerns about his officers, their families, and their problems, asking Donovan for advice on each issue.

Donovan was in a state of shock when he left the office. He floated through the other errands he had at headquarters. Later, he couldn't remember getting in his car or driving back to the stress centre.

Back in his office, he rehashed the meeting in his mind, assessing Roache's intent. For the first time, Donovan believed he wouldn't get the run-around. But there'd been so many broken promises in the past, he was afraid to accept today as good news, so he vacillated between controlled excitement and guarded apprehension. He called Mary and told her, then called George Leehan. After two individual counselling appointments, he finished his day at six and locked up for the night.

Rather than head straight to the freeway and home to Plymouth, he took a detour, the route through the Blue Hills Reservation. Still tense from the day's events, he drove along Randolph Avenue, then turned onto Chickatawbut Road, and began the winding trip up to the viewpoint. He gritted his teeth thinking about the superintendents who had given him the hard times and all the headaches and heartaches they had caused him. Then it dawned on Donovan. They were all gone, and he was still there.

"I won! I won!" he shouted. He banged on the steering wheel and then the dashboard with his right fist. "I beat the bastards! If I die tonight, I know I won!" he shouted.

Tears streamed down Donovan's cheeks as he pulled into the viewpoint. He turned off the engine and wiped his eyes, then looked out at the soft beauty of Boston at night. Slowly, a feeling of serenity overcame him.

"We won," he said softly. "We won."

EPILOGUE

A Wednesday evening, six months later, 7:30 P.M.

Max "Shaky" Shakura sat in a chair by the kitchen door, the same spot he had sat in at his first meeting. Around him in the main meeting room a dozen other officers drank coffee and talked as they waited for the regular Wednesday evening meeting to start. Max listened attentively to three men seated near him, occasionally offering a comment, or breaking into his shy, broad grin when they said something funny. He was neatly dressed, with his hair combed back, a look of contentment on his clean-shaven face. Since his arrest for drunk driving six months ago, he'd been sober and a regular attendee of both the Monday and Wednesday meetings.

Donovan was outside in the warm fall air, admiring the newly painted exterior of the stress centre. It was the first meeting since the work had been completed, and Donovan corralled everyone as they approached the house. He proudly held court, beaming like a new father as he leaned against his police car, a dark blue LTD, badly damaged in a police accident but completely fixed and assigned to Donovan. "Just like me," he said, pointing to the car and the house. "Once a wreck, but now new and improved." The group around him laughed. Donovan found it hard to believe the changes were real, and so did most long-time attendees and volunteers in the program. With their police officers' cynicism, particularly toward their own bureaucracy, they didn't expect Donovan to receive the things Roache promised.

Thirty-five officers were jammed into the main meeting room, and Donovan wormed his way to the back and took a seat. Long-time meeting attendees like Dr. John, Paul

Martin, Tommy Branigan, Charlie Gilham, Ernie Walsh, Bert Gee, Kevin Miller, and Shaky mixed in with a host of new people. The groups were always in transition.

Donovan asked Millie McCowan to run the meeting. She'd joined the program full time just the week before. George Leehan's assignment as a counsellor came within days of the meeting with Commissioner Roache, but Millie's appointment took time to clear red tape. However, she was here now, and Donovan was thankful.

Millie started the meeting by discussing a problem of her own. For the past year she had worked in the sexual assault unit and had seen many tragedies. Three months ago, she'd received a call from a fifteen-year-old girl saying her father was sexually molesting her and two younger sisters and beating their mother. Millie spent weeks on the case, setting it up to have the father charged, but doing it in a way that protected the family. She got the kids out of the home and eventually convinced the wife to leave.

Two days ago, Millie went to the preliminary court hearing, but the father and family didn't show. Millie called the wife, and a policeman answered. The man had shot and killed his wife. Millie was devastated. Now she was filled with doubts, agonizing about what she did wrong or could have done differently.

"Millie, it was going to happen sooner or later," Kevin Miller said.

"You probably saved the lives of the three girls," Shaky added.

"I know," Millie said dejectedly, "but it was me who convinced her to leave him, and that's going to be hard to forget."

Donovan put his hands behind his head and rocked back in his chair. He looked past the group at the cleaned and painted room. The smell of fresh paint suggested optimism and hope. The dingy look of a seedy meeting hall was gone, replaced by soft white walls and ceilings, newly tiled floors, and fluorescent lights. Character was added by the dark stain on the wood trim. Donovan, George, Millie, and some volunteers had done most of the work; the city provided the supplies. An unused part of the second floor had been opened up and painted to give both George and Millie offices.

The focus in the meeting moved from Millie to a long-time attendee of the meetings who had remarried three weeks ago and now bemoaned problems with his new wife and her teenage kids. Brian Connor, in uniform and on duty, brushed through the group and motioned to George that he needed to talk with him upstairs. Brian, a Boston municipal policeman, had been sober a year and a half now and in the last six months had brought fifteen other police-men into the program. The department that had been about to fire him now proudly boasted of him, had offered him a promotion to sergeant, and whenever there was a problem officer, turned to him for help and advice. With paint spots on his hands and pants, George went upstairs to assist Brian. A fellow officer had been suspended for drinking on the job, and Brian wanted George to help him convince the officer to get help. A year and a half ago it was Donovan and George who teamed up as "good guy–bad guy" against Brian when he needed help. This time George would be cast as the bad guy, and Brian would move up from victim to good guy.

Donovan breathed a deep sigh of contentment as his gaze returned to the officers in the room. With Millie confidently running the meeting, Donovan slipped into the kitchen and out the side door to the yard for some fresh air and another look at the house. But when he was about to go back inside, he saw a man standing on the other side of the parking pad behind some cars. Donovan walked toward him.

The man, fortyish, with rounded shoulders and a stooped posture, stared nervously at Donovan through thick, dirty glasses.

"Are you from the meeting?" he asked.

"Yeah, I'm Eddie Donovan. I run the stress program."

"I'm a Boston municipal policeman. Can I come to the meeting?" he asked through rotted teeth. His eyes were bleary and moist, his clothes rumpled. Donovan nodded.

"I'm a friend of Shaky's. I've seen the change in him. I used to drink with him all the time. I want a piece of whatever he's got now. He's a different person."

"Come on in, brother," Donovan said, putting his arm around the man's shoulder. "That's why we're in business."